THE FERMENT OF REALISM

THE
FERMENT OF REALISM

American Literature, 1884-1919

Warner Berthoff

CAMBRIDGE UNIVERSITY PRESS

Cambridge
London   New York   New Rochelle
Melbourne Sydney

Published by the Press Syndicate of the University of Cambridge
The Pitt Building, Trumpington Street, Cambridge CB2 1RP
32 East 57th Street, New York, NY 10022, USA
296 Beaconsfield Parade, Middle Park, Melbourne 3206, Australia

First published by The Free Press 1965

Reissued by the Cambridge University Press 1981

Printed in the United States of America

British Library Cataloguing in Publication Data

Berthoff, Warner
The ferment of realism.
    1. American literature – History and criticism
    2. Realism in literature
    I. Title
    810.9'004   PS214   80-42335
ISBN 0 521 24092 1 hard covers
ISBN 0 521 28435 X paperback

To LIBERALISM AND DEMOCRACY,
the good old causes, in whose ambiguous service the
work surveyed in this volume was mostly written

Contents

Preface to the First Edition

Chesterton, introducing his study of the Victorian age in literature, wrote that he felt wholly incompetent for the "delicate and entangled task" at hand, but that it was "rather reassuring than otherwise" to have undertaken "something that nobody could do properly." His remarks, I have come to appreciate, merely state the literal truth: literary history is an impossible genre. How is one to reconcile, in consecutive discourse, the requirements of historical accuracy and the just claims of the anthology; the multiplicity of events in sequence and the single-minded enterprise of a principled and discriminating critical order? Recently, moreover, Professor Northrop Frye has put it down as self-evident that evaluative criticism, on an objective basis, also is impossible. That hardly simplifies practical problems of organization and emphasis, but it does somewhat ease one's anxieties about the effort to keep both

responsibilities in view—the effort, that is, to write a specifically *literary* history.

I should like to suggest briefly what the present volume
undertakes and what it does not. It is designed primarily as a
survey of good work done, with regard to the formal motives
and characteristics that define it, rather than as a comprehensive record of individual histories and careers or of battles
and schools of opinion. There is no attempt to duplicate what
is better done by essential aids like the *Dictionary of American Biography* or *The Oxford Companion to American
Literature.* Neither has it been my concern to chart any great
evolutionary tendency in the national ethos. A survey of this
kind, even when covering only thirty-five years, probably
cannot take shape around a single main theme without serious
wrenching of the basic materials, which are likely—in their
actual historical emergence—to be irreducibly miscellaneous
and discrete. It can, however, have an interpretive or a
methodological center, to which the chronicler's judgment
continually refers itself back for certification. With the
present volume this center is a certain view of literature and
a certain view of history, and thus also a view of the special
amalgam that ought to result from doing justice to the claims
of both. Literary history is coextensive with social history,
cultural history, intellectual history but is not identical with
any of them, even the last, nor strictly determined by them.
This is because literature itself has its own purposes and
determinants. Though never wholly autonomous it is always
more accidental and eccentric than people think, whether
they choose to read it for symptoms or, going the other way,
to define it as an independent "institution." It draws its prime
motives from deep within the common culture, the life-
experience of its producers in their time (and can be in
turn a conspicuous agent in the formation of new motives and
new experiences), but it never speaks for the totality of that

culture. You cannot write intellectual, or cultural, history without reference to literature; neither can you write it solely on the basis of literature. Literary history, not less than literary criticism, is determined finally by the distinctive nature of the forms it examines, and these forms are unique in being at the same time, in varying proportion: (1) works of art, seeking self-completion; (2) documents in testimony, relating to the common consciousness of truths and probabilities; (3) acts of expression, more or less sustained and pitched at different intensities, in which we may see, among other things, how language, the genetic code-matrix of historical culture, is being "kept up." This uniqueness is the fact, at once formal and historical, before which every other consideration must finally give way. All lives and actions are symptomatic of the forms life takes, and all, ideally, deserve inspection; but very few transcend themselves to the point of defining concretely these life forms and making them intelligible, perhaps even reaching through them—in rare cases—to a projection of new forms. Literary history, as here conceived, is a record of such transcendences, according to the chances of a particular period and province.

The reader I have had in mind is one who already knows or will remember having read a good part of the writing here surveyed, who is already committed to an interest in literature in general and in modern American literature in particular. Specialists in the period treated will doubtless find matter to quarrel with, in the choice of names and titles, the pattern of emphasis, the critical judgments suggested. I have said too little about magazines, which throughout the period played a complex and shifting role in the promotion of new talents and new trends. I have said almost nothing about drama, since despite some worthy efforts in the right direction American drama did not effectively emerge from the morass of popular entertainment until the appearance at the very end of our period of playwrights like Eugene O'Neill and Elmer Rice. And though I have organized this survey loosely enough, I still have not managed to find a place for a considerable number of readable and accomplished works we should be the poorer for losing sight of. A random selection of these works—the *Personal Memoirs of U. S. Grant* (1885–1886), Thomas Sergeant Perry's *The Evolution of the Snob* (1886), Andrew Carnegie's *The Gospel of Wealth* (1889), Whistler's *The Gentle Art of Making Enemies* (1890), George Kennan's *Siberia and the Exile System* (1891), John Muir's *The Mountains of California* (1894), Walter A. Wyckoff's two-volume *The Workers: A Study in Reality* (1897, 1898), Charles W. Chesnutt's *The Conjure Woman* (1899), Captain Joshua Slocum's *Sailing Alone Around the World* (1900), Henry Adams's "Prayer to the Virgin of Chartres" (1901, 1920), Louis Sullivan's *Kindergarten Chats* (1901–1902), W. E. B. Dubois's *The Souls of Black Folk* (1903), Andy Adams's *The Log of a Cowboy* (1903), Lincoln Steffens's *The Shame of the Cities* (1904), Josiah Strong's *Our Country* (1907), Zona Gale's *Friendship Village* (1908), Jane Addams's *Twenty Years at Hull House* (1910), Horace B. Kephart's *Our Southern Highlanders* (1913), Walter Lippmann's *Drift and Mastery* (1914), Louis D. Brandeis's *Other People's Money* (1914), Logan Pearsall Smith's *Trivia* (1917), William Beebe's *Jungle Peace* (1918), John Reed's *Ten Days That Shook the World* (1919), Charles Ives's *Essays Before a Sonata* (1920)—may serve not only as a sort of blanket apology for all such omissions but also as a preliminary sampling of literary types and underlying historical changes characteristic of the period as a whole.

W. B.

Preface to the 1981 Reissue

When I began this book early in the 1960s and decided, a touch self-defensively, to open with a comment of G. K. Chesterton's, my intention was not to announce a stand in some intensifying literary-critical war. At the time no book by Roland Barthes had yet appeared in English, no book by Jacques Derrida had appeared anywhere, and centers of literary study such as Ithaca, New York, and New Haven, Connecticut, were still chiefly notable for careful scholarship in subjects like Chaucer, the eighteenth century, and English Romanticism. Much has happened since then. It is now common wisdom—even in the graduate schools, if not with everyone offering instruction there—that in literature as in other modes of activity the individual produced unit is, as a locus of value, a cultural fiction of dubious intent; that the word *literature* itself, as a classifier, begs too many existential and hierarchical questions, so that it is preferable all round to speak only of writing (écriture) and of texts; and that since no discoursing subject can be wholly present either to itself or to another observer, the category *author* stands exposed as a sentimental obstruction to clear thinking.

Such transformations having occurred, I am now fairly charmed, re-reading these pages, to hear myself talking along about *works* and *authors* as if they really had existed and deserved commemoration as such, under their own putative names. I am also unrepentant. Admittedly, were one now to undertake a book of this kind, modes of judgment and categories of consideration might profitably be introduced which would wholly discount the curious illusion that did somehow bring this or that historical personage to a definable "scene of writing": the illusion in the mind of writer and reader alike that what they were involved with was a single identifiable construct or form, a serial entity having a detectable beginning, a more or less extended middle, and some sort of end, or stop. It would be well worth trying, for example, to compose a history of literary activity over several decades as an account of one particular phase in language's incessant suprapersonal struggle to maintain itself as a living system. As chickens are said to be mechanisms whereby eggs deliver themselves of other eggs, and any natural creature is merely an instrument through which the gene pool secures self-continuance, so it is reasonable enough to consider authors, readers, and the objects they assert these identities in relation to, as incidental relay stations in the immense drama of linguistic renewal. Nevertheless I find it on the whole easier—and not without homologic truthfulness—to go on naming individual names and sorting out single titles. It certainly facilitates looking things up.

There is more than one reason for leaving the text of the first printing unchanged, but a chief one is simply that our basic picture of the historical period in question—who was important, and what publishing events mattered most—remains largely as it was. Looking back, I can regret oversights and moments of excessive cursoriness. A place should have been found for H. L. Mencken's *A Book of Prefaces* (1917), the appearance of which Edmund Wilson took to be "one of the cardinal events of the new American literature." I would not now leave W. E. B. DuBois's *The Souls of Black Folk*, with its rare blend of imaginative passion and disciplined sociological acumen, as an item on a supernumerary list, and I would at least record the existence of James Weldon Johnson's *The Autobiography of an Ex-Colored Man* (1912). In the bibliography S. Foster Damon's life of Amy Lowell should have been cited. But for the most part there seems little requiring revision. Many more titles from the period that were all but forgotten around 1960 have happily been revived, through a fresh concern for feminist literature, black literature, ethnic and special-interest literature generally; but (to cite a single instance) I have read nothing by the courageous Charlotte Perkins Gilman to convince me that omitting her from an extended essay in literary history was a more actionable oversight than omitting the Harvard bellettrist Charles Macomb Flandrau. In general, it still makes sense to me to cram the later Henry James into a mere twenty-three pages and allow Charles W. Chesnutt the luxury of almost a full line.

In support of a claim to have got the proportions basically right, the central evidence would be the secondary literature—biographies, critical studies, new editions, collections of letters and previously unpublished materials—that has accumulated since 1965. The mass of it is staggering, but when reduced to categories it fairly matches the allotment of space originally settled upon. James and Mark Twain, as before, lead by a sizeable margin, with Howells, Dreiser, Henry Adams, Edith Wharton, and Ezra Pound at the head of a strong second flight. The one kind of scholarly and critical production that has not kept pace is, interestingly, literary history itself. My disingenuous pro-

nouncement in the original preface about the impossibility of
"a specifically *literary* history" has to a degree been endorsed in
the aftermath. In the seven-volume series this book was originally designed for, only one other title ever appeared; and with
the brave exception of David Perkins's *A History of Modern
Poetry* we have had long essays advancing some fruitful bias
concerning the achievement of briefer periods (Hugh Kenner's
The Pound Era) or tracing the extended impact of a major historical event (Daniel Aaron's *The Unwritten* [American Civil]
War), but not comprehensive histories as such. Perhaps, with
the measureless expansion of information-retrieval systems,
literary and most other kinds of diachronic history have simply
become impracticable.

In any case, trying to update the bibliography would expand
my text inordinately and still give offense, I fear, to the many
scholars and critics excluded for reasons of space whose work
has nevertheless increased understanding. Fortunately, bibliographic aids, reference guides, newsletters, "critical heritage"
collections, have been multiplying at a comparable rate. In 1965
the first annual volume of the admirably edited *American Literary Scholarship* (covering the year 1963) had just appeared—and
it is worth noting that the separate chapters listing work on
James and Twain occupy, each year, between ten and twenty
pages. In 1967 the journal *American Literary Realism* began
publication, printing checklists and reviews of critical scholarship as well as interpretive essays. Both of these have become
indispensable to students and researchers, as have—for other
uses—Lyle N. Wright's tabulative *American Fiction, 1876–1900*
and Clayton L. Eichelberger's *A Guide to Critical Reviews of
United States Fiction, 1870–1930.*

On individual authors, certain outstanding titles deserve
notice, at whatever risk of inequity. Leon Edel's biography of
Henry James has reached conclusion—to a rising chorus of
critical dissatisfaction—while Maqbool Aziz's "variant" edi-

tion of the complete tales usefully supplements Edel's earlier one by indicating textual changes. An illuminating series of studies compares James to other major figures: Balzac (Peter Brooks), Nietzsche (Stephen Donadio), Flaubert (David Gervais), Conrad (Elsa Nettels), Turgenev (Dale Peterson), William James (Richard A. Hock); others—by Charles R. Anderson, Martha Banta, Jean Frantz Blackall, Peter Buitenhuis, Seymour Chatman, Jeanne Delbaere-Garant, Cristina Giorcelli, Kenneth Graham, Walter Isle, Carl Maves, Donald Mull, Sergio Perosa, Strother B. Purdy, Sallie Sears, Ora Segal, William Veeder, J.A. Ward, Philip Weinstein, Viola Hopkins Winner, Ruth Bernard Yeazell—explore formal, stylistic, intellectual, geographical, and hermeneutic aspects of James's (so far) inexhaustibly absorbing art. On Mark Twain, Justin Kaplan's fine biography, *Mr. Clemens and Mark Twain*, may be supplemented by Hamlin Hill's concentrated study of the final decade; Thomas Tenney's *Reference Guide* sets a standard for all such work; and James Cox's *Mark Twain and the Fate of Humor* brings an intensity of critical reflection such as, formerly, only James himself seemed regularly to elicit. The most substantial new work on Howells is Jean Rivière's Sorbonne thesis, *W. D. Howells: pionnier et coordinateur du mouvement réaliste américain*; on a smaller scale there have been reexaminations by George Bennett, George C. Carrington, Jr., Giuseppe Conti, Kenneth S. Lynn, and Kermit Vanderbilt. Dreiser has been profitably reconsidered by Ellen Moers, Richard Lehan, Donald Pizer, and, above all, Robert Penn Warren in a centennial monograph, *Homage to Theodore Dreiser*; Henry Adams by John Conder, Earl Harbert, Robert Mane, John Carlos Rowe, and (posthumously) R. P. Blackmur; Ezra Pound, particularly in his emergent years, by Hugh Witemeyer, Thomas H. Jackson, Ronald Bush, Richard Sieburth, and Timothy Materer.

In general, biographies, critical and otherwise, have made the most substantial contributions—on G. W. Cable (Louis D.

Rubin Jr.), Harold Frederic (Austin Briggs), Kate Chopin (Per Seyersted), Edith Wharton (R. W. B. Lewis and Cynthia Griffin Wolff), Henry Blake Fuller (Bernard R. Bowron Jr.), Robert Herrick (Louis Budd), Lincoln Steffens (Justin Kaplan), Jack London (Andrew Sinclair), Dreiser again (W. A. Swanberg), Gertrude Stein (James R. Mellow), Robert Frost(Lawrance Thompson—to another chorus of dissents), Ezra Pound (Noel Stock), T. S. Eliot in his early life (Lyndall Gordon). A scattering of primarily critical volumes has done something more than confirm existing valuations, in particular Frank Bergon, *Stephen Crane's Artistry*, and several introductions in the Virginia edition of Crane, especially those by J. C. Levenson; Richard Bridgman, *Gertrude Stein in Pieces*; Richard Poirier, *Robert Frost: The Work of Knowing*; Jules Chametzky, *From the Ghetto: The Fiction of Abraham Cahan*; A. J. Ayer's reconsideration of Peirce and William James in *The Origins of Pragmatism*; Olaf Hanson's monograph-length introduction to *The Radical Will: Randolph Bourne, Selected Writings*.

Finally, it is worth remarking that some of the most valuable recent commentary has come in books cutting through the period (and beyond it) along one diagonal or another, reassessing different aspects of its literary and imaginative character. Again risking inequity, I offer the following short list: Edwin H. Cady's reexamination of the idea of "realism" in *The Light of Common Day*; Jay Martin, *Harvests of Change: American Literature, 1865–1914*; Donald Pizer, *Realism and Naturalism in Nineteenth-Century American Fiction*; Robert Falk, *The Victorian Mode in American Fiction*; James Tuttleton, *The Novel of Manners in America*; Richard Poirier, *A World Elsewhere: The Place of Style in American Literature*; Richard Bridgman, *The Colloquial Style in America*; Gordon O. Taylor, *The Passages of Thought: Psychological Representation in the American Novel, 1870–1900*; several studies of American autobiography, in particular Thomas Cooley, *Educated Lives*, and Mutlu Konuk Blasing, *The Art of Life*; Harry B. Henderson III, *Versions of the Past: The Historical Imagination in American Fiction*; Richard Hofstadter, *The Progressive Historians*, and Marcus Cunliffe and Robin Winks, eds., *Pastmasters: Some Essays on American Historians*; Martha Banta, *Failure and Success in America: A Literary Debate*; Donald B. Meyer, *The Positive Thinkers*; Kevin Starr, *Americans and the California Dream, 1850–1915*; Henry Nash Smith, *Democracy and the Novel: Popular Resistance to Classic American Writers*; Bruce Kuklick, *The Rise of American Philosophy: Cambridge, Massachusetts, 1860–1930*; William H. Pritchard, *Lives of the Modern Poets*.

In the original preface I suggested that literary history (whatever else it does) ought to be a record of transcendences, in which—according to the chances of life in a particular period and province—certain acts of imaginative definition and origination took place within the shifting conventions of literary statement and found, somewhere, a responsive hearing. I am less sure now what "transcendence" means as a historiographic concept. But I should have added at the time that literary history is also, properly, a record of certain systematic uses of freedom. For this reason I am happy with the book's original dedication and wish to renew it here.

W. B.

THE FERMENT OF REALISM

But let fiction cease to lie about life; let it portray men and women as they are, actuated by the motives and the passions in the measure we all know; let it leave off painting dolls and working them by springs and wires; let it show the different interests in their true proportions . . . let it not put on fine literary airs; let it speak the dialect, the language, that most Americans know—the language of unaffected people everywhere. . . .
—Howells, *Criticism and Fiction*

I have disregarded all romantic traditions, and simply asked myself in every instance, not whether it was amusing but whether it was true to the logic of reality—true in color and tone to the American sky, the American soil, the American character.
—H. H. Boyesen, "Preface,"
The Mammon of Unrighteousness

Does the native novelist try to generalize the nation? No, he lays plainly before you the ways and speech and life of a few people grouped in a certain place—his own place —and that is one book. In time he and his brethren will report to you the life and people of a whole nation. . . .
—Mark Twain, "What Paul Bourget Thinks of Us"

Any point of view is interesting that is a direct impression of life.
—Henry James, "Deerfield Letter"

I would praise the work for its fine tone, its humanity, and its realism; for all good art is realism of one sort or another.
—Ezra Pound, review of
Prufrock and Other Observations

1. AMERICAN REALISM:
A GRAMMAR OF MOTIVES

The Emergence of "Realism"

*T*HE GREAT collective event in American letters during the 1880s and 1890s was the securing of "realism" as the dominant standard of value. But, as the postulations preceding this chapter suggest, it was a peculiarly indefinite standard. One can more readily say what kinds of writing the new American realists were in revolt against than what exactly they wanted to create. In the way of causes and movements in the United States, the cause of realism appears more exclusively a summons to some broad preliminary moral reformation than, as in French realism with Flaubert and after, not only this but also a systematic searching out, reasoned and progressive, of fundamental issues of expression and form, producing in its wake new experiments—symbolism, naturalism, expressionism, surrealism—in continuous and mutually instructive succession. Insofar as it constituted a movement at all, American literary realism was concerned less with problems of artistic definition and discovery than with clearing the way to a more profitable exercise of individual ambition. (Perhaps that is why, as a standard, it has been so remarkably long-lived; why it was as much the watchword in 1919 as it had been in 1884; why, even in the 1950s and 1960s, the great run of talents in American writing remains committed with a positively inhibiting single-mindedness to the premise of realism, the work of capturing the special immediate air of American reality in the familiar American dialect.) Embracing the cause of realism was much like joining an insurgent campaign in American politics. You committed yourself to a radical attack upon existing offenses, to honesty and a clean sweep, to partisan feelings of evangelistic intensity, but not to any clear conception of the proper actual conduct of operations and certainly not to any coherent program of business. It was as if swearing allegiance to the name of the movement and wearing its colors in public guaranteed solutions to all the fundamental problems of policy which, presumably, the movement had been created to deal with. As a critical standard, "realism" could thus as easily provide a way of evading the full creative task as of defining and prosecuting it: so Henry James (who stands as the signal exception to these opening remarks) had understood as early as 1870 in studying Howells's groundbreaking work.

When we take note of everything in 1884 and the succeeding years that did in fact satisfy the prevailing demand for a convincingly detailed account of actual experience, we may well ask whether "realism" in American literature was anything more than a name, a borrowed label which happened to come so strongly into fashion (in an era not widely distinguished by searching critical discussion) that no one could avoid deferring to it. Popular entertainment aside, what was not "realistic" in the heyday of Howells, Mark Twain, and Henry James? Documentary chronicles of city life and exotic legends of the remote and strange, horrific melodramas and placid genre sketches, works of social criticism and works of psychological analysis, novels written all in dialogue and novels in which the characters are barely capable of consecutive speech, prophecies of a transformed future and haunted daydreams of a visionary past—which is to say, Howells's *A Hazard of New Fortunes* and Lafcadio Hearn's *Chita: A Memory of Last Island*, Ambrose Bierce's *Can Such Things Be?* and Sarah Jewett's *The Country of the Pointed Firs*, Veblen's *The Theory of the Leisure Class* and William James's *The Principles of Psychology*, Henry James's *The Awkward Age* and Stephen Crane's *The Red Badge of Courage*, Edward Bellamy's *Looking Backward* and Mark Twain's *The Mysterious Stranger*—all could be identified as works of realism; all were in some degree conceived as such.

What do they all have in common? Not form, certainly, and not theme either, in any ordinary sense: to attempt to define American "realism" by classifying the particular books written in its name according to form and theme is to sink into a mire of inconsequential distinctions and details. But if we look instead to the fundamental motives to expression which direct these works, we come sooner to solid ground. We need to keep in mind the practical involvement of the work of writing, as of any art, with common life and history. For modern writers share in all the duplicity of behavior characteristic of an era which can fitfully remember the ideal of a life of high dedication and disinterested service but which increasingly measures virtue and achievement in terms of material success. Modern writers are as artisan-tradesmen,

competing for shares in a market not less contingent and
arbitrary than, broadly speaking, any other economic arena.
But they are also prophets of consciousness in a fundamentally
spiritual calling, willful instruments of moral reformation;
producers of objects which like sacred objects strive in the
making to become their own excuse for being and so to
affect the rest of us not merely in our habitual behavior as
consumers of marginal time but as seekers, in however limited
a way, of a truly better life. In the 1880s the standard of
realism was being raised in good part simply out of professional distaste for a polite literature that was rotten ripe with
idealizing sentiment and genteel affectation. Life, even at its
most ordinary, was simply more interesting than that—and
what was the point of a book if it wasn't as seriously interesting as life? At the same time realism spoke also for graver
dissatisfactions. More was at stake than the hostility (like
Hawthorne's hostility a generation earlier to Mrs. E. D. E. N.
Southworth and her works) of those who meant to say something worth saying toward those who had discovered the
trick of the modern middle-class best seller. The irritation out
of which literary realism developed in the United States was
as much with prevailing conditions of social and economic
life, with the latest forms of disorder and inequity (however
they might masquerade as progress), as with the insipidness
of other, feebler literary methods. That many realists were
also populists, progressives, sentimental socialists is not surprising. But life and history do not give way easily to books
and words. The same protest has to be made again and again;
the underlying conditions seem unaffected, perhaps grow
worse; the new generation, inheriting both its predecessor's
work and the regular failure of that work to transform the
conditions that prompted it, is summoned, if only to keep its
self-respect, to a new and more resolute, though probably
more desperate, effort. "Realism" in 1884 was thus also a

standard of profound though often sublimated rebellion, a movement of spirit directed against particular and identifiable new formations of civil culture and quickened by particular and identifiable fears, hopes, tensions, excitements, animosities, secessions, and visions of the future; it tended, furthermore, to become more intensely so throughout the period under examination in this volume.

Precedents: The Rise of the Novel

Formally the practice and general program of literary realism may be traced well back before our period. The writers of the '80s and '90s did not lack great precedents and supporting traditions. Throughout the eighteenth century, alongside neoclassical standards of decorum—formal propriety, dignified subject matter, correct diction, strictly reasoned design—there had coexisted an important body of popular writing which, precisely because it did lie beneath the notice of the principled criticism of that era, had been the freer to follow its own bent and develop its own methods for catching and holding attention. The novel in particular grew up in this popular limbo. Developed largely in response to vulgar as opposed to learned taste, the novel appealed to an audience already partial by settled habit to topical broadsides, to circumstantial chronicles of real events (including those biographies and journals of the soul's history that were the staple nourishment of the evangelical sects), and to the grossly sensational news, and newspapers, of the day.

Having thus begun with a strong footing in the observation of actual life, the novel has remained the chief genre for realism in modern literature. The actual in stories does not have to be the statistically ordinary. The reality documented by fiction, as by journalism, has been as often as not the strange, the exotic, the quaint, the sentimental, the sensational,

even the thoroughly improbable. The novel has always more
or less shamelessly appealed to vulgar curiosity and the bot-
tomless human appetite for gossip and sensation. What subtler
purposes its best practitioners have evolved have been super-
added to that primitive appeal. This special alliance of the
novel with the common consciousness operates formally too.
For the novel lives by implying a certain parity of spirit
between the reader on one hand and on the other the characters, the writer himself, or the mass of other readers in
their legions. (The passive relation of mass audiences to actors,
singers, film stars, and to one another in the presence of these,
is fundamentally different.) The result is that, from the first,
the more or less realistic novel has been the most egalitarian
of serious literary modes, the one that has most directly lent
itself to expressing the broad currents and undercurrents of
popular feeling and has most nearly reproduced, in D. H.
Lawrence's phrase, the common flow and recoil of our
"sympathetic consciousness." And it has been, as a consequence, the one most frequently brought under censorship.
Deliberately or not, it has again and again appeared radically
subversive of official standards of conduct and morality. Of
course it is also conservative of such standards: the point is
that its overriding concern for what the human creature
really is and how moment by moment or year by year he
feels and behaves, in his indestructible individuality, has given
the novel—like gossip, like curiosity—a certain built-in indifference to *ought* and *must* and a corresponding power of
interior resistance to official etiquette and certified moral
precept. Maintaining its existence largely beneath the notice
of respectable criticism (even in the 1880s Henry James could
assume, as Hawthorne had assumed forty years earlier, a
cultivated prejudice against the claims of storytelling to be
an art), the genre of prose fiction, the representational narrative of consequential happenings, could be so much the

more open and hospitable to unfranchised stirrings of feeling, to doubtful attitudes and anarchic states of mind. And when in recent generations there has been some widespread disturbance of human relationships and private morale—and when indeed has there not?—we can turn confidently to novels to find it vigorously and circumstantially, though not always coherently, not always appositely, expressed.

Precedents: Style and Truthfulness

This major popular tradition in modern letters has also been instinctively hospitable to plain speaking and the free use of common idiom: Howells's crude formula about the "language of unaffected people everywhere" points to this alliance. There is a realism of style and treatment as well as of subject matter, as admirers of Mark Twain, but not less of Henry James, do not have to be reminded. Here again the writers of 1880–1920 could draw on a solid inheritance. The first great manifesto of English Romanticism, Wordsworth's preface to the second edition of *Lyrical Ballads* (1800), is among other things a plea against affected diction and for the plain style; and disciples of Wordsworth's poetics could look back to the studied plainness of expression in Crabbe and in Cowper (both admired by Edwin Arlington Robinson), in Isaac Watts and Charles Wesley, and even to the ruggedly conversational style of Donne and certain contemporaries and of Shakespeare himself, for earlier precedent. In America, where a taste for seventeenth-century colloquial particularity in style had survived more hardily than in England, in part because supported by the dominant Puritan concern for plain and honest witness, such recent masters as Emerson, Thoreau, and Whitman had all promoted the voice of the natural man, speaking from direct personal experience and the self's inmost conviction, as the right basis for effective style, the surest means of securing that "veracity" of utterance which all the leading figures of their generation especially prized. It is worth remarking that all of these mid-nineteenth-century writers had sensed the presence of this natural veracity in the forms of popular humor and comic journalism, much of it in dialect, that Mark Twain was soon to exploit.

Indeed what there was of a theoretical program for "realism" in the '80s and '90s makes no essential advance over that of 1830–1860.[1] That earlier program is simply extended to the writing of novels and stories. Emerson's famous preference in "The American Scholar" (Howells quotes the passage in *Criticism and Fiction*, to justify realism) for the "common," the "familiar," the "low," and his request to be shown the meaning of the simplest, plainest things in life, defined for more than his own generation the attitude of the democratic, New World man of letters. What the corresponding forms might be Emerson had broadly suggested in sentences like the following: "Pictures must not be too pictur-

1. If anything there is a certain dilution and simplification. Few late nineteenth-century American realists shared the complex philosophic concerns of Emerson's generation: the sophisticated anxiety about style as an index to true knowledge; the moral reverence, in the face of religious breakdown, for truthfulness of expression as an end in itself. Henry James is the possible exception—and the degree of James's awareness of the philosophic implications of his fictional method is a matter sharply debated. The question opens down into the very foundations of specifically *American* literary tradition. An introductory chapter organized in another way might well take as its major theme the general indifference of American writers in this later period, compared to those of 1830–1860, to the cognitive aspect of form and style—there is nothing in American literature, for example, like the fundamental critique of "realism" indicated in Meredith's "Prelude" to *The Egoist* and in his *Essay on Comedy*— and it might also look ahead to the reaction against this indifference among our best twentieth-century poets.

esque. Nothing astonishes men so much as common sense and plain dealing. All great actions are simple, and all great pictures are." Whitman above all others sanctified for the younger writers who had opened their ears to him the general program of realism—the rendering of things as they actually appear, and in the language of natural feeling, the familiar dialects of a nation of free men—for he above all suggested that it need not result in any narrowing or compromising of the spiritual imagination: quite the contrary. So for writers as different as Robinson and Ezra Pound, Whitman could become one of the few durable native folk heroes of the new era, and one of the few American forerunners whose work did not have to be rejected out of hand.

The Resistance to Realism

Why then was realism a matter of controversy in the '80s? That it was scarcely needs demonstration. "Victorian" or "Second Empire" or "Gilded Age" hypocrisy is still notorious (and was first made so by the great nineteenth-century rebels against it, Flaubert, Baudelaire, Whitman, Zola, Ibsen, Tolstoy, Meredith, Hardy), but it is difficult now to imagine the hostility aroused in the high-minded by only a small degree of common candor in books. Wrapping up unpleasant facts in a thoroughly "moral" plot did not remove objections. Howells got into trouble for dealing with adultery and divorce in *A Modern Instance* (1882), Mark Twain for using bad grammar and natural morals in *Huckleberry Finn* (1884), Jacob Riis for documenting with actual cases his statement of how the "other half" really lives (1890). Even "Daisy Miller" was refused by the American editor to whom it was first offered. "Let only the truth be told, *and not all the truth*" (emphasis added)—so said Joseph Kirkland, a self-styled devotee of the new realism, in a *Dial* article in

1893. It would be wrong to attribute the resistance to realism entirely to prudes and Philistines. True, the audience for fiction was predominantly middle class and female, and most editors and publishers self-approvingly catered to the assumed tastes of that audience. Yet the double standard of a man like James Russell Lowell, who loved Chaucer and Fielding but doubted that they should continue to be widely circulated in unexpurgated form, was not altogether irrational. Men of worldly tolerance and of principle truly believed that essential standards of social order were giving way before their eyes—and could best be defended by literary censorship. That such men invariably reversed the logic of cause and effect, blaming literary realism for the decline of religion and morality and the instability of social relationships, does not lessen the seriousness of their concern. These views are chronic in modern culture and are held in subtler but nevertheless recognizable form by very discriminating minds. When Thomas Bailey Aldrich, who edited the *Atlantic Monthly* from 1881 to 1890, leveled a verse attack upon realism and "Zolaism," it was in metaphors that a later literary moralist, T. S. Eliot, still found appropriate to his more sophisticated but not dissimilar concerns in the 1920s and 1930s: "For have we not the old gods overthrown/ And set up strangest idols?"[2]

Such views are an expression of fear; and the fear that some book, some unsolicited work of compelling frankness and emotional directness, will contribute to social and moral dis-

2. The lines are in Aldrich's poem, "At the Funeral of a Minor Poet." Of Eliot's *After Strange Gods* (1934) one ought in fairness to say that it marks an extreme point of personal reaction against the tendencies of the age. His later tracts, *The Idea of a Christian Society* and *Notes Toward a Definition of Culture*, are more acutely reasoned. But the grounding of his thought in polite opinion of the '80s and '90s is always worth noting.

order is rooted in the deeper fear that the predicted disaster has already occurred. It is a shock response to some profound actual disturbance in the presumably settled order of things. Both the heavy shroud of middle-class parochialism under which serious literature labored, and the slow, faltering, frustrated rebellion against it which is so largely the social meaning of American literary history between the 1880s and the 1920s, derive from a common source: the constant and mounting disorder of common American life in the years between the Civil War and the First World War. Extraordinary changes, radical transformations, were taking place; the very foundations of life as supposedly established in the New World republic were being put in doubt.[3] It must be left to historians of another kind to describe all these changes —the rise of the industrial city and the mass society; the accelerating material complication and the impersonality of civil life; the cycles of financial and agricultural depression and of labor unrest, coinciding with what was understood by contemporaries as the closing of the frontier and the filling out of the national domain; the continual displacement of population from country to city and suburb and from region to region, East to West or South to North; the steady flooding in of immigrants without experience of the older Anglo-American traditions of culture and polity, their own traditions being wrenched and eroded in the process; the prolonged national advance in wealth and population; the corresponding redistribution of political power and authority; and above all

---

3. A more systematic analysis of the social background of American literature would surely show that disorder and disruptive change have been not merely the special burden of certain critical periods but something closer to the norm of the whole national history. Thus the greater service of certain books which first draw notice for their allegedly sensational treatment of some accidental condition of violence is that they more trenchantly define this persisting norm.

the ruthlessly disruptive incursions of capitalist enterprise, competitive and unrestricted, upon the organism of society and upon the continuities (such as they have ever been in America) of social behavior and expectation. Our concern here is with imaginative literature—and therefore with the contingent sphere of feeling, attitude, sensibility, opinion, sentiment, thought. The anxious human intelligence, seeing its own age as more problematical than any previous age can possibly appear to it, and its future more open to doubt, commonly underrates (though increasingly with good reason) the staying power of fundamental social usage and behavior. Yet around 1890 and after, the rate and degree of historical change did seem unprecedented to an extreme. The result, even for those who could somehow imagine it all as triumphant progress, was a crisis in consciousness and civil commitment that is of the first importance to any understanding of the literature of the period.

The City and Democracy

Different dates were suggested as marking the critical moment of change. To a character in Henry Blake Fuller's *With the Procession* (1895) the year 1876, a year marked by labor riots and agrarian insurgence following the Panic of '73 and, incidentally, by the Philadelphia Centennial Exposition, was the turning point: "the ending of [America's] minority and the assumption of full manhood with all its perplexities and cares." To Henry Adams the coincidence in 1893 of another great Exposition, at Chicago, and another shocking financial panic particularly concentrated impressions of the meaning of the era: of a "breach of continuity," a "rupture of historical sequence." The choice of such dates and moments is usually arbitrary. Nearly any other would serve as well. But what it was impossible for contemporary observers not to agree upon was that the patterns and the extremities of change were most vividly displayed in the crucible of the suddenly overgrown modern city.

"The nineteenth century is a century of cities," declares the temptress Isabel, herself a city woman, in Harold Frederic's upcountry novel, *Seth's Brother's Wife* (1887); "they have given their own twist to the progress of the Age." Metropolitan disorder and violence are the burden of no small percentage of the novels written in the three decades after 1885. Of the passages inspired by the Haymarket Square riot of 1886, Robert Herrick's brief description in *One Woman's Life* (1913) is fairly representative, except perhaps in being satirical in tone: Chicago on the night of the Anarchist bombing is a place of fear and street panic, and the organized counter violence of good citizens, defending order and privilege through management of law courts and newspapers and the hypocrisies of respectable opinion, is rather more shocking than the bombing itself. The signs of the times, above all the heterogeneous massing of men into cities, were such that more than a few writers of the period—decent men and women, charitable, naturally tolerant—had come to doubt representative democracy as a system of government. Xenophobia was a factor in these fears and doubts, which lay deeper than rational assessment and which infected politically radical as well as conservative opinion, the Populist Ignatius Donnelly (see *Caesar's Column*, 1891) as well as Aldrich (who in a poem on immigration entitled "Unguarded Gates" issued his eloquent warning against making America the "cesspool of Europe" in the name of "Liberty, white Goddess").[4]

4. Even Henry James can be shocking on such matters, as when, in *The American Scene* (1907), surrounded in New York by Jews, Italians, Armenians, and who could say what else, he registers the considered opinion that "there is no claim to brotherhood with aliens

Could the older ideals of the American republic, the vision of a new and more equitable order of the ages, continue to flourish under the new conditions? Among all the strange new breeds of voters and office holders and fortune-makers, were the freedom and stability necessary to the common pursuit of virtue and happiness still jointly possible? These questions were hardly new for committed observers of American life, but they were taking on immensely greater urgency in the '80s and '90s, and the weight of literate opinion was on the side of a negative answer. "I think as Mr. Arnold does, and as Mr. Lowell did," Sarah Jewett wrote in her quiet, definite way, in 1884, "that the mistake of our time is in being governed by the ignorant mass of opinion, instead of by thinkers and men who know something." Other writers, more sympathetic to the expansion of social democracy, were more particularly alarmed at the larger, the national, course of its development, the unregenerate barbarity of its opening ventures on the stage of great-power imperialism. The Spanish-American War and the snatching of the Philippines produced something like a solid anti-imperialist front among men of letters. Indeed, the force and eloquence of the attacks upon American policy and what it represented in the life of the nation, launched by Fuller (in verse) in *The New Flag*, by Mark Twain in "To the Person Sitting in Darkness," by William James in his letters to the Boston *Transcript* and

---

in the first grossness of their alienism." James rallies grandly, however; his imagination takes the decisive step—not only into compassion but into simple historical truth—as he asks: "Who and what is an alien, when it comes to that, in a country peopled from the first under the jealous eye of history?—peopled, that is, by migrations at once extremely recent, perfectly traceable and urgently required." James has been accused of lacking sociological awareness, but he saw in the plainest way that you cannot have an unrestrained, undirected business civilization without a correspondingly full dose of its characteristic social maladies.

William Graham Sumner in "The Conquest of the United States by Spain," by the derisive satire of Finley Peter Dunne's "Mr. Dooley" and the noble indignation of William Vaughan Moody's "Ode in Time of Hesitation"—all backed by the energies of outraged idealism—might well lead us to depressing conclusions about the decline of outspokenness and effective dissent in our literary life if we did not also happen to remember that this attack had no noticeable effect on policy and little enough on general opinion.

Material Success, Moral Panic

Among writers, there were doubts and fears most of all about the *quality* of life in the new age.

There was no denying, of course, the material success of the emerging conditions of industrial society or the approval these conditions met with among considerable masses of the population. Among those for whom it represented the chance for a new start, on the newest American frontier, the modern city exerted a magnetic attraction. It seemed a place not of chaos and impending barbarism but, at least at first, of opportunity and renewal, of a richer and freer existence. Like democracy itself, the city could oppress fearfully—but it could also liberate. The consent of the majority to expansion and change is not to be disregarded. The hopes of Dreiser's Gerhardt family, moving into Cleveland, are characteristic:

> If only they could all get work and do right. Here was no evidence of any of their recent troubles, no acquaintances who could suggest by their mere presence the troubles of the past. All was business, all activity. The very turning of the corner seemed to rid one of old times and crimes. It was as if a new world existed in every block.

These hopes, we notice, are built upon a very considerable "if." And in the novel they are only partially, ambiguously,

fulfilled. Dreiser himself, further along in *Jennie Gerhardt*
(1911), expresses in his ponderous, shrewd, detailed way the
darker aspect of modern city life and its crushing pressures
upon individuals. He pleads with us to withhold judgment
against the sinning protagonists of his story:

> We live in an age in which the impact of materialized
> forces is well-nigh irresistible; the spiritual nature is over-
> whelmed by the shock. The tremendous and complicated
> development of our material civilization, the multiplicity and
> variety of our social forms, the depth, sublety, and sophistry
> of our imaginative impressions, gathered, remultiplied, and
> disseminated by such agencies as the railroad, the express
> and the post-office, the telephone, the telegraph, the news-
> paper, and, in short, the whole machinery of social inter-
> course—these elements of existence combine to produce
> what may be termed a kaleidoscopic glitter, a dazzling and
> confusing phantasmagoria of life that wearies and stultifies
> the mental and moral nature. It induces a sort of intellectual
> fatigue through which we see the ranks of the victims of
> insomnia, melancholia, and insanity constantly recruited.

"Take a man who was born in 1860, and who is to die with
the century—what would be *his* idea of life?" The question
is asked in Fuller's *With the Procession*, and the answer given
is a curious one. "Contention, bickering, discontent, chronic
irritation": the indictment expresses not so much any clear
judgment of social disorder as a kind of inward frustration
at its effects upon individual persons, even the most privileged.
Few, apart from a fringe of radical polemicists, had reached
the point of roundly criticizing the fundamental norms and
laws of modern business society,[5] but almost every serious

5. These few, however, had a direct influence upon public opinion.
In the wake of Henry George's *Progress and Poverty* (1879) came the
Single-Tax movement; in the wake of Edward Bellamy's Utopian
romance, *Looking Backward* (1888), the Nationalist Party. Laurence
Gronlund's *The Co-Operative Commonwealth* (1884), which pushed
Howells toward a kind of sentimental socialism, became the bible of a

writer of the period testified in one way or another to a profound and epidemic crisis in private morale. "Why do we go mad? Why do we kill ourselves?" Fuller asked in another Chicago novel, *The Cliff-Dwellers* (1893). "Why is there more insanity and more self-murder to-day than ever before?" His answer is abstract, but it carries something of that authority of historical insight with which in the same year, in a paper entitled "The Significance of the Frontier in American History," Frederick Jackson Turner (speaking, he thought, at the fateful moment of its disappearance) redirected for a whole generation the study of the national past—and coincidentally helped to formulate the folklore of his own time.

> It is because [Fuller continued], under existing conditions, the relief that comes from action is so largely shut off. How has humanity contrived to endure so well the countless ills of countless ages? Because society has been, in general, loose-knit, so that each unit in it has had room for some individual play. What so increases and intensifies the agonies of to-day? The fact that society has a closer and denser texture than ever before; its finespun meshes bind us and strangle us. Indignation ferments without vent; injury awaits with a wearing impatience the slow and formal infliction of a corporate punishment; self-consciousness paralyzes the quick and free action that is the surest and sometimes the only relief.

Life was chaotic and formless but also constricted, oppressive, indifferently hurtful in its thickening complexity. The conditions governing ordinary social conduct—the conditions, generally speaking, of the culture of liberal democracy—were changing, had changed beyond recall; the safety valves

---

private co-operative movement. Henry Demarest Lloyd's *Wealth Against Commonwealth* (1894) set the pattern of Progressivism's subsequent attack on monopoly and legislative corruption. In the next decade, the writings of Daniel DeLeon and Morris Hillquit provided their respective Socialist factions with up-to-date primers for political agitation.

of free land and open yet self-sufficient community were
gone; the long dream of freedom was darkening into night-
mares of imprisonment and strangulation. What have the
prospects of life come to, the middle-aged Carl Linstrum
muses in Willa Cather's *O Pioneers!* (1913), for those who
like himself had gone in search of a wider opportunity out
of the drabness of countryside and village into the richer
culture of cities:

> Freedom so often means that one isn't needed anywhere.
> Here [back "home"] you are an individual, you have a back-
> ground of your own, you would be missed. But off there in
> the cities there are thousands of rolling stones like me. We
> are all alike; we have no ties, we know nobody, we own
> nothing. When one of us dies, they scarcely know where to
> bury him. Our landlady and the delicatessen man are our
> mourners, and we leave nothing behind us but a frock-coat
> and a fiddle, or an easel, or a typewriter, or whatever tool
> we get our living by. All we have ever managed to do is to
> pay our rent, the exorbitant rent that one has to pay for a
> few square feet of space near the heart of things. We have
> no house, no place, no people of our own. We live in the
> streets, in the parks, in the theatres. We sit in restaurants and
> concert halls and look about at the hundreds of our own kind
> and shudder.

To how many Americans would this reckoning apply? (Its
truth, of course, is not literal or statistical but prophetic, a
divination of tendency.) For the rich and those confidently in
pursuit of the new wealth, for those who lived openly according to the "main American formula," as Henry James described it in *The American Scene*, which is "to make so much
money that . . . you don't 'mind' anything"; or, at the other
extreme, for that larger class of persons not yet in possession
of the commonest fruits of opportunity and abundance, with
nowhere to go but up, it would be mainly irrelevant, though
not entirely so. But for the proto-"American" middle classes

—from whose ranks serious writers and their readers alike are almost exclusively recruited—it was very nearly the whole prospective truth. What does the analytic observer see about him, James asked, "if not a vast social order in which the parties to certain relations are all the while marvelously, inscrutably, desperately 'bearing' each other?" What does life amount to for those condemned to live under the "American pressure"—able neither to escape from it nor to surrender to it nor yet to find "a working basis" within it—but a "necessary vicious circle of gross mutual endurance?" Where the "rule of the bank-book" is absolute, who can escape paying?

The Condition-of-America Question

Novelists cannot set to work without becoming moralists, although those who make moral instruction their whole purpose rarely go on being read. The particular ways of human behavior are their enabling subject, and to observe social manners and note down the revealing gestures of personal conduct is to offer them for judgment. Furthermore, simply to put these data into the form of a story, with its establishment and resolution of possible courses of action and its fictive assertion of some serial rhythm of cause and effect, is to be discovered in possession of a definite view of life. Around the behavior of men and women and the assumed prospects of American life, in the fiction of the '80s and '90s, a whole new popular mythology full of moral judgment and insinuation was building up, and its message was not a flattering one.

A representative work of 1894, Howells's *A Traveler from Altruria*, is a case in point. As a critique of fundamental society Howells's contribution to the vogue of Utopian fiction is superficial. At times it appears that the critical issue facing

modern democracy is the servant problem—the setting is a
New England summer resort—and the Altrurian alternatives
of "neighborhood and brotherhood" are dreamlike and wishful in conception. Yet in this book we find the following
views of American life casually and freely set down, as if
beyond argument: that we live now more than ever as two
nations, with the separation of classes, rich and poor, genteel
and common, widening rather than narrowing; that the settled
attitude of those on top toward those beneath is fear and distrust; that only the poor know how to live for one another
in charity and true community; that the manufacture of
shoddy is sound business principle and the random despoiling
of the national estate the plain duty of good providers; that
hypocrisy and cant are the accepted language of social pre-
ferment (one well-heeled vacationer speaks soberly of the
"incivism" of the poor); that ministers of the gospel are as
likely to embrace such hypocrisy as are cynical plutocrats;
that nobody at all, neither rich nor middling nor poor, really
believes in education and liberal culture; that—an interesting
emphasis—above the working classes nobody in America is
really *well* ("you must pity our upper classes, too," the
ingenuous Mrs. Makely explains to the Altrurian); and finally
that nobody thinks anything can be done to change any of
these conditions except "a lot of crazy hayseeds": it is the era
of the Populist Revolt. Honest, generous, sharp eyed if mild
mannered, Howells was from first to last an astute observer
of the characteristic folkways of the middle classes. One of his
insistent topics—"themes" would be too positive a word—is
the coldness of the moneyed and leisured toward people not
of their own kind. Howells himself could see no solution to
the human troubles of his time. But he could not be complacent about what was forcibly brought to his attention, and
he was ashamed of complacency in others. Among all the
motives to realism and plain-speaking near the turn of the

century, democratic compassion and shame or anger at its being withheld have no small place. The sense of a generalized failure in feeling and sympathy, of a very conspiracy of restraint against ordinary human responsiveness: nothing lies closer to the heart of early modern American writing. Only with this in mind can the enormous importance of a figure like Dreiser in the years after 1900 be fully understood.

Howells's observations on this great matter were not new in American writing. They had been made with some frequency before; they are still being made. Perhaps no one has ever felt the paradox of democratic cold-heartedness and the national disgrace of it more keenly than Whitman, who in *Democratic Vistas* (1871) had noted that just in proportion as industrial democracy takes fair pride in the wonderful amelioration of life for the fortunate many, it seems to lose sympathy with the remnant (never so small as the majority chooses to think); it "looks with suspicious, ill-satisfied eye upon the very poor, the ignorant, and on those out of business." Howells by 1894 was hardly less disturbed by the evidences about him, but for all his instinctive personal optimism he was inclined to read them more fatalistically than was Whitman. In the decade of Turner's "Frontier" address and Brooks Adams's *The Law of Civilization and Decay* (1895), even Howells seemed to feel the massive development of industrial civilization not as free and progressive but as determined and catastrophic. Characteristically, the most honest and perceptive spokesman in *Altruria* is also the richest, the banker; and it was into his mouth that Howells put his own visionary analysis of where America now stood in the sweep of history. Formerly, the banker explains,

> if a man got out of work, he turned his hand to something else; if a man failed in business, he started in again from some other direction; as a last resort, in both cases, he went West, preempted a quarter section of public land, and grew up with

the country. Now the country is grown up; the public land is gone; business is full on all sides, and the hand that turned itself to something else has lost its cunning. The struggle for life has changed from a free fight to an encounter of disciplined forces, and the free fighters that are left get ground to pieces between organized labor and organized capital.

A public crisis of confidence concerning America's civil destiny, a private crisis of spirit and moral security for her middling and literate classes: so the writing of the period defines its historical co-ordinates. And if anything was clear to those who faced this double crisis directly, it was that the older attitudes and assumptions about progress, self-help, equal opportunity, manifest destiny, and the imminence of general happiness would no longer serve. At least, they could no longer go unexamined. In fact, where social and literary radical-realists could join forces most wholeheartedly was just in the attack on accepted notions, on the *idées reçues* of the general public consciousness. The very writing of a book was becoming, for the rising generation, a bid for freedom of mind and thought.[6] It is typical of the period that the tragic last section of Ellen Glasgow's first novel, *The Descendant* (1897), written at the outset of her long, decent, unequal struggle in fiction against illusion and barrenness, should begin with an epigraph from Ibsen (one of the master spirits of European realism to whom the younger Americans were learning to appeal):

It is not only what we have inherited from our fathers and mothers that walks in us. It is all sorts of dead ideals and life-

6. Turner's "Frontier" address and, twenty years later, Charles Beard's *An Economic Interpretation of the Constitution of the United States* (1913), shared in this more-than-scholarly motivation. Each seemed to convey a double implication: an indictment of the purblind, illusion-mongering clerkery of the historical profession and also a kind of prescription for the future well-being of American democratic virtue.

less old beliefs. They have no vitality, but they cling to us all the same, and we can't get rid of them. . . . And then we are, one and all, so pitifully afraid of the light.

The passage is clearly equivocal, a call to revolt but also a prediction of failure. But anything less desperate would not have done justice to the conditions of feeling and understanding within which American realism bore its witness between 1884 and 1919. The literature of this period, we may say, is a record of rebelliousness and liberation yet also of despair— at the human cost, and perhaps the ultimate futility, of the effort involved.

"The Way We Live Now"

In politics the response to these evidences of change and disorder made of the quarter-century between 1890 and the First World War a forcing bed of democratic theory and experiment. That response is broadcast throughout the civil history of the period. We find it in agrarian Populism; in the Progressivism of city and statehouse reformers; in the minority "insurgency" within the major parties but also in the slow creation of a stabler party machinery through a system of ward and precinct loyalties embracing the new urban masses; in campaigns, backed by a vigorous exposé journalism, for "good government"; in the establishment of settlement houses and the new realism of social workers; in new philosophies of education and nurture (John Dewey's *The School and Society* was published in 1899); in the opinions of certain distinguished "dissenters" in the judiciary, notably Oliver Wendell Holmes, Jr., and Louis Brandeis; in doctrines of "new democracy" or "new freedom" or "new nationalism"; in journals of opinion like *The New Republic* and *The Masses;* and in redefinitions of the very "spirit of American government" (the title of J. Allen Smith's influential book of 1907) or of the historic "promise of American life" (the title of Herbert Croly's of 1909). The same kind of response to the same conditions is conspicuous in the mass of realistic fiction of the time. As a consequence, most of this work belongs to the history of opinion rather than to the record of creative literature. Novels like Hamlin Garland's *A Spoil of Office* (1892), Paul Leicester Ford's *The Honorable Peter Stirling* (1894), Brand Whitlock's *The Thirteenth District* (1902), David Graham Phillips's *The Plum Tree* (1905) and even his *Susan Lenox: Her Fall and Rise* (1917), Winston Churchill's *Mr. Crewe's Career* (1908), and Ernest Poole's *The Harbor* (1915) have gone the way, to oblivion, of most topical writing and editorializing. Their interest is merely documentary, what they document being, of course, the queer organism of middle-class anxiety rather more than actual social relations.

The distinction such a judgment rests on, between art and document, cannot be drawn hard and fast. In fact the testimony of these topical studies of contemporary life is confirmed by the more scrupulously fashioned novels of the period; by (their very titles, however, suggest their more deeply imagined response) Edith Wharton's *The House of Mirth* (1905) and Henry James's posthumous *The Ivory Tower* (1917). The first concern in either case is the classic concern of the realistic novel: "the way we live now." And the point to make here is that both the novels written as tracts for the times and those fashioned out of the fullest ambition to master the subtler difficulties of the art of fiction and of truthful representation tell, on the face of it, the same melancholy story: of the corruption of public conscience and private spirit by the scarcely questioned values of an anarchically acquisitive society. But perhaps one significant distinction in fundamental argument between these two classes of performance may be offered. Where the competent general run of tracts and romances for the times tends to show how the salient conditions of contemporary life essentially *determine* the lives of individual men, the work whose power to command attention has survived the period of its making is more likely to suggest what it is that, given these inescapable conditions, individual men may still do or be within them. This distinction is not one between philosophical determinists (who were in the majority, up and down the scale of talent, in that era of scientific positivism and Darwinian analogy) and their philosophical opponents. It comes closer to the kind of distinction Henry James made in his preface to *The Spoils of Poynton*, between "fixed fools" and "free spirits"; between real "character," capable of emergence and change, and false, though perhaps materially triumphant, semblances of it. The finer the novelist's art, the more the characters will be seen to give form to their own history. And if any American author was convincingly optimistic and encouraging about the future of American lives, at least to the point of keeping his imagination open to that future's finer possibilities, it was Henry James. There is a nice irony in saying so, considering how much discussion of James's fiction by both disparagers and partisans has assumed his indifference to the larger historical world of his times, or his resignation from it. But to read through the mass of his work, particularly in his extraordinary last decade, is to find him a wonderfully persistent and undiscourageable moralist of human freedom and thus (so Eliot and Pound proclaimed him in 1918) an *American* novelist to the core.

The way we live *now:* there is an attractive concern in the writing of the period to bring its audience up to date, to deliver in fresh and full measure the news of the outlook for individual lives.[7] The most common species of serious fiction

7. The degree to which this purpose renewed the original efforts of Emerson, defining "prospects," and Thoreau, discoursing on "economy," made it more or less inevitable that the good writers of half a

all through these decades is the life history: the novel or story
(or verse narrative, as with Edwin Arlington Robinson) tracing through to its melancholy end the career of some exemplary single figure—a man of affairs corrupted into wrong-
doing; a poor boy or girl of special personal promise overborne
in the struggle to make a decent life; a potentially beautiful
soul, a woman's as often as not, victimized by the narrowness
and rigidity of its choices. In the process, the pieties and institutions of domestic life come off at least as badly as the
larger public ones. We meet egoistic husbands and polluted
ministers as frequently as covetous business men; right and
left the pretensions of individual pillars of society to virtue
and respect are violently put in doubt. Marriage especially, in
one novel after another, gets a bad name: in Fuller's, in Edith
Wharton's, in Robert Herrick's, in Dreiser's and Ellen Glasgow's. At best it is a state to be suffered and endured. Even
where the "unpleasant" social facts of divorce and broken
engagements are admitted into the field of action, the outlook
for those involved is just as bleak (see James's acrid "Julia
Bride" of 1908). Metaphors of shackles and imprisonment, of
cash appraisal and spiritual deprivation, are frequent and insistent for every phase of domestic relations.

The testimony of women concerning life's prospects is
especially severe. The figure of the sunny, freeborn American
girl of the magazine fiction of the '70s and '80s, flattered by
Twain and Howells and still to be apotheosized by Henry
James, no longer seems adequate to the reality of common

century later would have to find their practical models almost anywhere except in these direct spiritual precursors. Precisely as the
spirit of that earlier protestation was still alive and richly pertinent,
the letter of it had to be changed. On the other hand, a history of
American painting or music or architecture around 1900 and after,
particularly as it centered on figures like John Sloan (1871–1951), or
Charles Ives (1874–1956), or Louis Sullivan (1856–1924) and Frank
Lloyd Wright (1869–1959), would show Emerson and Thoreau, and
also Whitman, as acknowledged prophets of the new age.

existence. One of the significant developments in American writing around the turn of the century is the share of serious work, mainly in the novel and short story, contributed by women writers, and their newly articulate and resolutely candid point of view—and the point of view of their heroines: Mrs. Freeman's and Miss Jewett's nuns, widows, and spinsters; Kate Chopin's young matron in *The Awakening* (1899); Edith Wharton's innumerable hostages to social propriety; Gertrude Stein's Anna and Lena in *Three Lives* (1909); or, for that matter, heroines as different as Henry Adams's Esther (1884) and Stephen Crane's Maggie (1893)—offers a powerful and comprehensive indictment of the official creed of equal opportunity and generally diffused happiness in the land of the free. The plight of women speaks pathetically for the plight of all. No claim of progress can contradict it, and certainly no celebration of the beauty of wayside and disregarded virtue, virtue in hiding. A literature of shattered dreams and lost illusions: it is the predictable counterpart of that adventurous coming-of-age which, toward the end of our period, Van Wyck Brooks hopefully defined the times as preparing. And, though in such a literature there is always exhilaration that at last the truth is being told, this exhilaration invariably is overscored by the dreariness and sadness of much of the telling.

Nostalgia and Prophecy

In these circumstances, where could anxious spirits and free imaginations turn for relief? A conspicuous feature of the period is the network of reserve loyalties and counterattachments surrounding, and constraining, the central mode of critical realism. In most of the work so far mentioned, though the world it deals with is increasingly dominated by the industrial city, the older, narrower, simpler America persists as an active presence: the America of camp meeting and backyard neighborhood, of small farming and small shopkeeping, the "more or less handmade habitat" of regional tradition.[8] What this other, older society offers in contrast is a standard that exerts attraction as if in direct ratio to the certainty of its disappearance. From 1884 and earlier to 1919 and well after, there is a continuing and much-publicized "revolt" against the life of village and countryside, but there is also a powerful current of visionary nostalgia running, however ambiguously, in its favor. A way of life that has been willingly sacrificed by those who have come out from it returns insistently to mind in a glow of idealization as the whole grim character of the adopted new order of society reveals itself. A chief element in the crisis of spirit among the literate classes and consequently in all the literature of American realism is a haunting sense of loss, as at some irreversible falling away from a golden time. "Local color" writing especially is suffused with this feeling. Of course much local-color or regional fiction—and there was a remarkable quantity of it in the late nineteenth century—was condescending or satirical, as in the pillorying of upcountry Methodism in Harold Frederic's

8. The phrase is in the foreword by Harry B. Wehle to B. Cowdrey and H. W. Williams, *William Sidney Mount* (New York, 1944), where it is used to make a point about the importance of traditions of handicraft and independent artisanship for the fine arts in the United States during the nineteenth and early twentieth centuries. A number of realist novels point up the coexistence of these two orders of economic life, the artisan-individual and the corporative-monopolistic, drawing a contrast between the older self-made men of wealth and position, honestly successful marketers of some intrinsically superior product or skill, and the newer breed who deal in paper values and executive-suite mergers. Consider Augustus Kane and his sons in *Jennie Gerhardt* or old Brainard and his successors in *The Cliff-Dwellers*. A late novel by Brand Whitlock, *J. Hardin and Son* (1923), is about the defeat of the older merchant-artisan by the rising generation and its systematic production of shoddy. The resemblance to Veblen's categories of producer and profit-taker, engineer (good) and financier (bad), is worth noting.

The Damnation of Theron Ware (1896); or it chose to emphasize the quaintness of its subjects, as even Howells was inclined to do in describing, sympathetically enough, the manners of country people. The point is that good work of this kind is rarely single in attitude. And it is just in the most acutely observed and unidealized local-color writing that this sense of loss is strongest: in Jewett's *The Country of the Pointed Firs* (1898), in Masters' *Spoon River Anthology* (1915), in Sherwood Anderson's *Winesburg, Ohio* (1919). The harsh actualities of the vanishing older order are freely admitted, but the counterforce of an inexhaustible nostalgia holds this recognition in balance. Criticism, celebration, and lamentation go side by side. If there is a single formal genre that is native and peculiar to the American imagination in literature, it is perhaps the circumstantial elegy (even Owen Wister's wild West, in *The Virginian* of 1902, is treated elegiacally), the detailed narrative lament for a disappearing, though perhaps only recently and precariously established, order of life.

In much of this work the lament rises to a ritual intensity, as if the spirit's gravest concern and uttermost destiny were in question. This we may take, historically, as another vivid symptom of that irrepressible evangelicalism which lies at the heart of the older structure of American consciousness. Realism, we find, is not at all inconsistent with vision and prophecy. Even business novels, city novels, novels of sociological demonstration were likely to define their subjects in the language of scripture and gospel. Certain titles of the period are representative: Boyesen's *The Mammon of Unrighteousness* (1891) and *The Golden Calf* (1892), Robert Grant's *Unleavened Bread* (1900), Mrs. Freeman's *The Portion of Labor* (1901), William Allen White's *A Certain Rich Man* (1909). The same rhetoric was commonplace in movements of political reform—"crusades" they are usually called in the United States. (John Jay Chapman accurately defined

American socialism, around 1900, as "a religious reaction going on in an age which thinks in terms of money.") Even the marginal countertradition of religious unbelief relied upon this durable language. The raised evangelical voice that has never ceased to ring out across the American scene, lamenting, exhorting, prophesying, has had no more influential continuator than Colonel Robert Ingersoll (1833–1899), the "great agnostic," who personified the fight for intellectual freedom for a whole generation of dissident spirits.

Alternatives, Escapes

The deeper the sentiment of rebellion and innovation, the greater the need for traditional ways of expression: that appears to be a relevant formula for the mind's reaction to disturbance and change. At the end of the nineteenth century, the countermovements in an increasingly commercial and materialistic culture still tended to the formation of quasi-religious cults and sects. There was the cult of Bohemianism, and the accessory cults of the far away or long ago, the esoteric, the theosophic and occulto-cabalistic, all features of the '90s in particular. There was the cult of aestheticism—"art for art's sake" being art specifically not for the competition of the popular market. There was the aesthetic religiosity of incense, stained glass, music, and ritual (the instruments, among others, of poor Theron Ware's apostasy); Henry Adams wickedly labeled it the "religious Bohemianism" of "bric-a-brac and sermons."[9] There was, in another direction, the cult of "vagabondia," popularized in the poems of Richard

9. The phrase occurs in his novel *Esther* (1884), before he had begun to feel seriously, through its arts and the commitment of various friends, the fuller and deeper attraction of the Catholic Middle Ages. Aesthetic religiosity and spiritualism were nowhere more intense around the turn of the century than among the "Gallo-Roman" expatriate colonies in Rome and Florence, ancient tempting grounds of many a demobilized Puritan conscience.

Hovey and the Canadian Bliss Carman and exploited by Jack London, and the even heartier cult of the "strenuous life," endorsed between 1901 and 1909 by the White House itself. And there were the many, untraceable, homemade cults of fashionable decadents like Edgar Saltus (1855–1921) or of inspired autodidacts like Ignatius Donnelly (1831–1901) and General Homer Lea (1876–1912)—devoted to promoting the "philosophy of disenchantment" or to demonstrating cryptographically that Bacon wrote Shakespeare or to proving that the long "day of the Saxon" was at an end—all of whom operated according to the grand American tradition that every man should be his own prophet and lawgiver and if possible his neighbor's as well.

In the fiction of the day there was also (not surprisingly) a vigorous reaction against realism or at least a blurring of its fundamental loyalty to democratic unaffectedness and plain-speaking. The years around 1900 saw a profitable revival of "romantic" costume melodrama—a commodity which in fact had hardly been displaced by the vogue of realism. A skillful manufacturer of such merchandise like the best-selling F. Marion Crawford (1854–1909) could make a fortune producing it through the '80s and '90s. The champions of realism were annoyed, however, not so much by the huge sales of these books as by the evidence thus offered of the obduracy of public, and publishing-house, taste. The place of best sellers in literary history is a tricky problem. In any modern period, a certain large class of books can be found, bearing some resemblance to serious work, which nevertheless are "so disconnected"—the description is Henry James's—"from almost any consideration with which an artistic product is at any point concerned, any effect of presentation, any prescription of form, composition, proportion, taste, art," as to be fundamentally undiscussable, yet which evidently are pitched to the prevailing taste of the literate classes, and which, moreover, *are* somehow representative of the time's main bearings.

It may possibly come about that in the very long run scholarship will find more interest and value in such books—even in *Janice Meredith* (1899), in *The Little Shepherd of Kingdom Come* (1902), in *The Winning of Barbara Worth* (1911)—than is conceivable in our nearer view, just as we would look kindly now on popular trash that happened to be contemporary with Shakespeare, or with Vergil and Homer if we could find it: the further back the better. A more important point to raise, however, is that serious writers of the time were tempted by this revival of costume romance; Sarah Jewett's *The Tory Lover* (1901), Edith Wharton's *The Valley of Decision* (1902), Gertrude Atherton's *The Conqueror* (1902), and Stephen Crane's *The O'Ruddy* (1903) are all products of it.

Also, by 1900 the fashion of realism had itself settled into grooves of popular formula. The kind of writer who in an earlier day would have imitated Scott or G. P. R. James could now safely follow after Howells or Stephen Crane. Like any fresh impulse in the arts, realism could be made into a commodity and sold on the great public as unabashedly as Graustark or the old plantation. There was costume romance; there was also costume realism; and a competent market craftsman like Booth Tarkington saw no reason not to begin his Pulitzer Prize-winning novel, *The Magnificent Ambersons* (1918), with a twenty-page table of articles of middle-class consumption and ostentation from a period carefully chosen to coincide with the childhoods of middle-aged readers.[10] A little reluctantly one must include the gifted O. Henry in this category of pseudorealists. In the first half or two-thirds of more than a few of his stories he can still strike us as a

10. In his first success, *The Gentleman from Indiana* (1899), Tarkington made a somewhat more forthright attempt to deal with the prevailing conditions of actual society and mounted a blunt, though perfectly conventional, attack on political corruption at the county level.

skillful and observant fabulist of the way life commonly goes, particularly the lives of ordinary men and women in a mass society, only to throw away our interest with a trick ending that does not so much falsify the dramatic situation as simply abandon it.

New Subjects, New Opportunities

But for the more deeply ambitious writer, the man (or woman) who might want to do something more than make a saleable job of it, the need to take greater risks, to make some bolder strike for expressive freedom, remained and intensified. So also did the sense of a unique opportunity. As realism in these years represents a critical response to the era's multiplying social confusions, so it also involves the capturing of a whole new set of literary subjects and occasions that were being criminally neglected by the complacent professionalism of the day. A heady confidence in the opportunities for individual writers and artists is not a bit less characteristic of the years between 1884 and 1919—the "confident years," Van Wyck Brooks could reasonably call them—than disgust with most of their actual developments or pessimism about their prevailing drift.

The new subjects were chiefly those presented by the new order, or disorder, of society and by the toll it exacted from men and women caught up in it. For every kind of fictional realism—moral realism, psychological realism, social and circumstantial realism—there was material and to spare. Let some of it be noted. In general society, the drastic discipline of the modern economic process and the striving for success at the expense of more humane loyalties. In private life, the strain on personal conduct and personal relationships and all the extraordinary new manifestations of social mobility: freedom of career- and fortune-making, sexual freedom, divorce and breach of contract, chronic waste of capacities,

chronic frustration of powers, spiritual liberation indistin-
guishable from spiritual unemployment. And in personal consciousness, there was worse yet: the fear of an increasingly
uncertain future, the sense of injustice in worldly rewards and
punishments, and the morality-shattering intimations (backed
by popularized nineteenth-century philosophies of evolution
and determinism) as to the probable working out of life's
natural appetites and laws.

The problem for writers was to find the forms for exploiting these disturbing opportunities and not to be paralyzed by
them. The general standard of realism was clearer in suggesting what traditional forms would *not* serve than in indicating what new ones might. Also, the same broad impulses
that were making descriptive realists out of most aspiring
novelists and story-tellers had coincidentally produced a
formidable rival to imaginative literature itself in the enterprising, fact-devouring, image-squandering newspaper journalism of the day. (There is a parallel in the challenge to
painting posed by the emergence of photography.) It is
possible, in fact, to decide that, between the run of competent
realistic novelists and the run of good free-lance journalists
around 1900, the work of the latter is the more satisfactory.
Surer of the possible usefulness of their writing, the better
interpretive reporters—Jacob Riis and Lincoln Steffens,
Herbert Croly and, later, Walter Lippmann—were, if anything, imaginatively freer to follow their inquiry where it
led. They might at first approach the phenomena of city life
and business civilization with the usual high-minded assumptions about right and wrong, fair and foul; they remained to
continue the study as objectively as any social scientist. They
learned to write about the actual machinery of modern
society with the sympathetic enthusiasm of field anthropolo-
gists (another new breed of realistic observer more resource-
fully imaginative than most old-style men of letters).

Such writers were perhaps the first to see the new order of common life from the point of view of its "new men," its managers and agents, as well as of its victims; from the point of view, that is, of those for whom the culture of the modern city was all challenge, excitement, and opportunity. Following this course, not a few journalists, including some of the best-known "muckrakers," eventually became outright propagandists for the system of great capital wealth and concentrated business power. The more reflective, like Steffens, Croly, and Lippmann, broke through to discoveries and interpretations that contributed substantially to that inner reform of Progressive political thought which brought it forward into the nationalizing era of the New Deal and the Second World War. That is a story for political historians; the point here is that the novelists who addressed themselves to the same lively materials—Phillips, Herrick, Churchill, and, among younger men, Upton Sinclair and Ernest Poole—tended for all their show of disturbing new facts and impressions to remain mired in melodrama and sentiment and in increasingly irrelevant prejudices as to what at any moment might best be done. It is characteristic of their kind of rebelliousness to wander off into schemes for mind-cure (Herrick) or perhaps total abstinence (Sinclair) and pitch their reformer's standard there. The result is that they remain interesting now chiefly for the poignant insights they offer into the persistent frustrations and fantasies of cultivated middle-class feeling. In the historical drama of their times they figure as victims rather than as interpreters and prophets. But they do thus freshly remind us that the victimization of ordinary insulated men of principle and right feeling is a prime element in the historical transformations of our difficult century.

For the ambitious American writer, let it be said again, there was no "question of the opportunities"—to borrow the title of the first of Henry James's "American Letters" of 1898.

What he was doing with these opportunities or could ever learn to do was another matter. One glaring case of a great unexploited subject, James pointed out, was the American business tycoon. Here was a figure "whom the novelist and the dramatist have scarce yet seriously touched" (James did not rate his own early romance, *The American*, very high in this respect); and we may use James's example here as a lesson for literary history, an indication of what turns art may have to take to get its peculiar kind of hold on the conspicuous features of actual life and common knowledge. The American business man of the grander sort, James went on, would make a splendid subject, in both his public and his private life:

> an obscure, but not less often an epic, hero, seamed all over with the wounds of the market and the dangers of the field, launched into action and passion by the immensity and complexity of the general struggle, a boundless ferocity of battle —driven above all by the extraordinary, the unique relation in which he for the most part stands to the life of his lawful, his immitigable womankind, the wives and daughters who float, who splash on the surface and ride the waves, his terrific link with civilization, his social substitutes and representatives, while, like a diver for shipwrecked treasures, he gasps in the depths and breathes through an air-tube.

Clearly there is insight and point of view enough in this breathtaking prospectus for a dozen good novels. Yet it must be asked: who *did*, in the next twenty years, grasp the type of the man of great affairs in anything like the manner James outlines? Herrick, in novels like his *Memoirs of an American Citizen* (1905), tried as hard as anyone, but the combination he worked by of journalistic detail and soap-opera plotting was not equal to the task. Dreiser made a bolder attempt in his Cowperwood trilogy, of which the first two volumes, *The Financier* and *The Titan*, came out in 1912 and 1914; yet in comparison with his moving chronicles of the insulted and injured of modern city life, with *Jennie Gerhardt* above all, there is a fundamental implausibility about these books, which

surrender too much to private fantasies of power and afflu-
ence. Perhaps Thorstein Veblen, mixing analysis and caricature, came nearer to succeeding than any novelist, particularly
in the highly novelistic matter of the businessman's "terrific
link with civilization" through those vultures of conspicuous
consumption, his womenfolk, whose strange habits of life are
so persuasively defined in *The Theory of the Leisure Class*
(1899). Veblen saw as deeply into the character of contemporary life as any writer of his time and, with his ironic
tableaux of business civilization and the moral types who
flourish in it, broke much of the ground later occupied by
social fabulists like Sinclair Lewis and John Dos Passos, Fitzgerald and Nathanael West.

No writer, however, communicated the paradoxical sense
of the businessman as epic hero more picturesquely than
Henry James himself, through Adam Verver of *The Golden
Bowl*—but it has become a commonplace of critical opinion
that James failed to imagine this character in the round and
with regard to the plain gross data of getting and spending
which (so the insistent metaphor of ownership reminds us)
remain the shaping principle of his being. In this respect the
characters in the unfinished *Ivory Tower* are more solidly
built up. But perhaps the job of "doing" the American businessman was impossible. The breed itself was "unreal," unimaginable, precisely not rooted in the common humane life
of feeling and behavior upon which the notations of fiction
depend.[11] Perhaps only outright fantasy could capture so
fantastic a social phenomenon—and it may well be that the
most fully achieved image of the business tycoon in American

11. Dreiser himself advanced the view that the American financier
was not a human being at all but a kind of animal force or, more
precisely, "a highly specialized machine for the accomplishment of
some end which Nature has in view" but which is unimaginable to
men: see "The American Financier," *Hey Rub-a-Dub-Dub: A Book
of the Mystery and Wonder and Terror of Life* (1919).

literature (the one best fitting the wonderful wildness of James's metaphors) is the looming ghost figure at the climax of "The Jolly Corner" (1909), who has no women and, except in the fearful masquerade of his evening dress, no link to civilization at all but is a pure demon of hallucination.

The Prestige of Intellect: Pragmatism, Experiment, Science

If "The Jolly Corner" is thus, among other things, a brilliantly inventive response to a particular challenge from contemporary life, the very expertness that brings it off, merging ghost story with social and psychological fable, makes it a thoroughly characteristic production of the "confident years." So in a sense was the whole of James's remarkable later career. His increasingly freehanded and original exploitation of the opportunities of his craft became, for young men like Pound and Eliot after 1910, a critical rallying point, a demonstration that an English-speaking writer could indeed take full and heroic part in the great modernist renaissance of art and thought. It was in technique, experiment, new work addressed and original performance carried through, more than in any particular set of themes and arguments, that the creative confidence of these years most typically expressed itself.

A factor as nebulous yet fundamental as intellectual morale, even in a relatively brief period, is difficult to discuss with precision.[12] But what seems more and more to distinguish the larger scene of literature and thought around the turn of the

12. In civil life, some positive estimate of its effective energy is possible, in terms of particular laws, policies, debates, issues, and reforms. The general confidence of the years preceding the First World War as to the efficacy of "progressive" political action is a matter of record. So, too, is the excessively prolonged reaction against this active optimism, a reaction that is still painfully working itself out.

century is precisely its broad confidence in the efficacy of the mind's effort—the imaginative, formal effort of writers and artists; the systematic, principled effort of political theorists, social engineers, community educators and planners; the exploratory and synthesizing effort of scholars and scientists. Various effects of this confidence can be listed: the founding of new universities and the systematizing of new intellectual disciplines like sociology and anthropology; the multiplication of professional societies and scholarly journals; the forwarding of such great collective enterprises as *The Cambridge Modern History* and *A New English Dictionary*, among which, in the United States, the *Encyclopedia of Social Reform* (1897; revised 1908), edited by W. D. P. Bliss, deserves mention. But perhaps a better way, in a volume of literary history, is simply to recall some of the works of disciplined inquiry and scholarship published during this era—Holmes's *The Common Law* (1881), Professor Child's *English and Scottish Popular Ballads* (1883–1898), Woodrow Wilson's *Congressional Government* (1885), Henry Charles Lea's *A History of the Inquisition in the Middle Ages* (1888), William James's *The Principles of Psychology* (1890), Henry Adams's *A History of the United States During the Administrations of Thomas Jefferson and James Madison* (1889–1891), Captain Mahan's *The Influence of Sea Power Upon History, 1660–1783* (1890), Berenson's *Italian Painters of the Renaissance* (1894–1907), Brooks Adams's *The Law of Civilization and Decay* (1895), Josiah Royce's *The World and the Individual* (1900–1901), Edward Eggleston's *The Transit of Civilization* (1901), Santayana's *The Life of Reason* (1905–1906), William Graham Sumner's *Folkways* (1907), H. O. Taylor's *The Medieval Mind* (1911), Breasted's *The Development of Religion and Thought in Ancient Egypt* (1912), Ernest Fenollosa's *Epochs of Chinese and Japanese Art* (1912), Veblen's *The Instinct of Workmanship and the*

State of the Industrial Arts (1914), H. L. Mencken's *The American Language* (1919)—and ask whether a comparable list can be drawn up for any other era in American letters.

It seems impossible now, so little do we share the broad faith in applied intellect embodied in these works, to over-rate its generative power and stimulus. Beside it the *fin-de-siècle* vogue of cosmic pessimism appears shallow and theatrical. Always, with particular works, we need to look beneath theme and stated attitude (though not ignoring them) and observe the governing method, the imaginative sweep, the play of executive intelligence, the reasoned authority of the design. The composed argument may turn out bleak and despairing in its conclusions, yet it may involve the most invigorating display of intellectual mastery. The literature of neo-Darwinist determinism is typical. Fears that the system of evolution must deny mankind any real freedom to act or power to control are widely expressed; they represent one of the deeply characteristic positions of argument in the writing of the period. Yet nothing opposes such fears so forcibly as the vivid impression created in one book after another of the human mind's power to thread its way through labyrinths of data, not omitting the formidable evidences of its own bondage to irreversible laws of nature, and come to ordered and usable conclusions. In every case a distinction has to be made between the burden of the findings and the temper and energy of the inquiry.

The philosophy that, in the United States, most nearly expresses this manifold confidence in the creative mind's sufficient capacity is pragmatism, in particular the open-minded, affirmative pragmatism associated with the thought, and voice, of William James. Has innovation in philosophy ever quite so directly given aid and comfort to innovation in the arts, and with less inclination to dominate and dogmatize? All students of the *anni mirabiles*, for the arts, of the earlier twentieth century are bound to discover at some point the enabling presence of two underlying attitudes, in close conjunction: on the one hand that free, opportunistic outlook on all contingencies of life and thought which is at the heart of pragmatism and, on the other, a corresponding appetite for technical experiment and invention, an undaunted readiness to line out new work and then get it done. This alliance deserves fuller investigation than is possible here. Certain results, however, seem clear enough. The rough pragmatic test of truth, accepting operative performance as a sufficient verification, served as a morally inspiring warranty that truths did exist and could be established and acted upon—and that the evident pluralism and inconsistency of particular truths and of particular forms of truth ought only to delight the healthy-minded, the true bearers of civilization. Against the continuing erosion of traditional culture and belief, pragmatism could give men of letters a new courage, as well (for it was first of all a critique of knowledge) as a surer basis in reason. The pragmatic intelligence looked doubt in the eye and glared it down, in calculated offense. It asserted against the specter of intellectual paralysis a "will to believe" embodied in the whole nature of man; against the observed chaos of the phenomenal world a countervailing appetite for the sheer vital abundance and variety of experience. So, in an essay that Whitehead later singled out as a turning point in philosophy comparable (as a symptom if not as an influence) to Descartes' *Discourse on Method*, we find William James ungrudgingly demonstrating that no such entity as human "consciousness" really "exists"—and then proceeding to make the flooding succession of particular conscious events, and the tracing of that succession, as heroically preoccupying to the reflective intelligence as any Promethean or Faustean myth of human power.

A further point. Whatever the exact terms of their conjunction, it is clear that pragmatism in philosophy and free experiment in the arts were both beneficiaries of the enormous contemporary prestige of science. This prestige was never higher than around the turn of the century. For many humanists and men of letters, of course, all science appeared to pose a wholly unprecedented threat—to the arts, to the habit of faith, to civilization itself. Even among persons not irretrievably committed to received doctrines of religion or, equally, to the doctrinaire attack upon religion—persons for whom the widely publicized "warfare" between science and theology (solemnly recorded in President White's bulky *History* of 1896) was largely a sham—the scientific intellect and the humanist-poetic imagination were thought to be deeply opposed: rivals for the mind's allegiance, dark and light angels of humankind's conceivable destiny. But that view (renewed in our day in the bugbear of "the two cultures") is plainly sentimental, and the writers and artists who knew their own minds had little sympathy with it. Industrial, technological, bureaucratic complication was another matter, of course, and took a heavy toll in waste and demoralization with every new incursion upon the received fabric of life. But scientific inquiry—what could it be but profoundly inspiring to creative minds? In its technical excitements, its discipline, its extravagant success, it had become the great contemporary example of that disturbing faith long known to mystics and poets (and renewed in the emergence of European symbolism): that the world belongs to those who find the right words or formulas for it, who learn to speak most purely and efficiently its intricate secret language.

Freedom

For writers with the wit or nerve not to be intimidated, the astonishing advances of scientific inquiry served as both model and moral support. The intrinsic realism of the scientific concern with nature shored up the cause of realism in the arts. Equally important, the sciences provided, with regard to form and workmanship, operative analogies of great authority. Certain minimal standards of performance in literature and the arts became easier to enforce: precision, thoroughness, economy of statement, elegance (in the mathematician's sense) of formulation, mastery of technique, conceptual seriousness and point. Coincidentally the old and clouded Romantic commandments to originality and sincerity were redefined and restored to use—an enterprise central to the opening critical efforts of Eliot and Pound, for all their distaste for "Romanticism." Pound's critical injunctions, of purest 1910–1912 vintage, are typical. "Consider the way of the scientists," he advised the poets of his time, "rather than the way of an advertising agent for a new soap. The scientist does not expect to be acclaimed as a great scientist until he has *discovered* something. He begins by learning what has been discovered already. He goes from that point onward." A first corollary of this for the writer was the command to apprentice himself as if without any mental reservation whatsoever —so much for merely *personal* sincerity—to the long technical tradition of his craft: that is the chastening implication of Eliot's influential essay, "Tradition and the Individual Talent" (1917). A rather different corollary, expressing more directly the practical confidence of the time, was the stimulating notion that *no* achievement could be proved impossible to a mind that had liberated itself from ignorance and prejudice and taken command of its proper tools; that no authority living or dead could say what might *not* be "discovered" if an effort, any effort, was properly made. Pound's schoolmasterish edict that poems should be at least as well written as good prose was meant to clear the way for a deeper ambition: that the craft of poetry become once again at least as intelligent, as freely exploratory, as capable of interior discipline, and thus in its way as greatly influential, as the craft of science.

A pragmatist *à outrance*, Pound became a major critical

force in the decade after 1910 by playing to the hilt a classic
role in Anglo-American letters: the role of the revolutionary
moralist-adventurer recodifying fundamental law (upon a
new gathering of precedents) and redefining the history of
that law's descent and present continuance. By an assertive
and yet critically tactful personal effort Pound arbitrarily
dragooned most of the best new work of his time into the
cause of modernism and coincidentally manufactured a tradition—"platform" would be nearer the mark—for it to campaign upon. His principled quirkiness, broadcast in letters,
pamphlets, manifestoes, and editorial sorties, makes his whole
career fascinating as a rendezvous of historical symptoms. In
all this effort his essential Americanness is hardly to be questioned. Pretending, as Whitman had seemed to, to dismiss all
the past as wholly outmoded, irrelevant to one's present duty,
is not greatly different from pretending to swallow that past
whole by means of an efficient selection of exemplary instances. It may be taken as a tribute to the integrity of Pound's
lifework that the reason and logic of its various undertakings
so persistently mirror the reason and logic of so many familiar
positions and attitudes of the American consciousness. "Life
is action, the use of one's powers. As to use them to their
height is our joy and duty, so it is the one end that justifies
itself"—if we put forward this well-known affirmation of
Justice Holmes's, with its matter-of-fact verbal heroics and
also its considerable moral ambiguity, to represent the spirit
in which the durable work of 1884–1919 got accomplished,
we must grant that it expresses fairly directly Ezra Pound's
infectious passion for the making, and "justifying," of works
of art. Who else, we may ask, reveals so distinctly in the
pattern of his "life and contacts" the lines of development
that in Anglo-American letters join the '80s and '90s to 1912,
and 1912 to the ebullition of the 1920s?

Characteristically, it is Pound himself—writing in *The*

Little Review about Henry James—who, at the very end of our period, gives us a clue to perhaps its deepest and most persistent common motive. (There is a lesson in this, the cogency of the insight of one master of his art into the work of another, for the writing of literary history in general: that beyond anything else it is accomplished art that makes for representativeness and that only the very best work and very best workmen of any period can be relied on for accurate insight into its historical meaning.) "What I have not heard," Pound complained, "is any word of the major James"—and, ignoring arguments about the opaqueness of the master's later style, he proceeded to say who this major James really was:

> the hater of tyranny; book after early book against oppression, against all the sordid petty personal crushing oppression, the domination of modern life; not worked out in the diagrams of Greek tragedy, not labelled "epos" or "Aeschylus." The outbursts in *The Tragic Muse*, the whole of *The Turn of the Screw*, human liberty, personal liberty, the rights of the individual against all sorts of intangible bondage.[13]

Criticism of James, and in general American criticism of modern literature, has not notably followed this remarkable lead. Yet Pound's striking judgment has a ring of fresh and rather heroic truth about it. Such authority as it carries is drawn in no small part from the moment of its formulation. The second decade of the twentieth century had human liberation on the brain, and the unnerving crisis of the First World War gave a hysterical edge to that fixation, the etiology of which involves, at the least, the whole span of history surveyed in this volume. Touch and go from the start, the long struggle which American realism most consistently bears witness to was, at its core, a struggle for free-

13. The passage is characteristic of Pound: a valuable general perception sharpened by intense moral commitment but worked out through an oddly inconvenient selection of examples.

dom of mind and development against whatever might stand
in the way. And the evident fact by 1920 was that this struggle
was hardly closer to resolution than it had been in 1880. The
indictment of the whole drift or slide of modern civilization
implicit in Pound's early work and elaborated in Veblen's
and Randolph Bourne's contains little not specifically anticipated by Henry George and others in the '80s or, for that
matter, by *Democratic Vistas* in 1871 (and by Carlyle and
Ruskin in England). There is only a geometrical accumula-
tion of new ills to take account of—the First World War
being, of course, a particular disaster—and a corresponding
intensification of shame and outrage.

It can seem most impressive now, this intellectual struggle
for freedom, where the residual confidence it rises from is
shadowed if not wholly put in check by an apprehension of
what may most deeply oppose it—the apprehension recorded
in the air of fatality surrounding Edith Wharton's or Theodore Dreiser's best characters, for example, or in the much-
publicized "imagination of disaster" claimed by Henry James.
By contrast, the progressive hopefulness characteristic of the
period often seems shallow and brittle, and the literature
directly expressing it lacks weight. The very slant of Pound's
terms for defining what was "major" in James's achievement
—terms denoting only resistance and opposition and a wholly
individualistic conception of "liberty"—is open to obvious
objection and may suggest where this common imaginative
effort of American realism fell short. Let it succeed, let human
liberation come: what then? Then must follow that deeper
and (because endless) more savagely taxing struggle which,
it may be argued, all the remarkable historical privilege and
immunity framing the long American settlement for its
favored members had been postponing for generation upon
generation (the generation of the Civil War partially ex-
cepted)—the struggle not *for* freedom but *with* freedom;

the struggle to find a decent and manageable footing for human life and work (including the work of art) within the mass secular society and ungoverned technological order of modern times.

But it would be misleading to end this survey of tendencies on a note solely of reproof and alarm. The actual creativity of the period in view deserves full credit. If the realist impulse in American literature, following its chief motives, came to a kind of dead end morally, it got there only after an impressive forward progress. The literary life in the United States around 1880 was more soddenly parochial and unambitious than it had been for half a century; and the actual broadening of taste and practice during the next forty years, the breaking down of arbitrary and irrelevant barriers to honest work, the increasing intelligence of critical judgment, the deepening capacity to express actual feeling, the renewed openness (as in the 1830s and 1840s) to Europe and the major intellectual currents of the times are all beyond dispute. By 1919, in fact, the traditionally dependent relation of American to English and European letters was on the point once again of becoming more than a little reciprocal. What the best American writers would accomplish now was no longer interesting merely as an index to the precise degree of American provinciality; in the work of Eliot and Pound, O'Neill and Dos Passos, Faulkner, Fitzgerald, and Hemingway—the inheritors of "realism"— modern American letters began, so to speak, to make regular payments on its immense foreign debt.

There are no tendencies worth anything but to see the actual or the imaginative, which is just as visible, and to paint it.

—Henry James, "Deerfield Letter"

2. NOVELS AND NOVELISTS: THE ERA OF HOWELLS AND JAMES

$\mathcal{I}$N AMERICAN literature, the 1880s and 1890s are a watershed of particular distinctness. Longfellow and Emerson died in 1882, Emily Dickinson in 1886, Lowell, Melville, and Bancroft in 1891, Whitman and Whittier in 1892, Parkman in 1893, the elder Holmes in 1894—poets, essayists, monologuists, journal-keepers, narrative historians. The impression of a historical division is heightened by the fact that the leading younger figures of the early '80s were all novelists: Howells, Twain, Cable, Henry James, even (in disguise) Henry Adams. That earlier generation had of course produced its masters in prose fiction. But the work of Poe, Hawthorne, and Melville, though separated by a mere two or three decades from the new era, somehow seems more remote than that. Reading James's critical study of Hawthorne and his milieu (1879), we seem to be listening to a contemporary, a mind of our own time whose interests are coextensive with our own, reimagining rather distant history.

The history of modern literature involves much more than the history of the novel. But the novel itself is a distinctly modern form. Its modernness is especially evident in the impression it gives, formally, of freedom, of opportunism, of indefiniteness. Perhaps this impression is the secret of its continuing hold on modern letters. Operating between the poles of gossip and documentary truth—and remaining in fashion more by its refusal to cut away from the first than by any slavish commitment to the second, it remains the "great form," as James declared, for "a direct impression of life." It is the medium best suited to satisfying our infinite curiosity (increasingly on short rations in the dehumanizing circumstance of modern society) about one another's essential lives and, of course, about the prospects for our own.

William Dean Howells (1837–1920)

Howells in the mid-'80s was in the full stride of his long and productive career. He had resigned the editorship of the *Atlantic* in 1881, and he continued throughout the decade to cut his ties, so far as he wished to, with what seemed to him most restrictive in the old Brahmin tradition of polite letters. The promise of his trenchant study of middle-class manners in *A Modern Instance* (1881) seemed expertly fulfilled in the widely popular *The Rise of Silas Lapham* (1885). In 1886 he began writing for *Harper's* the series of critical essays that, collected in the volume *Criticism and Fiction* (1891), were to constitute a defense of the kind of realism he preferred in the novel, a realism that treats of life according to "the measure we all know."

For several years more, Howells's output was extraordinary. He was publishing (after serialization) at least one substantial novel a year and at least one volume of travel sketches, reminiscence, or criticism; he wrote a long string of farces that were great favorites with amateur theater companies; he worked away as an editor and publishing-house associate, speaking out on public issues, sympathetically encouraging a whole new generation of American writers, supporting the right of talents as different as Lafcadio Hearn's and Hamlin Garland's to write as they pleased and calling the attention of the public he now commanded to one after another of the contemporary European masters of realism, in a way that could not fail to be deprovincializing in American letters. Of Howells as a novelist, judgment seems bound to remain divided. For many it is impossible now to read him without feeling the force of Henry James's remarks in a letter of 1884: you are "in the right path," James wrote; you are already "the great American naturalist"; but, "I don't think you go far enough, and you are haunted with romantic phantoms and a tendency to factitious glosses." But about Howells's essentially liberating services to American letters in the '80s and '90s there is much less ground for doubt. In the view of H. H. Boyesen he bestrode the field, defiant of "public opinion" and the timidity of editors. It would be unfair not to remember that in 1885 he was being attacked as an immoralist. *A Modern Instance*, in treating divorce, commercial venality, and scandal-sheet journalism, had been widely criticized as sordid and disgusting. Howells's realism, so the old-guard critic Hamilton Wright Mabie wrote in a review of *Silas Lapham*, was nothing less than "practical atheism applied to art," profaning the temple of the arts and the proper understanding of life with the destructive methodology of "materialism."[1]

Attacks of this sort made no real dent in the popularity of *Silas Lapham* with the novel-consuming public. The genuinely attractive qualities of Howells's fiction were seldom so well displayed: the plentiful succession of lifelike scenes playing off one set of social manners against another, the humor and easy irony of exposition, the tolerant rendering of the commoner sorts of human weakness, the genuine interest in the material circumstance of everyday life, the completeness of the world described. What can be said in Howells's favor has not been said better than by Rudyard Kipling, who spoke admiringly of the "large undoctored view," in *Silas Lapham*, "into lives which did not concern or refer themselves for judgment to any foreign canon or comparison, but moved in their own proper national orbit, beneath their own skies and among their own surroundings." That self-sufficiency was the instrument of its own acceptance. "Subjected to the severest test,—that of every word being spoken aloud,—the truthful and faithful fabric of his presentments," Kipling continued, "showed neither flaw nor adulteration, pretence nor preciosity, and the immense amount of observation and thought that had gone evenly into its texture shot and irradiated, without overloading, each strand of the design."

The Rise of Silas Lapham shows Howells at the top of his bent. Yet it is as likely as any book he wrote to suggest

1. "A Typical Novel," *Andover Review*, November, 1885. Historically, the interesting thing about Mabie's critical argument, a literate and reasoned polemic based solidly on the classical position that the function of serious literature is to present an ideal world occupied by ideal figures of conduct, is that it stands very near Henry James's fundamental critique of Howells's work as insufficiently imaginative. Mabie, however, carelessly lumps James and Howells together as practitioners of one and the same fictional method.

doubts and reservations about his stature as a novelist. The main scheme is clear and serviceable: the worldly rise of a decent, self-made, conventionally self-esteeming businessman by means (hard work aside) of the kind of ambiguous business transaction that the "world" looks upon with favor so long as it succeeds and its perpetrator is not himself embarrassed by it; the moral rise of the same man as he later accepts bankruptcy rather than save himself by another such transaction, the thought of which has come to be an intolerable burden on his developing conscience. It promises the pleasures of that morally serious social comedy which is the classic field of the English novel. And it may be precisely because so much is promised that the execution disappoints. The trouble is not that the various layers of the narrative are not perfectly fused: the affectionate satire on ordinary social climbing, the ethical dilemmas, the element of romantic farce with its misapprehensions of sentiment and apparent reversals of fortune. The trouble is rather with what the characters are permitted to do, what is imagined for them, as participants in the story. In a word they act "small"—smaller than the moral truths the story supposedly endorses; smaller even, in feeling, than what is required by the romantic subplot of young love and its silly-sweet trials. And what Howells has done is what in all his novel-writing he was never able to keep from doing; he has dodged off the potential dramatic life of his chronicle by refusing to allow his characters to respond adequately to its developed pressures. In fact, the winning and undoubtedly "realistic" personal weaknesses he attributes to these characters become his own means of escape as well as theirs. Invariably, in Howells's fiction, those who have been dealt with unjustly as individuals sooner or later behave badly as persons—an arrangement that somehow absolves everyone concerned from any necessity of intervening in the interests of justice. It is a way of proving over and over again that things always come out pretty much as they should, whatever we feel and do about them. And it is this compromising of his own apparent themes that is at the heart of the case against Howells, who never wrote a novel that does not somewhere, usually at its climaxes, suggest the core of truth in Ambrose Bierce's angry diatribe against his "smug personality and his factory of little wooden men and women on wheels."

The same radical fault undercuts the otherwise charming *Indian Summer* (1886). This romance, set in the American colony in Florence, is full of the kind of mellow domestic comedy of which Howells was so nearly a master. Though the situation—a man passing forty, who should know better, falls in love with a glowing girl scarcely twenty, who is attracted to him because of the story of an unhappy love affair in his youth—is perilously near the stuff of soap opera, we go along with it, and Howells's usual skill at scene-building keeps us happy until, once more, at the very end, the novelist dodges out of the net of all that is serious and touching in his story with a piece of vulgar wisdom. Mature human feeling, it is shown, always *does*, in such cases, settle into the groove of sensible self-interest; the right marriage *will* be made, with the always available older woman whom the hero really loved all along and whose own self-approving scruples vanish on cue. Besides, the girl was stupid and insensitive anyway. The objection is not that nobody has been hurt by what has happened; it is rather that nobody appears even touched by it.

A similar kind of moral rigging flaws *Annie Kilburn* (1888), the first of Howells's novels to take as its main subject the contemporary "social question." The basic datum of this novel is that the minister who challenges his parish to apply true Christian charity to the problems of an inequitable society is too eccentric and unpolished to compel respectable citizens to choose for or against him. (His chief supporter is the town alcoholic.) It is as if the authority of moral principles depended on the propriety of their adherents. To clinch things, Howells kills off the minister in a railroad accident—a final proof of his unsuitability. Gratuitous accident also resolves *The Shadow of a Dream* (1890), a psychological thriller of considerable intensity that draws upon Howells's lifelong interest in visionary phenomena; again the device enables him to end the book without having to finish it. In a curious novel about the race problem and miscegenation, *An Imperative Duty* (1892), going off to Europe serves the same purpose; in the Ibsenesque design of *The Son of Royal Langbrith* (1904), it is death by typhoid. Even on the impressive canvas of his New York novel, *A Hazard of New Fortunes* (1890), this abuse of serious structure finally undermines all the rich observation of middling city life. The strike at the novel's climax is introduced without warning; twenty pages later it is all over—but not before it has served the purpose of killing off precisely those two characters (the intransigent old Socialist and the rebellious son of the business tycoon) who are beyond accommodation in the tidying-up at the end. We are not in the least prepared for this pivotal event, despite several hundred preliminary pages dealing with everyday life in the modern industrial metropolis. *A Hazard*, and indeed all the work of this fertile period in Howells's career, suffers in what finally is the most damaging way—with respect to our taking its themes and actions quite seriously—from the tendency that Henry James warned him against in 1886, his appearing "increasingly to hold composition too cheap."

Howells freely admitted his difficulties with endings and with composition in general. A passage in his *Imaginary Interviews* (1910) recalls those days in his life "which were mainly filled for him with the business of writing fiction, and when the climax of his story seemed always threatening to hide itself from him or to elude his grasp." But this difficulty, he thought, was in the nature of his materials. It proved the integrity of his commitment to realism. So he might have justified his handling of the strike in *A Hazard of New Fortunes:* such an event would in fact have erupted upon his middle-class characters as if from a wholly alien world, and their unpreparedness for it would precisely exemplify their probable relation to it in life. If the novelist is to write true social history, he must respect real probabilities. There was, of course, a basic confusion at this point in Howells's critical thinking. The essential soundness of the campaign for realism, the fussy irrelevance of most of the opposition to it, kept him from ever quite breaking through to the realization that art, whatever its materials and occasions, is first and always a making of forms and that its clinching relation to reality is not simply a matter of accuracy in particular details. The fault of Howells's realism is that it is an arithmetical realism. In the crisis, it refers us merely to the flat average of behavior and consequence. In getting at the truth of the life of the man-in-the-street (a great aim for a democratic writer), it mistakenly adopts the man-in-the-street's way of seeing—which is "like memory," so André Malraux has remarked, "at once synthetic and incoherent." In brief, Howells conceived of the novel as a segment of actuality extracted from life, a segment that ought to re-produce life's ordinary inconsequence and disconnectedness; whereas it is in fact a form imposed upon life, or upon our sense of life, a segment not of actuality but of erected con-sciousness.

As they apply to his own work, Howells's theories of fiction have the air of rationalizing inconvenient habits. It is worth remembering how he came to the writing of novels: not by way of story-telling, as did both Mark Twain and Henry James, but by way of books like *Venetian Life* (1866) and *Suburban Sketches* (1871). As a novelist he remained essentially a descriptive writer, expert at every phase of the art of fiction except the primary one of composing and sustaining a coherent action.[2] He saw what was in front of him, what presented itself to his leveling glance, but it was not in his nature to look deeper or to see matters through to an end. From first to last his travel sketches are efficient and readable, and his several books of reminiscence, notably the charming *A Boy's Town* (1890), *Literary Friends and Acquaintances* (1900), and *Years of My Youth* (1916), contain some of his most agreeable work. But as early as 1871 Henry James had recognized the truth about Howells— "He seems to have resolved himself, however, [into] one who can write solely of what his fleshly eyes have seen"—in which respect he never really changed, though his experience of life widened a little.

The consequence can be seen very clearly in his plays. He was a skillful writer of dialogue and of stage directions (Bernard Shaw found this work genuinely refreshing, given the general state of English drama at the time). But not of whole plays, not of rounded dramatic actions: Howells's comedies and farces read pleasantly but positively resist performance. It was not only that he fatally believed, as he wrote in *Criticism and Fiction*, that character is more important than plot. He simply did not accept what is at the very basis of the art of narrative fiction, of story, of drama—the truth that participation in *actions* is the form of our existence as

2. See Richard Chase, *The American Novel and Its Tradition*, p. 177: "His stories are full of unbridged gaps, and he is seldom able to give that indispensable impression . . . of a coherent action that includes and relates all the elements of the fiction."

beings and that every action does in some measure transform its leading agents: they will never again be exactly as they were. Howells's characters give an appearance of acting; they fall in love, marry, take jobs, lose jobs, get into trouble, get out of it; but their experience passes over them, they are not alive to their own histories. And this, we may say, is the lie about life, the denial of life, that in book after book cancels out all Howells's exceptional talent for realistic observation. The generous form of the novel can, of course, tolerate a great deal of such falsification, which is fundamental to the art of caricature. Dickens is the master of it in English and a proof of its centrality to a robust art of fiction, but Dickens never extends it to *all* his characters; the key figures at the center of his great chronicles are always subject to the full pathos of change and consequence.

It never seemed to occur to Howells that good temper, a sharp eye, and a candid tongue were not sufficient equipment in a writer of novels. The impressive virtues of his kind of realism are in the end negative and accessory virtues. It is not that we want him to come out resolutely for some positive solution to his characters' problems. We only want him to follow through as a novelist, to accept the responsibility of connecting one thing to the next. "Moral complicity": that was Howells's favorite theory (announced first in *The Minister's Charge*, of 1887); but all it seems to have meant to him was that since nobody is *un*involved in what goes wrong, there is consequently no ground for any one person's assuming responsibility, no individual reason to feel guilt. It is a way, really, of condescending to his characters—which was indeed Howells's habitual attitude as a novelist—and it amounts to a denial of actual human nature that all his genuine kindliness and egalitarianism cannot retract. Even his criticism of modern society, though rising from a decent indignation at its characteristic wrongs, too often comes down to a kind of nagging about cases of rudeness and incivility.[3]

All this concerns Howells the writer of novels; it would not be a fair account of Howells the man, and man of letters. He never did lose the democratic tolerance of the Ohio towns of the 1840s and 1850s—though we know how easily that cast of mind could pass over into the envy and cynical distrust of populism. He liked to say, "I don't believe in heroes," a remark in keeping with his rather assertive "anti-Romanticism," but he did revere Lincoln, Grant, Tolstoy; and despite a lifetime's opportunity to be both envious and condescending, he revered his friend Mark Twain—which is one reason why his memoir, *My Mark Twain* (1910), is as good a book, as adequate to its subject, as any he ever wrote. And he never lost the generous vision of the good society, the better life, that came to him out of the

3. There is a noticeable trick of style that accompanies these flaws in attitude and shares in their unpleasantness, a trick that can make Howells painful to read for very long at a stretch. For narrative exposition he loved the long sentence-unit divided into short, rapid, declarative statements parallel in syntax (to give an effect of rhythmic advance) and joined by semicolons (so that one is invited to hurry through it). By this means the component parts of what is being presented—the motives, reasons, feelings of the actors—are run through in quick succession, after which the dialogue can begin again. The effect of this style is to suggest that no one motive or reason or feeling is more or less important than several others and that, therefore, the observer is released from the responsibility of discriminating. Any component in the general pattern for which a short clause in a long series of short clauses is not definition enough appears to make Howells impatient.

Another disagreeable mannerism is a kind of petty facetiousness in describing the particulars of human conduct. It must be noted, however, that most of Howells's contemporaries found his humor charming and just.

Swedenborgianism and Utopianism of his childhood—his family had in the 1840s briefly joined a co-operative community, as described in *New Leaf Mills* (1913)—even though in his later years he could not disentangle the remnants of this vision from his everyday satisfaction with polite society and the best company. In a letter of 1903 he exclaims, "How charming and interesting people are! I wish I could live a thousand years, and see more and more of them," and we find ourselves believing him; we remember, too, how he struck Theodore Dreiser, who had no great reason to flatter him, as a thoroughly decent and honest man.

Year after year, well into the new century, his books, his observation of the life of his times, continued. When a social or moral problem caught his attention, he put it into a novel, so that, in the twenty-odd works of fiction he published after 1890, we have a virtual encyclopedia of the problems and anxieties of the day: the problem of class relations in a democracy, the problem of labor, the problem of business dishonesty, the problem of conservation, the servant problem, the problem of amateur theatricals, the problem of well-brought-up girls who have not married by thirty, the problem of charity, the problem of justice, the problem of alcoholism, the tramp problem, the race problem, the problem of the social responsibility of artists or of ministers, the Ibsenesque problem of egotism and the unconscious selfishness of idealists, and again and again the peculiarly, touchingly American problem of how to surround oneself with "the right sort of people"—and what then to do about the wrong sort—without actually giving offense or sinning against the common democratic good. Inevitably younger writers, and readers, turned away from him. His late years were shadowed by the sense of having been passed by; and several attempts to start Howells revivals have not yet proved that James's assurance in 1912, that his "really beautiful time" of high critical favor was still to come, was more than a birthday compliment. It is characteristic of Howells, however, that he kept in his chosen track right to the end and in the last year of his life brought out one of his pleasantest novels, *The Vacation of the Kelwyns* (1920), in which the fundamentally comic problems of the middle-class social conscience form the screen upon which a touching nostalgia for an earlier, simpler America— the novel is subtitled "An Idyll of the Middle Eighteen-Seventies"—shines out undimmed.

Mark Twain (*1835–1910*)

In his memorial tribute to Mark Twain, Howells wrote, "[he] was sole, incomparable, the Lincoln of our literature." That judgment, translating its subject out of the realm of literary criticism into the mysteries of mythmaking and national idolatry, is a tribute to Howells's critical discernment. With Mark Twain the fundamental questions—what kind of writer the man was, and where and what are his works—remain open and unanswered. This is true even in the case of *Huckleberry Finn;* surely no other American classic has so perfectly resisted coherent critical analysis. A part of Twain's unique service to American letters is the affront his work continues to offer to schooled understanding —an affront registered as sharply in the uneasy rationalizations of recent comment as in the notorious condescension of cultivated opinion during his lifetime.

To admit the real peculiarity of Mark Twain's work is at least a first step. We think of the writer (even the popular writer like Bunyan) as a maker; we imagine him probing after his subjects, defining them in imagination, carrying through a more or less rounded account of them, according to his developing conception, by means of some kind of organizing design. With Twain, however, another analogy is needed.

We sense that we are in the presence of a great bravura actor; except in a few singular instances, what he does is really incidental to how he conducts himself in doing it. Most of the time we take him more seriously than the work he puts before us. His art, in a word, is the art of the performer. It is nearly always inseparable from the presence of Mark Twain himself, projected directly or through a more or less sustained impersonation, and it creates, through its repeated flourishes of performative skill, a special kind of indulgence. The expectation that some such flourish will be there for us on the next page never quite leaves us in reading him. There is always the chance—and the fantasy of exploiting it was perhaps Twain's most durable working motive—that the occasion will produce yet one more sovereign *tour de force* or *coup de main;* that it will lead again (the words are in *Pudd'nhead Wilson*) to "some crowning act, now, to climax it, something unusual, something startling, something to concentrate . . . the company's loftiest admiration, something in the nature of an electric surprise." "The most consummate public performer I ever saw," was Howells's verdict.

The paradox, to literary history, is that for all his apparent indifference to the model of dedicated craftsmanship presented by his greatest native contemporary, Henry James, Mark Twain brought to his career in letters an incomparable technical training. By 1875–1876, when he was publishing "Old Times on the Mississippi" and beginning *Huckleberry Finn*, he had served a twenty-year apprenticeship in his craft; he was as thoroughly professional a workman as any American author of the day. It was, of course, a special sort of apprenticeship and in a special sort of performing tradition: essentially a popular tradition, journalistic and theatrical, developing in newspapers and sporting magazines and on the popular stage. The art it fostered was an art of putting something across, holding an audience's attention for the space of a few columns or a couple of hours. It was not in any sense an art of inquiry, interrogation, definition, discovery—which is why it is reasonable to think that Twain's great influence on subsequent American writing has been in the main a technical and not an imaginative influence.

Like Poe before him, who also had come into literature through professional journalism, Twain conceived of the writer's work as pre-eminently a manipulation of responses, a staging of irresistible effects. The result in both cases is an art that in many of its most serious undertakings is self-defeatingly mechanical. Absorbed in the machinery of performance, it does not know how to break its fundamental dependence on stereotype and pastiche. Yet this absorption is also, now and then, the means to an effect that compels us to rank both men among the few original masters of our literature—and that effect is a certain trance-like directness and integrity of enacted vision that comes upon us with the force of unarguable revelation. The significant gestures of such an art have indeed a visionary authority. So, in the great case of *Huckleberry Finn*, the secret logic of dream, wish, and fear—the mysteriously unifying logic that so confounds attempts to apply a moral calculus to either its structure or its narrative argument—is released with hallucinatory purity and power, although that logic is in a sense as much "outside" the author's practical consciousness as are the comic stereotypes he relies on for incident and seeks only to make more efficient. All this is why with both Edgar Poe and Mark Twain criticism has been inclined to turn quickly to psychoanalysis; nothing else seems likely to penetrate their baffling artistry. But it is also why psychoanalytical explanations tend to be adequate only to their third-rate and fourth-rate performances, their artistic failures. The mystery remains: how every so often the work of each of these powerfully disturbed spirits passes out of the mechanically sensational or self-expressive into a visionary truth and beauty, releasing and concentrating rather than obstructing and diffusing the free flow of objective perception.

In *Life on the Mississippi* (1882) and *The Adventures of Huckleberry Finn* (1884) Mark Twain had plumbed as deeply as he ever would the double setting that had given him, in his youth, his imaginative measure of the life and ways of men—that setting of river and village which was at once the ambiguous Arcadia of his childhood and the first proving ground of his coming-of-age, and whose literate culture (such as it was) gave him the language and the forms from which his work is constructed. These two were in fact the last of his books to be built primarily around his own remembered experience. Howells had remarked in a *Century* essay of 1882 that in one form or another Mark Twain "has told the story of his life in his books." For the succession of titles from *The Innocents Abroad* (1869) through *Huckleberry Finn* that judgment is only slightly inaccurate, but after 1884 it no longer applies.[4] We have the sense at this point of a shift of direction, a turning and readjustment. In Mark Twain's career *Huckleberry Finn* is a climax and also a terminus. Thereafter, potboilers aside, personal recollection gives way to other forms—romances, fables, tracts, each written to substantiate some predetermined theme. The maker of images mostly retires behind the pronouncer of opinions; the public figure, whose every word and action are immediately broadcast to the nation, usurps the artist. (The parallel to the career of an artist-performer like Charlie Chaplin is worth noting.) The shift is relative, of course. From first to last in Twain's writing there is a marked con-

4. Mark Twain's "autobiography," which he worked at throughout his later years, never reached the final stages of composition. Its various editions represent the selections and arrangements of successive editors.

tinuity of attitude and impression. Certainly the harsh, excited, distrustful picture of the common world and of common human behavior that Mark Twain offers never radically changes. What does change, as Twain passes fifty, is the manner of presentation, above all the degree of the author's own imaginative involvement in work in which we are increasingly conscious of a fundamental evasiveness and substitution in the actual development of the indicated themes.

For several years after *Huckleberry Finn*, Mark Twain published only magazine sketches.[5] He was as full as ever of larger schemes and projects—books, sequels to books, parodies of books—but was too occupied with other business to carry them past the first outpouring of his enthusiasm. In his thickening involvement with business ventures—lecture tours, the fantastic Paige typesetter, the marketing (successfully) of *Huckleberry Finn* by advance subscription, the great project of Grant's memoirs, the disastrous one of Pope Leo XIII's biography—and in his wholehearted absorption in the role of international social lion, he seems less a man of letters than a whole corporation; he becomes a figure out of one of his own Gilded Age extravaganzas. He is the first in a still lengthening succession of American writers whose careers seem to pass altogether out of the sphere of literature into that of salesmanship and publicity.

One ambitious work, begun in 1885–1886, that he did finish was *A Connecticut Yankee in King Arthur's Court*

5. The most notable, prompted by his involvement in publishing General Grant's memoirs, is "The Private History of a Campaign That Failed," in which an amusing self-deflation in remembering his own brief and unheroic part in the Civil War leads to certain grittier emphases—"themes" would claim too much for them. There is the shock, when a man is killed, of discovering that war is not only bushwhacking but also bloodshed and fratricide; and there is also more than a touch of that populist derision of great reputations and noble attitudes that was never far out of sight in Mark Twain's comedy.

(1889). It was the first and most accomplished of a series of books, all of rich promise, all finally disappointing, that Mark Twain published over the next seven years and that assessments of his later career as a writer must come to terms with as they can; the others are *The American Claimant* (1892), *Tom Sawyer Abroad* (1894), *The Tragedy of Pudd'nhead Wilson* (1894), *Personal Recollections of Joan of Arc* (1896), and *Tom Sawyer, Detective* (1896).[6] Howells immediately took *A Connecticut Yankee* to be Mark Twain's masterpiece to date. It is the book, he said, in which "our arch-humorist imparts more of his personal quality than in anything else he has done"—by which Howells meant his passion for justice as well as his caracoling humor; "there is a force of right feeling and clear thinking in it that never got into fun before, except in *The Biglow Papers*." Characteristically, the book first took form in Twain's mind as a rather mechanical farce of contrasts such as would follow from putting a creature of settled nineteenth-century habit back into what was assumed to be sixth-century civilization. "Dream of being knight-errant in armor in the Middle Ages," a notebook entry reads. "No pockets in the armor. No way to manage certain requirements of nature. Can't scratch. Cold in the head and can't blow. Can't get a handkerchief. . . ." and so forth. Characteristically, too, the book, as it went along, began to gather up a quantity of more serious motives and themes, above all an irritable concern to defend the civilization of industrial democracy against highbrow disapproval. The focus of this concern was Matthew Arnold's criticism of democratic leveling and the general lack of distinction and reverence in American life (*Discourses in America*, 1885) and particularly certain equivocal remarks in Arnold's *Civilization in the United States* (1888) about the prose style of Grant's *Memoirs*.

6. Dates are of book publication. The second, third, and fourth were also serialized, in *St. Nicholas*, the *Century*, and *Harper's* respectively.

Arnold's views epitomized that continuing condescension among enlightened foreigners which was as galling to Twain as it has always been to Americans in general. Not that he disagreed with such criticism. He had said worse things himself and would continue to say them. It was rather that this criticism, coming from Europeans, seemed to him in bad faith; certainly the American way of life could be faulted but not half so easily as the old hierarchical orders of systematized injustice and impoverishment from which it had broken away. As a contribution to the long post-Civil War debate over the prospects of democracy, *A Connecticut Yankee* has the potential advantage (which it shares with *Democratic Vistas*) of presenting a richly drawn double view of the matter. It ridicules the cult of medieval feudalism, as endorsed by books like *Ivanhoe* and Carlyle's *Past and Present*, but it also keeps a certain distance from the point of view of its hero, the parody figure of Hank Morgan, the Yankee foreman: "a perfect ignoramus," as Twain himself described him. The book exults, like any eulogy of modern progress, in the thoroughgoing supersession of a bad old past, yet in the relentless holocaust of its closing pages it projects the darkest of premonitions about where exactly the present age must eventually lead. Utopia and apocalypse finally merge in Twain's deeply equivocal imagination. The title of Hank Morgan's manuscript, we note, is "The Tale of the Lost Land," and alongside the sacred democratic rage against despotic oppression runs a dreamlike current of nostalgia and elegiac regret, equally powerful. In Mark Twain's later work it is still this current, the great force behind "Old Times" and *Huckleberry Finn*, that produces the most touching effects.

A Connecticut Yankee is full, energetic, inventive, brilliantly executed. But in terms of its further aims, it must be called a failure. The narrative intention flies all over the place.

The book takes a stand, at intervals, against a score of disagreeable matters—bigotry, clerical dogma, flunkeyism, vested authority, the *Idylls of the King*, the awful German language, Jay Gould, social bores and second-hand story-tellers, charlatanism, art (or rather gushing art-lovers), cant of any kind, hypocrisy, slavery of mind or body, meanness of spirit, cruelty and thoughtlessness—all of which are reasonable antagonisms; most of them are still doing service in the satirical realism of the present day. The miscellaneousness of the list suggests what goes wrong, however. The book becomes a catchall for what was on Mark Twain's mind while he was writing it. At the same time, his ignorance or indifference concerning the full nature of the things that irritate him makes it impossible for him to develop a serious imaginative critique of them, even through the free indirections of fantasy. There is, as always with Twain, a continual return of pleasure in the vivid clarity of particular scenes and incidents and in the racy, pungent, economical prose style. But the book as a whole will not seriously follow up its own best openings. The standing joke of the "practical Connecticut man" set down among Tennysonized Arthurians, with the matter of Britain presented in the language of a Hartford petty bourgeois, is always there to fall back on, and though its incongruities are as suitable to major irony as to mechanical farce, the farce is what Twain gets carried away by—as if, in a parallel instance, the account of Gulliver's voyages to Brobdingnag and Lilliput *were* only a matter of big men and little men.[7]

7. Even so, it is always possible to see method in Twain's fooling. Hank Morgan's point of view opens the door to an element of economic realism that makes his creator's Arthuriad truer in its way to the probabilities of actual human history than was Tennyson's, or the decorative version for children that Howard Pyle (1853–1911) began to produce in 1903. In this respect it may call to mind the economic interpretations of medieval history advanced soon after by Brooks Adams for his brilliant *Law of Civilization and Decay* (1895).

The American Claimant, based on a play Twain and Howells had written ten years before, is a slighter affair. The need to offset financial losses was what mainly compelled Twain to carry it through, and the result is one of his most slapdash performances. This is a pity—for the scheme of the book is a better one, potentially, for the purpose of "answering" Matthew Arnold than is that of *A Connecticut Yankee*. (Twain's originality never ceases to be remarkable; the mere outlining of these unfinished projects is worth the finished labors of all but a few of his American contemporaries.) Alongside the frenzied comedy of Colonel Mulberry Sellers, a character brought down from *The Gilded Age*, and his discovery that he is rightful Earl of Rossmore, there is the figure of young Lord Berkeley, with the "fresh air of freedom in his nostrils," casting title and prerogatives to the winds and starting at the bottom in order to climb the ladder of New World opportunity by his own virtuous effort. Of course he cannot find honest work, of course he discovers an instinctive servility and conformism among the free American masses; but the chance for a satire on the illusion of democratic freedom is wasted as the narrative bogs down in elaborate corpse-and-ashes jokes and in a long farce sequence about materializing dead spirits, which the objections of every actor and manager who had read the original play could not persuade Mark Twain to give up. Colonel Sellers himself is in top form, however, "sodden with grief and booming with glad excitement—working both these emotions successfully, sometimes separately, sometimes together." "Feel my pulse," he says, to show the coolness with which he goes out to make a fortune, "plunk—plunk—plunk—same as if I were asleep." If only for the Colonel's great speech in praise of the spirit of the new age, *The American Claimant* deserves to be kept in print:

Ah, well [he meditates], we live in wonderful times. The elements are crowded *full* of beneficent forces—always *have* been—and ours is the first generation to turn them to account and make them work for us. Why, Hawkins, *everything* is useful—*nothing* ought to be wasted. Now look at sewer-gas, for instance. Sewer-gas has always been wasted heretofore; nobody tried to save up sewer-gas—you can't name me a man. Ain't that so? You know perfectly well it's so—

and he rattles on to describe his latest money-making invention, the "decomposer." The fact that the temper of this speech begins, at least, very near to that of the progress-exalting letter that was Twain's contribution to the celebration of Whitman's seventieth birthday, in 1889, only increases our sense that *The American Claimant* is a piece of work into which Twain could have put the full duplicity of his heart and mind if he had felt like making the effort.[8]

The two published Tom-Huck sequels of this period are also manifest potboilers. Twain himself thought well of them, and *Tom Sawyer Abroad* in particular has had its defenders, notably Bernard DeVoto. Style, however—Huck narrates both—gives them away. The debasing mimicry of the style of *Huckleberry Finn* only Mark Twain himself could have invented. Indeed, to come upon a paragraph like the following, in *Tom Sawyer Abroad*, is more than disheartening. It forces us to ask again exactly how much of the creative breakthrough in *Huckleberry Finn* can in fact be ascribed, as it has come to be in recent Twain criticism, to the narrative idiom of the book and the creation of a so-called "vernacular hero":

Then we laid into it. It was mighty hot work, and tough; so hot we had to move up into cooler weather [they are empty-

8. Is it possible to decide whether Twain's eulogium, in his Whitman letter, on the triumphant modern age is in earnest, on the model of Whitman's own modernist exuberance, or a deadpan burlesque of that model?

ing sand out of the balloon's basket and have tricked Nigger
Jim into doing an unfair share of the work] or we couldn't
'a' stood it. Me and Tom took turn about, and one worked
while t'other rested, but there warn't nobody to spell poor
old Jim, and he made all that part of Africa damp, he sweated
so. We couldn't work good, we was so full of laugh, and
Jim he kept fretting and wanting to know what tickled us
so, and we had to keep making up things to account for it,
and they was pretty poor inventions, but they done well
enough, Jim didn't see through them. At last when we got
done we was 'most dead, but not with work but with laugh-
ing. By and by Jim was 'most dead, too, but it was with
work; then we took turns and spelled him, and he was as
thankful as he could be, and would set on the gunnel and
swab the sweat, and heave and pant, and say how good we
was to a poor old nigger, and he wouldn't ever forgit us.
He was always the gratefullest nigger I ever see, for any
little thing you done for him. He was only nigger outside;
inside he was as white as you be.

Tom Sawyer, Detective, which wisely returns to the Arkansas
village setting and gives us the interesting figures of the
Dunlaps, Jake, Jubiter, and Brace (prototypes of Faulkner's
Snopeses and Gowries), promises better, but again the chance
is wasted for lack of serious workmanship.

The novel *Pudd'nhead Wilson* is another matter, however
—or it tended to become so after getting disentangled from
the Siamese-twin absurdities of its companion piece, *Those
Extraordinary Twins*. It is Mark Twain's last full-dress examination of the country of his early life. Slavery, miscegenation, and double identity, the sterile pretensions of first families
and the squalor of back-alley life: it can hardly be said that
the matter of the book lacks interest. Nor, obviously, given
these elements, is the changeling mechanism of its lurid plot
inappropriate. "*Pudd'nhead Wilson* should be recognized,"

F. R. Leavis has written, "as a classic of the use of popular modes—of the sensational and the melodramatic—for the purposes of significant art." That judgment is half right but flattering to an excess, though one may regret not being able to share it. "Significant art" is precisely what the book is not. Twain's method, as he candidly described it, of "listening [to the story] as it goes along telling itself" was simply inadequate to the job of managing effectively all that he dredged up in the process. Significant statement it undoubtedly is: rich in theme, in emotional suggestion, in social and moral implication, in all the usual complexity of Twain's extraordinarily poised and clairvoyant apprehension of things. But its compositional design is as crude and forced as that of a television western, and—more important—the narration is careless and undeveloped. Is there really any question about this? The profound archetypal symbolism—black and white, guilt and innocence—that has been claimed for this novel lies out in it only as the rhythm of breathing lies out in the vivid waste of natural speech. Such symbolism is intrinsic to language itself, presented with such an occasion; it can well up in the most casual story-telling—and Twain remains a master, nothing less, of language and of anecdote; but in any strict sense it composes, in *Pudd'nhead Wilson*, no clear meaning. It simply has not been coerced into doing so. So, too, the slave mother, Roxy, might indeed have become the great figure of "passion and despair" that Professor Leslie Fiedler finds in her, but Twain will not let her. The job of sustaining a major dramatic characterization put too great a strain on his limited store of artistic patience; it was irresistibly easier to turn aside into minstrel-show comedy turns and blackface jokes about claiming descent from the line of the Smith-Pocohontases. We need only compare Twain's handling of Roxy's part with certain directly contemporary English cases—Hardy's Tess Durbeyfield, George Moore's Esther Waters—to recognize his failure.[9]

If anywhere in this book there is a "tragic dialogue" that "will always haunt our minds," as Richard Chase asserted, it surely concerns not Roxy and the changelings, Thomas à Becket Driscoll (free but "colored") and Valet de Chambers (slave though "white"), but Pudd'nhead himself—though it is hardly "tragic" as presented. But how else can we make sense of the full title: *The Tragedy of Pudd'nhead Wilson?* If there is a truly "haunting" episode, it occurs at the end of the splendid first chapter (the one thoroughly composed chapter in the book), when poor David Wilson, the fortune-seeking American stranger, comes into town and gets his indelible public name from the caucus of village idiots who have been standing around, in the American way, waiting for him to make his move so that they will know how to think about him. It is to this archetypal episode of democratic victimization more specifically than to the melodrama of the main plot that the sardonic ironies of "Pudd'nhead Wilson's Calendar," heading each chapter, typically refer. The episode and its outcome are deeply characteristic. The best part of Mark Twain's work involves his setting before us, with great circumstantial distinctness, one after another representative type-character or fragmentary life history. The stories adumbrated are seldom really *told*, but they are invariably taken from life. What indeed was Mark Twain but a kind of inadvertent Plutarch of the democratic American undercon-

9. For a shrewd contrary opinion see "Lena Horne: An Interview," *Carleton Miscellany*, Winter, 1963: "I have often said that my favorite Clemens story is *Pudd'nhead Wilson*. It's the greatest mystery story in the world, and it was, even for its time, a most satirical scathing kind of pronouncement about our swallowing the camels and gagging at the gnats." The critical point is well taken. To see Mark Twain's later books as "pronouncements" is to see the best in them.

sciousness, a stockpile of fundamental though undifferentiated racial history?

The last in the series of books written as he approached sixty, his *Joan of Arc*, Mark Twain himself (*and* his loyal family, *and* his excellent biographer, Paine) honestly considered his finest work. Of course it is not. Of Twain's Joan, Bernard Shaw remarked, sympathetically enough, that "she makes her creator ridiculous, and yet, being the work of a man of genius, remains a credible human goody goody in spite of her creator's infatuation." "It is the description," Shaw continued, "rather than the valuation that is wrong"—and we notice that Shaw's idea of Saint Joan pays Mark Twain's the special tribute of imitation. Both heroines are given to us as transcendent geniuses whose visions and voices are simply the form in which a great mind's stunningly unarguable intuitions flash upon it. The damaging rightness of the rest of Shaw's comment, however, must be conceded. The Joan Mark Twain's imagination rises to is a figure to whom Washington Hawkins's open-mouthed admiration of Colonel Sellers in *The American Claimant* would exactly apply: "Prodigious conception! I *never* saw such a head for seeing with a lightning glance all the outlying ramifications and possibilities of a central idea." The view is not unrelated to the view of Mary Baker Eddy that develops in *Christian Science* (1907; serialized 1902–1903). What begins there as contempt soon turns to fascination: Twain could not help admiring the genius of anyone who "with a limitless confidence and complacency" offered to clarify in a phrase Biblical texts and theological issues which had confused popes and archbishops for centuries. His conclusion that Mrs. Eddy is "in several ways . . . the most interesting woman that ever lived, and the most extraordinary," does not seem wholly ironical.

To the work of the final decade and a half of Mark Twain's life, critical commentary seems inappropriate. Much of it reminds us simply of his unique status as a national dignitary, whose word was sought on every conceivable subject. Even in a piece like "To the Person Sitting in Darkness" (1901) there is scarcely any reasoned argument, and there does not have to be; the great fact of this decent and beloved man's enormous anger at America's "pacification" of the Filipinos is enough. "What is Mark Twain saying now?" was what people wanted to know—and the pleasure of tracing these late pronouncements is in observing how pungently, with how few professional inhibitions, he continued to have his say.

As for the "Gospel" of determinism and despair in which, no longer the mere entertainer, he would tell mankind the whole pitiful truth about its life and character, demolishing at last the "sweet-smelling sugar-coated lie" that there is such a thing in the world as moral independence or even personal identity, the most that can be said is that the bits and pieces he wrote of it are often stylish and nearly always touching— touching partly because we know that their dark views were being put into words coincidentally with the last nostalgic passages of childhood reminiscence he was dictating for his autobiography—but they are not seriously persuasive. They chiefly refer us to the private sorrows and apprehensions of the writer, the genuineness of which is of course not in question; Twain's personal losses were real and shocking, and he bore them courageously. Even in the best of this later work there is a serious disproportion between the writer's intensity and his actual accomplishment. The simple point of "The Man That Corrupted Hadleyburg" (1899), that all men have their price, is too grossly contrived, and the characters are too cypher-like, to be either impressive or disturbing, though Twain's personal absorption in this point has the rich biographical interest of all the notable gestures of his career. The same is true of *The Mysterious Stranger* (1916), a more ambitious work even more heavily freighted with personal feeling. The version we read (published posthumously, in

Paine's editing) builds through a number of poignant scenes to what is meant to be an overwhelming revelation: that life, and all the superimposed apparatus of God, universe, heaven, and hell, is nothing but a dream, "a grotesque and foolish dream." Well, we say, worse revelations than that can be imagined. Dreams, at least, perfectly hold and satisfy the attention; one is never really bored in dreams; more than that, one is never wholly let down, abandoned, cast loose; dreams have rarely been called a waste of time. In any case what difference would it make—so Emerson, we remember, wrote at the outset of his career—whether life and reality are all a dream, "the relations of the parts and the end of the whole remaining the same?" The spectacle of Mark Twain's last years —all that "intensity of common sense, passionate love of justice, and generous scorn of what is petty and mean" that Howells celebrated in him turning inward upon the specters of private anguish—rightly stirs our compassion, but there is little point in making false claims for the importance of the writings conveying it. They belong, surely, to the tortuous natural history of the American spirit but not to the creative record of American literature.

Bierce, Hearn, Cable, Kate Chopin

Describing the curious amalgam of Mark Twain's humor, with its whiplash expertness of expression and its melancholy and inner rage, Marcus Cunliffe has placed it squarely against the special, half-legendary context of the old-style newspaper office and city desk:

> American newspapermen have long been a special group, the licensed jesters and cynics at the court of public opinion; budding authors, budded authors, blown authors; consumers of late-night coffee, smokers of cigars, singers of ribald songs; lie- and cliché-detectors, disenchanted men; men somewhat detached from the world they watch.

Somewhat detached, yes—but also strictly dependent, as writers, upon the inexplicable mass and persistence of that world. Only in reaction against it do they function at all; they require its repetitive miseries and follies to keep them going. They are in the purest sense "men of the crowd," deeply and ravagingly out of sorts with what, day after day, they see before them, yet spellbound and otherwise voiceless.

It is a memorable type and—given the great number of American writers who from the time of Howells and Twain, and earlier, served their apprenticeship in city rooms, editorial offices, press boxes and press galleries, and in filing feature columns and field reports—a significant one in American letters. Adding to his account of it the elements of personal bitterness and, in style, a strong bias toward "economy and witty phrases," Cunliffe cites Ambrose Bierce and Ring Lardner as characteristic examples. They are well chosen. Since his disappearance in Mexico in 1913, Ambrose Bierce (b. 1842) has maintained a curious kind of underground reputation, less as a maker of books than as a personal legend, a minority saint for the cynical and disenchanted. (A passion for taut, precise, desentimentalizing English is a special part of this legend.) Growing up into the holocaust of the Civil War, in which he served with honor and was badly wounded, he became a writer whose voice and outlook are more impressive than the literary uses he managed to put them to. He survives as a figure of bitter dissent and disaffiliation—from the bluster and prodigality of the Gilded Age, from its daydreams of comfort and success, from all its gross connivance in hypocrisy and untruth. It was as such, a scarifier of his times and an honest measure of their moral shabbiness, that the critic Percival Pollard celebrated Bierce in *Their Day in Court* (1909) as "the one commanding figure in our time."

The very peremptoriness of his naysaying, however, limited Bierce's authority as a satirist and moral critic. Nonetheless his *Fantastic Fables* (1899), sardonically reviewing the rules and conditions for success in contemporary society, do pungently underscore the more formidable critique of the sociology of the leisure classes that Thorstein Veblen published in the same year; Bierce's indictment is less substantial but rather more absolute. His point of view is even more starkly expressed in *The Cynic's Word Book* (1906; reissued as *The Devil's Dictionary*), a book worth keeping in print and commending to the young and their teachers, although by reason of its piecemeal form this collection of "old saws fitted with new teeth" loses bite when read straight through. Bierce's major achievement is rather in his two volumes of stories, *In the Midst of Life* (1891; also issued as *Tales of Soldiers and Civilians*) and *Can Such Things Be?* (1893). Even these stories are perhaps most impressive as emotional gestures. The second title suggests their essential form: a shocked outcry against the horrors and violations of life in what is called peace as well as in war. There is not much invention or variation in these stories. Eventually the ironies they turn upon appear mechanical: the Union soldier on picket who must shoot his Confederate father; another who must carry out orders to bombard his own house, knowing that his wife and child are in it; another who steels his nerves to put out of suffering a mortally hurt comrade whose exposed entrails have been rooted by wild pigs (he fires his pistol only to find that he has used up his bullets and must do the job by sword thrusts); a captured spy who coolly, philosophically, states his contempt for death but panics and runs amok when his execution is advanced a few hours. We begin, in fact, to see that the fidelity of these savage anecdotes is not to the way "things are" in the world but to the shocked and haunted consciousness of the writer himself. Yet the feelings he writes from—outrage, despair, desolation, grim resignation—do him credit. The monstrous thing would be to have written about such subjects without being somewhere overborne by their raw terrors.

Always tightly made, Bierce's stories renew a standard of form set by his master, Poe. Like Poe's they are distinguished by descriptive intensity and a strict economy of means; they are as compact and bare as mathematical equations—which is partly why they are not greatly interesting as stories. Where they are most effective is in indicating the weariness and the barbarism of men in the front lines of war; and, as we sense that for Bierce these front-line conditions are somehow only an intensification of the norm of human life, we must grant that we cannot easily argue him wrong. Perhaps the real terror of his work is in suggesting how naturally men can be brought to give to the anguished question, "Can such things be?" the numbed answer, "Yes, of course."

The vision of life in Bierce's work, though intensely personal, is also very much of its time. It is close to that of the school of "naturalism," which was entering American literature around 1900 with the generation of Norris, Stephen Crane, and Dreiser. Under the assault of the mindless, amoral forces of nature—or of a society equally savage—men are seen as victims and casualties of agencies beyond their control. If they survive, it is by some crippling process of dehumanization. Interestingly, the same general vision of life figures strongly in the best work of Lafcadio Hearn (1850–1904); all the qualities for which he is more usually remembered, the aestheticism, the sensuous feeling for the exotic pleasures of earth, the psychological acumen, are disciplined by it. The resulting tension is one measure of Hearn's superiority to Bierce. The pull of immitigable violence upon all that stirs sensibility: this apprehension directs the vivid scene-painting of the newspaper stories of catastrophe and squalor that Hearn was filing in Cincinnati and New Orleans in the

'70s and early '80s; it fills the legend-haunted canvases of his fine short novels, *Chita* (1889) and *Youma* (1890); and it shapes the argument of the last and most deliberated of the dozen books he wrote about his adopted homeland—*Japan: An Interpretation* (1904)—as he makes plain his sense that the cost of the transformation into a modern industrial order which history and social evolution are forcing upon the Japanese people will be nothing less than the obliteration of most of the strange, self-sufficient beauty he has admired in their way of life and has defended against Western prejudices.

In choice of subject Lafcadio Hearn's bent was always toward the exotic. (It does credit to Howells's critical sense that he saw Hearn's work as also, in its own way, a contribution to realism.) The Irish-Aegean inheritance his name spells out, the homelessness of all his early years, and the personal torment caused by his disfiguring half-blindness combined to make him incurably restless and vulnerable in sensibility and acutely responsive to the existence of certain fluctuating and extreme states of mind. It is his own case he describes at the beginning of the compact sketch, "A Ghost" (1889):

> Perhaps the man who never wanders away from the place of his birth may pass all his life without knowing ghosts; but the nomad is more than likely to make their acquaintance. I refer to the civilized nomad, whose wanderings are not prompted by hope of gain, nor determined by pleasure, but simply controlled by certain necessities of his being,—the man whose inner secret nature is totally at variance with the stable conditions of a society to which he belongs only by accident.

The whole sketch deserves comment in a further respect. As Hearn develops its touching theme—the wanderer's lifelong experience of estrangement and the corresponding sense of becoming haunted more and more by the composite presences of his own scattered past—his language appears to echo directly an influential passage in Poe's "Marginalia," one that had been of special significance to Baudelaire; indeed Hearn's precisely modulated evocations of "those sudden surprises of sensation *within* us, though seemingly not *of* us, which some dreamers have sought to interpret as inherited remembrances —recollections of pre-existence" may be read as an effort to fulfill Poe's ambition to put into words a certain elusive "class of fancies, of exquisite delicacy, which are *not* thoughts" and which "arise in the soul only at its epochs of most intense tranquillity," the recording of which, by the really adventurous stylist, would surely "startle the universal intellect of mankind." There is much of Poe in Lafcadio Hearn: not the machinist of terror that Bierce's tales look back to but that other Poe whose pursuit of the margins and rarities of consciousness made him one of the gods of French symbolism and so of "modern" literature in general. It was, in fact, in translating some of Poe's French contemporaries and successors—Gautier, Flaubert, Pierre Loti, Anatole France— as well as in retelling Chinese and Caribbean tales and legends that Hearn did perhaps his best sustained work in English prose.[10] Hearn was before anything else a maker of verbal shapes and forms. In all his writing we sense his hold upon a wider literary culture and also a more discriminating feeling for style than in almost any other American of his time; these are the saving virtues of his risky dream of a "poetical prose." We sense also, in Hearn, a natural command of the colloquial ease, the idiomatic purity, that is supposedly the special resource of Irish and of Southern writers. Pages of

10. His translations are superior to those of the Parisian New Englander Stuart Merrill (1865–1915)—whose *Pastels in Prose* (1890) was his one publication in English—simply by virtue of their unmannered firmness of diction and prose cadence.

the psychological recital, "Karma" (1890), would not be out of keeping in Joyce's *Portrait of the Artist*.

Simply to mention certain themes and emphases in *Chita* and *Youma*, the best of Hearn's fiction, is to suggest what makes him a more impressive figure than is usually granted. It is to show him, moreover, surprisingly close to some of the harsher, deeper currents of the major literature of the time. The drama in the dreamlike *nouvelle*, *Chita*, is all in the scene-painting. Its Gulf Coast setting of shoreland and waterway, high sky and wide ocean, is caught in a panoramic-geological view prefiguring Hart Crane's powerful vision of some "seething, steady leveling of the marshes" and slow "alluvial march of days." Out of this context the hurricane that engulfs Last Island rises with an extraordinary naturalness, and so also does the perception, by the protagonist of the second half of the book, of his true human relation to "the vast and complex Stream of Being," in which "he counts for less than a drop." *Chita* is not a Darwinian tract; yet nowhere in our turn-of-the-century literature is there a more intense evocation of the Darwinian fecundity and savagery of Nature than in Hearn's descriptions of swamp, forest, and sea. The Martinique romance, *Youma*, on the other hand, shows him in touch with themes characteristic of the important social and political realism of the period, though he treats them in his own fashion. *Youma* turns on a paradox defined in the opening pages—a paradox Hearn's writings on Japan would renew—that what there was of beauty and virtue in the older pattern of island life, the play of loyalties, the simplicity and steadiness of human relationships, had been founded on slavery, and that, with the coming of freedom and its changes, that beauty and that virtue had disappeared: "generosity and prosperity departed together; Creole life shrank into narrower channels; and the character of all classes visibly hardened under pressure of necessities previously unknown." The terrible dissolution, in the fury of a slave revolt, of Youma's and her lover's vivid dream of an escape to freedom carries this paradox through to a consistent end.

If we add to Hearn's the work of George Washington Cable, who was in mid-career in 1885; of the story-tellers Ruth Stuart, Grace King, and Kate Chopin; and of the older Creole writer C. E. A. Gayarré, it becomes reasonable to speak of a New Orleans renaissance in the '70s, '80s, and '90s. (Nothing contributed more to it than the critical essays Hearn wrote for the New Orleans *Item* and *Times Democrat* between 1878 and 1887, week by week defining problems and broadening taste.) The movement, if it may be called that, produced no masterpieces and was not especially influential elsewhere in the country. But the books it left behind have kept their savor better than the work of any other regional school in late nineteenth-century American writing. These books can still give pleasure and command respect; in contrast to most local-color writing, they are works of specifically literary imagination. Their quality, and also the knowledge that New Orleans produced them, the contact they hold with rumors of gay carnival graces, cosmopolitan manners, cosmopolitan cookery, folklore and folk music, helped to give that attractive city an aura of possibility for artists and writers that was still strong enough in the 1920s to draw Sherwood Anderson and William Faulkner there.

The New Orleans stamp upon its writers in the '80s and '90s is not confined to the sensuousness and erotic languor that supposedly derive from the climate and latitude. The city was also a thriving modern port where fortunes were to be made or lost. Entrepôt for both the North American heartland and the Caribbean and Latin provinces to the south, New Orleans was a cauldron of social, racial, economic, and imperial history. The polyglot variety of the population—

Spanish, Creole, Acadian, Negro (with gradations of field hand and house servant, octoroon, quadroon, and mulatto), Indian, German, Yankee, Sicilian, mountain white and river tawny—and, still more, the density and energy of actual society and then the whole city's participation in the collective disaster of the Civil War all lay richly to hand for the New Orleans writers, who could not have escaped the influence of these conditions even if they had been foolish enough to try.[11]

With Cable, this special backing is even more evident in *Dr. Sevier* (1884) than in his better-known *The Grandissimes* (1880), which is more complexly fashioned but also, as a historical romance, rather more conventional in treatment. Lafcadio Hearn, in fact, thought the later novel distinctly superior as a work of art, less satisfactory than Cable's first book, the collection *Old Creole Days* (1879), only by reason of the author's difficulties with the more demanding structure of a 500-page novel. Certainly in *Dr. Sevier* the city and society of New Orleans are full-bodied presences, vivid, substantial, *and* dramatically validating. The New York scene in Howells's *A Hazard of New Fortunes*, even the brilliantly indicated settings of James's *Bostonians* and *Princess Casamassima*, seem incomplete and a bit manufactured in comparison. The tension of the period just before the Civil War and the wearing attrition of the war years, operating upon various breeds and classes of men, compellingly underscore the commonplace plot, which involves the struggle against

11. An interesting parallel case is that of Constance Fenimore Woolson (1840–1894), certain of whose novels, like *East Angels* (1886), were much praised in their day for their renderings of the South, particularly of life in the marshlands of the Carolinas and Florida. They strike one now as tourist work, however. They offer lively opinions on the differences between North and South, and northern and southern character, but lack the firm interior grip on an actual social order that the New Orleans writers all possess.

poverty and separation of an attractive, young, high-minded couple and the corresponding struggle out of "untenderness" and moral rigidity by the austerely withdrawn and bereaved doctor of the title. It must be granted that the main drift of this double story is rather floridly sentimental in its lesson-pointing. *Dr. Sevier* is not alone among Cable's novels in suffering the warp of his dedication to moral improvement. But this fault has been made too much of and need not put readers off. Sentimental apologue occurs in Cable as it does in Dickens, and it is shored up in the handling of individual scenes by a positively Dickensian verve and prodigality. Parts of the novel are indeed quite extraordinary in American realism of the '80s: in particular, the detailed study of poverty and want and the delicate understanding (eminently "novelistic") of how, in a society pledged equally to human fellowship and to the rigors of self-help, differences in worldly fortune may both destructively inhibit and curiously stabilize the relations of persons. The closing episode of *Dr. Sevier*, describing Mary Richling's tense journey through the loosely strung fighting lines to rejoin her husband, shows off Cable's special talent for chronicle-narrative to particular advantage. Through the fears and alarms besetting this one character, we get a brilliant representation of the whole immense disorder of the war—an achievement bringing to mind similar journey passages in Tolstoy and in Faulkner, and equally inventive.

Cable's fiction never entirely freed itself from some of the worst conventions of his period. He had as perilous a taste for sentimental quaintness as did any of his readers and cheerfully surrendered an exceptional mastery of dialect characterization to its demands. The idealizing of human character seemed to him the novelist's proper instrument of instruction. As for plot, he seldom could resist weakening it for the sake of artificial mystification and suspense (we may note again an influence from Dickens). But if his editors and publishers had

had their way, these objections would make up our whole account of him. Cable paid the price, as a novelist, for the fears and hypocrisies of late nineteenth-century gentility. He was constantly under pressure to remove unpleasant details of subject matter and to soften the disquieting painfulness of particular scenes and actions; several of his best stories—the powerful Bras-Coupé episode in *The Grandissimes* is the best-known instance—were rejected by the magazines. The Cable whose charming platform recitations more than held their own in competition with Mark Twain, when the two were on tour together in the '80s, was one thing; the Cable who wanted to write the social history of his extraordinary province and aimed at both honesty and completeness was quite another, and distinctly less saleable.

Around 1885, in fact, this ambition had got Cable into public difficulties. The plight of the freed Negro in the South after Reconstruction and the spreading white conspiracy to re-establish a *de facto* condition of slavery seemed to him a social danger as well as a moral wrong. In a steady succession of letters, addresses, and articles—collected in *The Silent South* (1885) and *The Negro Question* (1890)—he carried out a pioneering inquiry into the race problem in the United States. Inevitably Cable's closely reasoned defense of Negro civil rights made him *persona non grata* in the South of the 1880s; speaking engagements were canceled, and his decision to settle in Northampton, Massachusetts, took on the appearance of an exile. Indeed it would make him so in the 1960s. For in the phrase, "the silent south," he had defined one act in the larger drama that still has its bitter course to run, and that is the whole long dismal scandal of the self-silencing of decent white southern opinion.

The remaining two works of Cable's major period—*Bonaventure* (1888) and *Strange True Stories of Louisiana* (1889)—are not directly burdened with these issues and involve, no doubt, concessions to the terms of his popular acceptance. Let it be said that such concessions (quite apart from what editors pruned away) were willingly made. Cable loved to spin out long passages of dialect mimicry, and he loved, in the high Victorian manner, to exhibit the saints and angels of common life. Albert Bigelow Paine's account of the Twain-Cable reading tour describes Cable going around to Sunday schools and churches wherever the pair stopped and making a little improving speech at each one—and this is what he tends to do more and more in his later fiction. At each climax a twist of explanation is put in, a moralizing emphasis, an editorial curtain scene. In *Dr. Sevier* and *Bonaventure*, however, as opposed to the half-dozen attenuated romances he wrote after 1900, the general design contains these interpolations without essential damage.[12] *Bonaventure*, in fact, turns the looseness and digressiveness of Cable's fiction into positive virtues. This episodic work, a celebration of the power of goodness though humble, is cast from the opening pages in the mold of some romantic folk chronicle of far away and long ago (though one key character is a thoroughly up-to-date Yankee drummer). Much of the action is seen as in a ballad vision of events at once intimate and legendary, and much of what Cable wishes to show in the lives of his old-fashioned Acadians comes to us through the irregular rhythm of change and alteration in the loosely joined succession of developed scenes. A "prose pastoral," Cable called the book, and this subtitle

12. The ambitious Reconstruction chronicle, *John March, Southerner* (1894), quite fails as a novel, on the other hand—but not because it is stuffed with social problems and editorial sentiments. The reason is simply that Cable's eye and ear have gone dead in it. The region it is set in, the southern Appalachian fringe, Cable knew only on the basis of field trips, and no amount of note-taking could overcome this disadvantage. The dialect in *John March* is indicative. For once in Cable it seems faked. As a writer of stories he left Louisiana at his peril.

and the slightly mannered style confirm one's impression that its quality resembles nothing in Anglo-American fiction quite so much as W. H. Hudson's *The Purple Land That England Lost* (1885). (The parallel might be worth pursuing. Both Cable and Hudson were of New England descent, and both responded to the Latin South with a special idealizing intensity of feeling and perception.) Like Hudson's charming, elegiac evocation of pastoral Uruguay, *Bonaventure* is most impressive in setting and atmosphere: the "prairie tremblante" out beyond the bayous; the terrifying power of nature in flood and hurricane; most of all, the firm, history-creating pattern of persons and lives moving year by year back and forth across a low, wide, hospitable, yet still wild and unmastered landscape.

One returns to the suggestion of what New Orleans could give her writers, even those who like Grace King might dodge social issues and soften outlines wherever possible. Their best work can seem quite artless, yet it has an unforced imaginative roundness and body in its show of life that sets it apart from the work of their realist contemporaries north, east, and west. The order of life these writers report on has given way significantly less to the erosions of democratic individualism; it has not gone so far over into the war of each against all that is the discovered norm of life in "our time." The sense, indeed, of a conflict between two distinct ways of life is woven into the fabric of *Bonaventure*, in which even the Yankee salesman, G. W. Tarbox, becomes a humble convert to pastoral simplicity. In Kate Chopin's remarkable novel, *The Awakening* (1899), this conflict steadily underscores the main action, giving dramatic force to its psychological probings. The heroine of *The Awakening* is a young, well-born Kentucky woman who has married into Creole society and who, in response to the languor, sensuality, frankness, and erotic sophistication of Creole manners, gradually finds release for the "deeper undercurrents of life" that begin to stir within her; in the process, she "casts aside that fictitious self which we assume like a garment in which to appear before the world." It is, of course, a New Orleans version of the familiar transcendentalist fable of the soul's emergence, or "lapse," into life (it is also, with its talk of "mother-women," "animalism," and the moral neutrality of Nature, a period piece of post-Darwinian ethics). In detail, *The Awakening* has the easy candor and freedom appropriate to its theme. It admits that human beings are physical bodies as well as moral and social integers and that the spirit acts not only by sublimation but directly through the body's life. Not many English or American novels of the period had come so far. And its successive scenes—of household, country place, café garden, dinner party, and race track—are vividly realized. Kate Chopin seems to have paid some attention to the recently translated *Anna Karenina* and its extraordinary clairvoyance of observation. (Her short stories—collected in *Bayou Folk* of 1894 and *A Night in Acadie* of 1897—are less remarkable, being rather more constrained by current magazine conventions. But the people in them are real physical presences; invariably they strike us as having actual body, breath, color, and temperature.) That *The Awakening* caused a scandal is not surprising. But its irregular theme was not the main reason. Its deeper offense was in presenting the phases and consequences of the heroine's history—withdrawal from her duties as a wife and mother, adultery, the contemplation of divorce—without cautionary emphasis and without apology (Dreiser's offense, too, a year later, in *Sister Carrie*). The fact that her "awakening" ends in tragedy did not lessen the offense, for the description of her suicide is not less sympathetic in its simple intensity (so that it is psychologically, sensually, convincing), yet it is matter-of-course, unarguable.

Regionalism, Local-Color Realism

In the decades before 1880 something like a systematic regionalist movement had come into being in American letters. In the main its conventions were impromptu and self-taught (the New Orleans writers are exceptional in this respect); it was fundamentally a popular movement. Discovering its forms by way of capturing the dialect and common manners of back-country New England and the older southern frontier, it rapidly expanded its field of attention until almost every distinct section and local pattern of life in the United States had found a literary spokesman. "There are scarcely a dozen conspicuous states now," H. H. Boyesen wrote in 1892, "which have not their own local novelist." The liveliest local-color writing, however, continued to come mostly from those regions that had been settled and built up earliest but were now being left behind in the economic and social revolution of the post-Civil War years. If from the years between 1870 and 1900, when local-color writing chiefly flourished, we take away the work of Cable, Hearn, and Kate Chopin; of the New Englanders Mary Wilkins Freeman and Sarah Orne Jewett; and, of course, of Mark Twain, whose visionary Mississippi Valley homeland had vanished forever in the Civil War, not much of more than antiquarian value remains. The prime source of imaginative energy in American local-color writing was in the tension put upon the older agrarian-mercantile order of life by its triumphant industrial successor. And that tension gained the degree of permanence that imaginative art seems to require of its occasions only in those districts where the older order was, first, solidly rooted down and, second, not so directly under attack: thus, in these years, Louisiana and upper New England rather than New Jersey or the trans-Appalachian plains.

In the Middle West, whose towns and villages had existed

for barely a generation before the double force of railroad and metropolis shattered whatever they had of societal integrity, the process of social change was not a bit less dramatic, but as a subject it tended to resist the indirections of imaginative treatment. If the classic judgment reached separately by Fenimore Cooper, Hawthorne, and Henry James—that American society is in its very formation fundamentally inhospitable to the art of fiction—applies anywhere, it must be in the democratic heartland of the Middle West. There the inevitable rawness and disorder of first settlement gave way to the rawness and disorder of industrialization almost without interval. (The region, or pockets within it, eventually did produce its elegists and fable-makers but not until another thirty or forty years had passed and the generation of Edgar Lee Masters, Willa Cather, and Sherwood Anderson had reached the threshold of middle age.) To historians the progress of this section is of the greatest interest. For American society as a whole it had become perhaps the dynamic center of late-century change and consolidation. Indeed, precisely this sense of a special historical role is reflected in the earliest specifically middle-western books. It is as social historians first of all that the older novelists of the region—Edward Eggleston (1837–1902) and Joseph Kirkland (1830–1894)—present themselves.[13] And it is noteworthy that both men eventually gave up fiction for history proper: Kirkland with his *Story of Chicago* (1891) and the larger *History of Chicago* which his daughter completed after his death; Eggleston with

13. So, too, a generation before, did Joseph Kirkland's mother, the novelist Caroline Stansbury Kirkland (1801–1864). Her first book, *A New Home—Who'll Follow?* was presented as a "veritable history; an unimpeachable transcript of reality; a rough picture, in detached parts, but pentagraphed from life; a sort of 'Emigrants' Guide.'" Fifty years later Joseph Kirkland told Hamlin Garland, who had reviewed him with high excitement, that he conceived of his own work as following the example his mother had set.

his two ground-breaking volumes of sociological history, *The Beginners of a Nation* (1896) and *The Transit of Civilization from England to America* (1901). For both, "realism" was a function of patriotism and of their citizen's interest in the special circumstances of American development. More particularly, it was a way of showing their loyalty to the distinctive local pattern of life they had grown up within. The egalitarian motive we sense in their writing—the desire to show that this pattern of life was just as good, or bad, as any other known to men—is fundamental to the first phase of midwestern regionalism.

By the mid-'80s Eggleston's work as a novelist was nearly done (the last of his "Hoosier" books appeared in 1883). Increasingly, research in the field of social history absorbed the attention of this busy and attractive writer, in whom a special interest in the American dialect had broadened into a liberal respect for the unobtrusive continuities of human culture. His historical romance, *The Graysons* (1888), turning on an episode from Lincoln mythology, is better made than any of his earlier books, yet, precisely as there is less of direct personal recollection in it than in his Indiana writings of the '70s, it has been more completely forgotten. (Reissued, however, as it ought to be, *The Graysons* could take on new life as a children's classic; it is at least as good a book as *The Prince and the Pauper*.) Eggleston's last novel, *The Faith Doctor* (1891), deserves special comment. In it he remains the conscientious social historian, but now the field he surveys is contemporary New York City. Local-color writing, it was discovered, did not have to confine itself to rural backwaters. This interesting novel Eggleston called "a study of human nature under certain modern conditions," and he made a point of defending its fidelity to contemporary fact. And though its observation of social climbing, literary jobbing, mission work, and other such phenomena of metropolitan life is rather baldly presented, it remains amusing as a record of manners and seemingly authentic in detail; Eggleston, who had been a metropolitan journalist and editor for twenty-five years, remarked in the preface that he had known no other way of life "more intimately and . . . for so long a period." Moreover, in its disapproving yet objective account of various kinds of faith-healing and "aerial therapeutics," including Christian Science, *The Faith Doctor* develops a notable intensity of feeling. The dramatization of these newest, city-spawned demireligions necessarily involved Eggleston in presenting with some force the pain and vacuity of life that were driving people of all classes to embrace them.

Of the commoner, county-seat species of local-color fiction, Kirkland's *Zury: The Meanest Man in Spring County* (1887) and a celebrated precursor, *The Story of a Country Town* (1883), by the Kansas editor E. W. Howe, were minor sensations in their day. What interests us now about these books is their expression of the newer, *critical* spirit of midwestern realism; there is no idealization here of the democratic picturesque. It must be granted that the "realism" of these novels is rudimentary. Plot and action defy credibility; by comparison, life along Sinclair Lewis's Main Street is domestically civilized in the extreme. This is not to say that repression, greed, civic corruption, rape, insanity, mob violence, murder, suicide, and a general desolation of the human prospect were not actual characteristics of American village life in the middle and later nineteenth century (nor of American life only: Kirkland wrote in a preface to the second edition of *Zury* that his novel was "a palpable imitation of Thomas Hardy's *Far from the Madding Crowd;* an attempt to reproduce, on American soil, the unflinching realism of the picture, given by that remarkable work, of English low life down in actual contact with the soil itself"). The evident falsity is rather in the wholly arbitrary way in which the pieces of the story fall into place, and—more important, since novels can survive a good deal of improbability of this kind—in the almost total lack of psychological truth. A certain dallying in each book with dominant passions and uncontrollable phobias, in the manner of naturalism, is no substitute. The sequel to *Zury*, *The McVeys* (1888), is of no account, Kirkland admitting that his resources of local color had been used up; but some interest attaches to his last novel, *The Captain of Company K* (1891), inasmuch as the realistic battle scenes of this Civil War tale, along with its deromanticizing dedication, may have contributed to the scheme, four years later, of Stephen Crane's *The Red Badge of Courage*.[14]

The New England story-tellers, too, functioned as local historians, but less methodically. Their first concern was craftsmanship. With the example before them of the *Biglow Papers* and Mrs. Stowe's carefully drawn studies of provincial life, and with the literary standards of Boston and the *Atlantic Monthly* close at hand, they worked harder for good form and clean finish than did the midwestern writers, and took pride accordingly in the commendation of Howells and the approval of Henry James; they were more deliberately men —or women, mostly—of letters. The best among them, Sarah Jewett, had very nearly the narrowest range; but it is in her

14. The dedication reads: "To the surviving men of the firing line; who could see the enemy in front of them with the naked eye, while they would have needed a field glass to see the history makers behind them."

The involvement of midwestern realism with the egalitarian-populist outlook is as obvious and as constant as its results in any given instance are unpredictable. The populist spirit is strong in Kirkland. Yet his political opinions were distressingly illiberal: he abhorred nothing in modern life so much as labor unions and social reformers, and considered George Pullman's company towns the best solution to what was known in the 1880s as "the social problem."

work that local-color writing distinctly emerges as not an end in itself but the natural means, for certain talents, to a more precisely measured and disciplined art. Sarah Jewett began as an imitator of Mrs. Stowe's genre studies; she ended as, in the best sense, the master rather than servant of her materials, a realist after the manner sanctified by Flaubert, whose injunction to write about "ordinary life" with all the scrupulousness of the great historian she made her working motto.

Her nearest rival among the New England regionalists, Mary Eleanor Wilkins Freeman (1852–1930), was more distinctly a novelist and story-writer than Sarah Jewett (for whom plot and drama were incidental to the precise rendering of emblematic scenes and voices). A strong-minded, somewhat quirky woman, Miss Wilkins (as she was until her fiftieth year) was vigorous and direct in attacking her themes. Perhaps for that reason she is at her best in the shorter forms of story and tale, where she can follow her first impulse through to a satisfactory end, without attenuation. Her two early collections, *A Humble Romance* (1887) and *A New England Nun* (1891), raised local-color characterization to a new plane of expressive seriousness. There is not much subtlety or imaginative shading in these firm, compact, poignant studies of village repression—her regular subject—but there is compassion and, even more important, emotional solidity; her definition of blighted lives and their muffled gestures toward freedom may still compel recognition and assent. In novels, on the other hand, like *Pembroke* (1894), *Jerome, A Poor Man* (1897), and *The Portion of Labor* (1901), she is merely heavy-handed. The singleness of tone which is a strength in her short stories turns into perfect monotony; moreover, with the freshness of first treatment now behind her, her reliance on magazine formulas of plot and sentiment becomes suffocating. The creditable fact that in the second and third of these

novels she made some effort at a sociologically accurate examination of poverty and industrial servitude does not save them
as novels. She went on into the 1920s producing stories and
novels (by then her late marriage to a younger, weaker man
had succumbed to the strains apparent in it from the first), in
most of which a radical imbalance between her close knowledge of village manners and a curiously wise-blind obsession
with psychological abnormalities is increasingly evident. Some
of this later work, like the morbid melodrama, *The Shoulders
of Atlas* (1908), cries out for psychoanalytic unraveling, the
author's own explanation of what takes place being patently
inadequate.

Mary Wilkins Freeman's accomplishment was to bring a
greater concentration of treatment to a reigning popular
fashion, that of the picturesque regional tale. This she did
with her first stories, which she never improved upon. By
contrast, the slow, steady advance of the art of Sarah Jewett
(1849–1909) from the miniature competence of her *Atlantic*
sketches of the '70s, collected in *Deephaven* (1877), to the
formal perfection of her masterpiece, *The Country of the
Pointed Firs* (1896), indicates a writer of a different, and
superior, order. This advance is an event of special significance
in American literary history. As much as Mark Twain's
breakthrough in *Huckleberry Finn* or the towering example
of Henry James—for all obvious differences in scale—it
marks the crystallization of the broad undifferentiated impulse
toward realism in American fiction into the durable forms of
an objectively valid art. The special quality of Sarah Jewett's
achievement can best be suggested in her own words. In a
letter of 1896, defining what it may be that makes good work
good, she provides formulas for defining her own success:
she speaks of "the reticence or the bravery of speech, the
power of suggestion that is in it, or the absolute clearness and
finality of revelation; whether it sets you thinking, or whether

it makes you see a landscape with a live human figure living its life in the foreground."

This is what her own stories and sketches move toward: exactly revealed figures, standing or moving in a landscape that is itself a vivid theater for the endless dialogue between human beings and the enclosing conditions of their straitened lives. Increasingly Sarah Jewett learned to isolate the major tones of this dialogue, stripping narrative down to the emotional burden she heard in its unhurrying repetitions. There were as many temptations to sentimentality and archness in her materials—the lives of villagers and country people along the economically moribund Maine coast: mostly old, mostly single, invariably quirky or quaint in some picturesque way— as in the materials of most local colorists. In the best of the stories she was writing in the '80s and early '90s, as in the collection *Tales of New England* (1894), these temptations are more and more firmly mastered. The deeper common themes of American local-color writing in general—the loss of vitality, the huddled courage of resistance to a fundamentally ruthless and destructive pattern of outward history —emerge more and more sharply defined. There is no change in subject matter or emotional attitude. It is simply that the art, the composition, clears itself of irrelevancies. The quaint in human behavior is stiffened by revelation of the harsh historical necessities underlying it; the sources of sentiment are plumbed so directly that they well up with surprising force, though the presentation is muted and oblique; the archness is objectified into the tart humors of dissent and resistance that are her people's natural armor against sour fortune and diminished opportunity.

The odd thing about these stories—"A White Heron," "Marsh Rosemary," and "A Lost Lover" stand out—is that they make their impression almost in spite of their form. Plot and the succession of incident, as Sarah Jewett handles them,

tend to be mechanical at best, or else melodramatic and fundamentally implausible. So in the beautiful book that all her
development as a writer seems now to have pointed toward,
The Country of the Pointed Firs, it is interesting to see that
she abandons the conventions of dramatic fiction and impro-
vises something else. In this novel-length chronicle of remembered episodes, two dominant features bring the whole
loose sequence into an exceptional unity, and both involve an
imaginative submission to her materials. One is the firm, unforced evocation in chapter after chapter of the setting named
in the book's title—the rocky shoreline and green forest; the
shrunken village (always disappearing from sight, as in the
book's closing sentence); the restless, untamable ocean. The
other is her allowing her chief characters to tell their own
stories, in their own voices and at their own pace of dis-
closure. It is this last device that is at the heart of the illusion
the book gives us of circumscribing a complete actual "world,"
though a small one. We hear of these episodes in the very
accents of those who have themselves been party to them and
for whom they have already taken on the absoluteness of
legend; and that is the practical source of the book's quiet
power, the formal means through which we discover the
residual fullness of feeling beneath the pathetic deprivations
of social circumstance.

Once imaginatively secured, this legendary world became,
for Sarah Jewett, more actual than that of her own time. It
thus renewed the risks of sentimentality. She wrote more
Dunnet Landing stories, three of which came to be included,
but only after her death, in new printings of *The Country of
the Pointed Firs:* a publisher's mistake, it may be said, for in
their renewed concessions to quaintness and charm these additional stories jeopardize the delicate yet strict unity of the
original book. But a fourth, and much the longest, is quite
another matter. Entitled "The Foreigner," this extraordinary
story may truly be called one of the mislaid treasures of

American writing; until its recovery by Sarah Jewett's most recent editor, it had been buried in the files of the *Atlantic* since its publication in August, 1900.[15] Not least because it briefly moves us back into the vanished world of masculine enterprise which Dunnet Landing has bleakly come down from and yet is still haunted by—and shows Sarah Jewett in easy control of that world, too—"The Foreigner" confirms one's sense of the authority of *Pointed Firs*. It is, for one thing, a masterly instance of narrative framing. The storm perils and ambiguous reassurances of safety with which it opens introduce the bold combination of tones through which it goes forward: on the one hand there is the broad masculine humor of the four Yankee shipmasters, out on the town in the West Indies and "three sheets in the wind," gravely interposing their persons between a mysterious guitar-playing lady and some unmannerly mistreatment of her; on the other, the shadowy pathos building up around the lady herself, French-born and French-mannered, after she had been taken as a bride into the austerities of seafaring, Calvinist New England. These tones, moreover, are perfectly fused in the rising and falling rhythms of Mrs. Todd's patient, precisely detailed narration. It is all lively, charming dialect comedy—and it is also a ghost story summoned up out of a strangely heroic past, legendary, elegiac, and only reluctantly recalled and renewed. Its resonances are, one may say, peculiarly "American." In the figure of the gay, sensual foreign lady widowed (inevitably) and wasting, her exotic tastes and ways isolating her in Dunnet and becoming fixed into a permanent warp of queerness; in the half-grotesque episode of the lost treasure supposedly hidden away in her house; and finally in the faultlessly rendered climax, when her mother's ghost comes to take her home and, as Mrs. Todd has seen plainly, the doors suddenly open wide, out of the losses and deprivations of the

15. See *The World of Dunnet Landing: A Sarah Orne Jewett Collection*, edited by David Bonnell Green, Lincoln, Nebraska, 1962.

world of time into a redeeming outer world of timeless spirits —in all this Sarah Jewett found the right occasion for setting out once more her deepest knowledge of her fictional world and its fundamental human history, in a story no part of which (to use Mrs. Todd's words) seems in any way "beyond reason."

At its most compelling, American local-color realism thus points toward an imaginative sociology that is at once objective and visionary. The images it yields up compose the fragments of a book of the people, an essential history of their lives' common conditioning. Paradoxically, at this level of realization the particular local circumstances begin to appear incidental. The same stories are told, in more or less detail, on all sides. Indeed it is in the nature of American life, heterogeneous and disorderly and yet oppressively uniform, that any sector of it, honestly examined, is likely to reveal a logic of occurrence (or nonoccurrence) that holds true for the whole national experience. Yet at different times, different particular sectors seem to lie nearer the center; or— since much of what appears as variation in the design of American social life is a matter of accidental local differences in the rate of development—certain sectors lie spectacularly further along, closer to the mold-shattering vanguard of change. In the 1880s the modern city itself, the vital center of industrial capitalism, played this part. Inevitably it was also the locale that most writers of books, city-oriented by occupation, knew in most detail. And it was proving, on first inspection, to be as colorful and picturesque a locale as any rural backwater, to say the least, and consistently more challenging to those realists who wished not only to write marketable sketches but to make some bolder and more direct impression upon the extraordinary life of their extraordinary times.

One such new realist, in his last years, was the Norwegian-born novelist and critic, H. H. Boyesen (1848–1895). (In the 1870s he had written poems and florid historical romances, but, following Howells, he gave these up and embraced the new cause.) Before coming to New York in the '80s to teach German and Scandinavian literature at Columbia, Boyesen had acquired a certain experience of provincial American life teaching in the little Swedenborgian college at Urbana, Ohio, and then at Cornell University in rural New York—an experience, specifically, of that interesting juncture where a half-formed village order of life is crossed by aspirations toward some higher and purer culture. As a writer Boyesen has the interest of a man who has learned the lessons of his experience, though only just. An element of evangelical moralism—indicated by the titles of his best-known novels, *The Mammon of Unrighteousness* (1891) and *The Golden Calf* (1892)— weighs down his work, at the expense of the imaginative freedom it would have needed to fulfill its own best ends.[16] Nevertheless the first of these two chronicles of petty career-making and venal temptation is a genuinely interesting document. There is a spirited caricature of Ezra Cornell in the person of Obed Larkin, founder of Larkin College; there is much lively observation of local manners and types; the interest in social conflict is sufficiently serious; and there is psychological acumen in the characterization of those whose busy consciences unfailingly produce convincing reasons for serving the god of worldly success. In this book, in fact, more than in those of E. W. Howe and Joseph Kirkland, the

16. Note also the closing sentence of Boyesen's essay, "The American Novelist and His Public" (1886; reprinted in *Literary and Social Silhouettes*, 1894): "Art can engage in no better pursuit than to stimulate noble and healthful thought on all matters of human concern, and thereby clear the prejudiced mind and raise the average of human happiness." It is a fair academic statement of a view that is not so much mistaken as incomplete. The real business of criticism begins just beyond this point: exactly how do the peculiar forms of "art" accomplish this great service?

conventions of fictional behavior that eventually receive proper habitations and names in *Main Street* and *Babbitt* take clear form for the first time.

The interesting variation in Boyesen's last and best novel, *Social Strugglers* (1895), is that its setting is metropolitan. The title seems uninviting—until we discover that it is ironic; the book's "strugglers" are not only the poor and the shabby genteel but also the snobs and social climbers who move between Fifth Avenue townhouses and villas at Easthampton. Boyesen's ironies are hardly subtle, but the underlying seriousness of his inquiry into the culture of money-making and society-adventuring gives the whole book some strength of backbone. The great question it raises is put by the conscience-ridden young hero (later shown reading Henry George's *Social Problems*): what exactly is going to be the human result of our society's absolute commitment to the standard of wealth and leisure?

> If it means, as in this country it seems to mean, the loss of vital contact with humanity, the contraction of one's mental and spiritual horizon, a callous insensibility to social wrongs and individual sorrows, a brutal induration in creature comforts and mere animal well-being, the loss of that divine discontent and noble aspiration which alone makes us human—if it means this or any part of it, it is the greatest calamity which can befall a man.[17]

This was Howells's decent concern in the '90s (and *Social Strugglers* is dedicated to Howells): that the bitter conse-

17. The exchange immediately following this declaration is symptomatic. The young hero goes on in the usual manner of such indictments to cite the gospel text about the camel and the needle's eye. But the bright American girl he loves, daughter of a self-made millionaire, assures him that this text refers—so she has been told—merely to a certain gate in ancient Jerusalem. When even the American daughter takes her stand upon the Higher Criticism, the evangelical flank must consider itself turned and routed.

quence of our society's astonishing material progress has been a withering away of community and brotherhood, a brutalization of the moral consciousness. The incidents of Boyesen's novel bear out the rhetoric of the passage. In one striking episode, of a slum-party organized by uptown people to see for themselves how the other half lives, the gulf between classes is cataclysmic; the "other half" in this instance very properly resents being condescended to, and the members of the party, in danger of violence despite their police escort, have to retreat into a nearby slum mission, where, ironically, their own class is more firmly in charge than on the open street.

The episode is vivid and authentic and integral to the book's rich subject. Moreover, as an episode that might have been described by Jacob Riis or Stephen Crane, it incidentally confirms a suggestion implicit in Boyesen's essay of 1892, "The Progressive Realism of American Fiction": that the future of realism lies with those writers who have taken the city as their scene and its life and manners as their great subject. So the closing emphasis in this essay is upon certain nearly forgotten figures, Philadelphia's Thomas A. Janvier, New York's Edgar Fawcett and Henry Harland, who by one means or another—Bohemian comedy, satire of the *beau monde*, lower-depths sensationalism—had all accepted the metropolis as the characteristic environment of their age and had set themselves as a matter of course to be its intimate historians.

Henry James (*1843–1916*)

The American master of the metropolitan setting in this period, however, goes unmentioned in Boyesen's essay. His indifference to Henry James's work of the 1880s no doubt marks a failure of critical intelligence. Beside *The Bostonians* and *The Princess Casamassima* (both 1886) every other American city novel of the time seems pale and (except for *Dr. Sevier*) scarcely half furnished. Yet Boyesen's omitting them in the kind of survey he offers is not entirely unreasonable. Obviously these novels were something more than instances of a new trend. With their weight and brilliance of composed detail, it is not to local-color writing but to the great nineteenth-century masters of metropolitan realism, to Balzac and Dickens, that comparisons (for the first time in this chapter) are strictly required. In the manner of these predecessors, *The Bostonians* and *The Princess Casamassima* impose themselves on readers most of all through a power, continuity, and circumstantial exactness of social description; they impose themselves (in terms that Balzac and also George Eliot used for characteristic works) as "scenes from life."

In this respect each is a prime example of what in the '80s James had settled upon as a first rule for serious fiction: the rule of *saturation*. Opening chapters plunge us thickly into the distinctive organisms of Boston and of London, putting the narrative on a footing of realized social fact, which, even through the curious second-half difficulties each novel falls into (difficulties of a kind that must increasingly be noticed in James), never quite gives way. Each in its own manner thus confirms the point, made half a century ago by T. S. Eliot, that the real focus of attention in James's best work is always "a situation, a relation, an atmosphere, to which the characters pay tribute," and that "the real hero, in any of James's stories, is a social entity of which men and women are constituents."

To an unusual degree for James, moreover, the social entity in each of these books is coextensive with the common social world, the world addressed by the daily newspapers. The main characters stand out against this world but not apart from it. In a naturalistic sense *The Bostonians* and *The*

Princess Casamassima are James's most worldly novels. In writing them he drew upon his own most abundant personal impressions. The Boston and Cambridge of horse cars, winter slush, "causes" and relentless "improvement," and all manner of high-minded provincial busyness, he had known from childhood; and two visits to America in the early '80s had both refreshed his observation and sharpened his satirical detachment. As for the setting of *The Princess*, in "the great, roaring, indifferent world of London," that had been for nearly ten years both home and studio for him. He had adopted London as his place of work coincidentally with his determination to become nothing less than what the American novel had so far lacked, a *master*, and he had devoted several winters to the process of saturating eye and ear with London impressions. Neither book involves James's "international" theme—but what other writer has ever made himself so much at home and at ease, imaginatively, in two different national societies? The firm definition of character and action in these novels, against settings that beg no exemption from the strictest measure of descriptive realism, is surely one of the fine ful-filling achievements of the nineteenth-century novel.

Yet these two novels were failures. They put, James himself said, a blight upon his career from which it never recovered. And though recent defenders have explained this failure in terms of the rare seriousness of their themes and the generally low state of public taste, it must finally be admitted that the trouble is inward as well. For all their wit, humor, insight, compassion, and high workmanship, for all their obvious involvement with James's great lifelong theme of the moral use or exercise of the blessed gift of life, they are seriously flawed compositions. We come here head-on against the "James problem." Why *are* these strong, substantial novels— "major" in ways that nothing he had previously done quite

matches; composed in the fullness of his power and assurance
as a prose writer (as all his letters, travel essays, and literary
and dramatic criticism of the period abundantly confirm);
truly Balzacian, as they were meant to be, in scope and
seriousness; and propelled by a literary intelligence the characteristic mark of which is that every sentence counts toward
the forming of central impressions and the forwarding of
essential action—why are they nevertheless unsatisfactory?
How is it that they fall short of that virtue which James
himself, in his magisterial lecture on "The Art of Fiction"
(1884), had recently defined as supreme in the novel: the
virtue of possessing the "air of reality"?

(Such questions are not really suited to volumes of literary
history. If *The Bostonians* and *The Princess* are failures, what
shall we say of *A Hazard of New Fortunes*, of *Dr. Sevier*, of
Maggie? Across everything that follows in what may seem an
ungenerous account of James's fiction, this truth ought to be
blazoned: that uniquely among American writers in the period
surveyed in this book Henry James has the stature of the
grand écrivain; the producer of a genuine *oeuvre* the very
mass of which dignifies and informs every particle of it; the
creator of norms—their mostly having to be rejected does not
alter the case—and the forwarder of fundamental literary
history. It is a rare tribute to be able to say of a writer, as
must be said of Henry James, that he refuses to let us make
special allowances but compels us instead to re-examine the
whole nature of the art he practices and the morality he communicates.)

Curiously, the trouble in these novels occupies the ground
where partisans of James, and where James himself, most often
take their stand critically—the ground of form, the discovery
and execution of right content. The simplest way of suggesting what is amiss in *The Bostonians* and *The Princess*—and
in their more obviously flawed successor, *The Tragic Muse*

(1890)—is to say that at a certain point in each, roughly midway, the developing structure falls out of sorts with the pressure of the indicated content. The author appears to lose hold of the story he has brought forward; we have a sense of his groping this way and that for the wherewithal to bring his work to a proper resolution.[18] In *The Bostonians* the satire (not unsympathetic) on the old Transcendentalist reforming spirit turned sour and driven into holes and corners, and the harsher satire of the New England demimonde of spiritual quackery and Paul Pry journalism (the newspaperman Matthias Pardon is one of James's triumphs of realistic caricature) are firmly projected in early scenes, and the sour dramatic contest at the center—between the neurotic bluestocking, Olive Chancellor, and the shallow gentleman-egoist, Basil Ransom, for possession of Verena Tarrant, daughter of platform charlatans, with her strange, ingenuous gift of tongues— is developed initially with force and economy. Projected and developed—but toward no clearly imagined end. A Hawthornesque tale of soul conflicts (resemblances to *The Blithedale Romance* have often been noted) has been crossed with a naturalistic comedy of representative social types and tensions; and though James is evidently in technical command of both modes, he can neither reconcile them nor choose between them, nor does he appear to see that he must.

The same kind of interior division and displacement dissipates the taut drama of *The Princess Casamassima*—concerning which James confessed that he had got well into serial publication without a clear sense of what lay ahead. The strength and interest of this novel, dramatizing the systematic disorder, the class antagonism, the competition for power characteristic of modern society, are chiefly in its compact

18. In point of fact, *The Bostonians,* contracted for as a six-part monthly serial, sprawled on through seven additional installments— for which James was paid nothing extra.

sociology of motives for revolutionary commitment. James is particularly effective in anatomizing the self-serving motives of those who from outside and above the working class adopt its cause and pre-empt its leadership, the very willfulness of their fervor implying eventual betrayal. Though Hyacinth Robinson is the protagonist, the emphasis of the title is well chosen. The Princess stands forth as the first and most un-principled of these subverters from within of the cause of social justice. Her cry is, "The old ferocious selfishness *must* come down," but her behavior contradicts her; invariably it is "more addressed to relieving herself than to relieving others." (How explicit James is, and how intelligent! how responsive in nar-rative detail to the pressure of his governing themes!) Little Robinson's deepening misery and the pathos of his being trapped by his own singular integrity into suicide are poig-nantly rendered. Alone among the characters he has not *chosen* estrangement and divided loyalties but has been born to them. (James makes him the illegitimate child of an English peer and a continental demimondaine who has worn out her life in prison for murdering her noble seducer.) Like his mythical namesake, but without resource or hope of rescue, Robinson is cast away—into the cannibal wilderness of modern London. His consciousness is the book's tonal center. But that center is just what blurs in the later stages, and the blurring comes, paradoxically, with James's rising concentration upon his hero's bewilderment. What happens is that this bewilderment is torn loose from its frame: the whole abundant metropolitan context of poverty, injustice, dispossession, self-serving, con-spiracy, and betrayal. Instead, a new, counterfeit motivation is introduced. Hyacinth receives a legacy and uses it to expose his sensibility to the artistic splendors of Paris and Venice, the result being that his passion for social justice cools and he becomes, for aesthetic reasons, a troubled convert to a sentimental conservatism. What price revolution if it destroy these treasures? From a realistic drama of social anguish and betrayal the novel veers arbitrarily toward the form of an ironic problem-parable of value judgment and choice: it is Godwin's stale old problem (in *Political Justice*) of Fénelon or the valet. James substantiates this new departure with his usual thoroughness and intelligence; he is, as Lionel Trilling remarks, personally absorbed in the problem raised; but it is nevertheless, given the novel he had built up, a serious formal mistake.

By 1886, twenty years along in his career, James strikes us as having mastered the arts of exposition as few American novelists ever have—and as not knowing what further use to make of them. He composes now with an ease that, in Ethel Mayne's words, "threatened to, or actually did sometimes, turn into slickness." Some of his work at this time, like the novellas *Lady Barbarina* (1884) and *The Reverberator* (1888), polished, rapid, adroit, is nevertheless disturbingly shallow and tinny in its moral resonances. More so, the point is, than James seems to have realized; the objection is not to the persistent "unpleasantness" of these tales but to insensitivities in tone and treatment. Certain other stories from this same period, on comparable themes, are among his finest—the disquieting parable of "The Author of Beltraffio" (1884) and, even more, the long "Aspern Papers" (1888), both intensely engaged with central Jamesian ironies of moral corruption and betrayal; the witty and vivid novella, *A London Life* (1888), in which the egotistical characters shout, quarrel, express passion, and gratify impulses with a shamelessness that quickly reduces the impossibly high-minded heroine to a state of "stupefied suspense"; and such touching and masterly tales as "The Pupil" (1891) or, though slighter, "The Real Thing" (1892). But even some of these fall into odd short cuts and evasions. Climaxes are hurried through, efficiently but mechanically, or omitted altogether. The danger of such lapses is in fact built into James's art of fiction now, and henceforth the interest of his successive works is in no small part whether or not, and in what ways, they are avoided. It is as if his power to judge the actual weight and value of his subjects was incommensurate with the intelligence of his plans for putting them on display, as if this power were somehow turned off prematurely at the source. For all its assured brilliance of treatment, some fundamental failure in imaginative definition afflicts Henry James's work in the '80s, and is a main cause of the crisis overtaking his career.

It is typical of James that he had already, at the time of *The Portrait of a Lady* (1881), defended his procedures in a notebook entry which gives us words to deal with this matter. He would be criticized, he said, for not seeing his heroine through to the end of her situation, for leaving her, dramatically, in mid-air. "This is both true and false," he went on. "The *whole* of anything is never told; you can only take what groups together." The point of this casual formulation —which, broadly, is axiomatic for most of modern literature and particularly for the aesthetic of Symbolism—corresponds to the point of Yeats's doctrine that in art will cannot do the work of imagination. But there is also a sense in which it affirms the weaker side of the late-Romantic aesthetic, the side of moral passivity and architectural negligence. Thus it indicates a cause of these curious failures of handling in James just when his mastery of workmanship has proved itself secure. For the effort of the greatly original artist is to do something more than make the best of "what groups together"; it is—in Pasternak's extraordinary phrase—to break out of this "chaos of workmanship" with the hammer blows of intellectual passion and to aim at some *substantial* completeness of demonstration, a completeness the ideal of which, though the thing itself may always escape, is nevertheless an indispensable condition of major artistic success.

Perhaps nothing is more characteristic of the general interest of James's long career than his seeming to recognize the difficulties he had got into. After *The Tragic Muse*, which addresses a variety of promising themes—the life of true vocation, for example, against the life of career-making—with wit and intelligence but without sufficient artistic persistence, he abandoned the novel for several years.[19] When he returned to it, it was as an out-and-out experimenter, an explorer of forms and types of narrative that would better suit the "groupings" of his restless imagination than had the big, world-anchored, realistic novel. That perhaps is the real service of his increasing concentration upon "point of view" (the refraction of events and impressions through the focus of a single participating consciousness). In any case, nothing contributed so much to making his career exemplary to the generation of Pound and Eliot as this critical responsiveness to the developing problems of his own art.

On the plane of expediency, however, it was largely the hope of making more money than his novels were bringing in that led him, after *The Tragic Muse*, to launch a second career as a writer of plays (though long before, in a notebook entry of December, 1881, he had called this "the most cherished of all my projects"). The failure of his campaign to make his way as a dramatist, culminating in the "abominable quarter of an hour" when he was jeered off the stage after the opening night of *Guy Domville*, is a matter of biographical record. But he had not given up prose fiction altogether. During this same period, 1890–1895, he began to publish certain stories of an exceptional metaphoric intensity, the themes of

19. See, however, Pound's judgment of *The Tragic Muse:* "Excellent text-book for young men with ambitions, etc."

which, moreover, refer with an unusual directness to his immediate personal situation: stories about the glory of art and the trials of artists ("The Death of the Lion," "The Figure in the Carpet"), or about the psychological crises of middle life ("The Altar of the Dead"), or about both together ("The Middle Years," with its hero's great deathbed affirmation of the "doubt," the "passion," the "task"—and the "madness"— of art).

Then, with his wholehearted return after 1896 to the writing of novels, a return celebrated in notebook entries of an extraordinary sacerdotal fervor, the James whose singular quality no comparisons to Balzac or George Eliot or Hawthorne or any other nineteenth-century forerunner can quite suggest comes storming into view. The style turns richer and subtler, more fanciful and elaborate yet also more rankly colloquial. The composition curls closer around its imaginative centers. The states of consciousness that were formerly attached to the outward data of realism now seem to well up directly and create their own data, their own "worlds" (for which the free, irresponsible world of the wealthy and leisured that James now almost exclusively deals with provided peculiarly appropriate detail). The result of these changes is a series of works—from *The Spoils of Poynton* (1897) and "The Turn of the Screw" (1898) through *The Awkward Age* (1899) and *The Sacred Fount* (1901) to the massive triad of his "major phase," *The Ambassadors* (1903), *The Wings of the Dove* (1902), and *The Golden Bowl* (1904), not to neglect stories like "The Beast in the Jungle" and "The Great Good Place"—which are remarkable first of all for the extreme differences of evaluation and interpretation they have inspired. Here the James "problem" has its true locus. Does this phase of his work represent a fulfillment and transformation of the main practice of Anglo-American fiction? Or is it the aberration of an excessively insulated creative mind whose irrepressible gifts of expression (James's

Irishness is worth remembering) had always exceeded its understanding of life and of the right use of form? Is it greatly original, or is it just monumentally peculiar? These questions do not seem possible to settle by ordinary critical explication. But the burden of proof has long since passed to James's detractors. Even Edwin Muir, a particularly severe critic of James's aesthetic, did not think to question his immense intelligence and inventiveness. Though *The Ambassadors*, which James himself considered his masterpiece, seemed to Muir, in form, a "minor offshoot" of the significant tradition of the English novel, he went on to say with his usual acuity that it was "in a tradition exactly as important as its author"—and he made no cheap effort to pretend that its author's mind was not one of the great shaping forces, for better or worse, in modern Anglo-American writing.

James's themes now appear to take hold of him with obsessive power. That may partly explain why his artistic control can seem so uncertain from one work to the next. Nearly every survey of the whole *oeuvre* agrees that there are notable ups and downs in his later performance. There is less agreement which is which. Motifs, however, are singularly consistent. The successive novels and tales seem to be joined in some vast *roman fleuve*, the stages of which overflow and commingle. Again and again the center is an action of moral violence or spiritual outrage, involving victimization, sacrifice, betrayal; the mortal struggle of fine consciences against dullness or corruption; the taking or not taking the cup of life at one's lips, or its being dashed away. "I have the imagination of disaster," James wrote to A. C. Benson in 1896, "and see life as indeed ferocious and sinister." These late works richly bear him out.

One of the few to win fairly uniform critical approval is the compact novel, *What Maisie Knew* (1897), concerning a girl caught between her two sets of divorced, remarried, and unreconstructibly selfish parents. Has any other been so often reclaimed as James's most neglected triumph? Technically interesting as a pure case of point-of-view experimentation ("the one presented register of the whole complexity would be the play of the child's confused and obscure notation of it, and yet the whole, as I say, should be unmistakably . . . there"), it has been called, by D. W. Jefferson, "the perfect example of method as a liberating factor, the means of placing the novelist on the happiest terms with his subject." Of course there is another reason than the technical why Maisie's consciousness serves so effectively as the "ironic centre" James was seeking. Like Huckleberry Finn, Maisie as a figure to build out from is immediately sympathetic, a child living estranged in a world she never made which incessantly lays its crooked claims upon her, without explanation and without remorse; and the intense emotion this situation arouses—James's later "Preface" names it: "the death of her childhood, properly speaking"—excites his moral vision to an exceptional intuitive clarity. At the same time we notice that this "liberating" pragmatism of method, as we may call it, carries over into a kind of pragmatic optimism of feeling, quite different from the darker tones of *Huckleberry Finn* and more than a little forced. This effect contributes to a nagging impression that *Maisie*, though very efficiently made, rings a little hollow morally. The result of the formal concentration on Maisie's own understanding of events and relations is in effect that her poor parents' lives (as we know them) get narrowed down to what her knowing makes of them. There is a sense in which the novel shows her raw energy of awareness and responsiveness triumphing gratuitously at their expense. If this is so, we probably applaud twice over (for the triumph of this child over these adults would appear to be in the interest of the essential human succession) and thus we seem to confirm for at least once the moral rightness of the basic design—even though we coincidentally see that by the same token *What Maisie Knew* quite subverts the moral logic of the traditional "education novel" describing the young person's entrance into the world. For the world Maisie enters has been reduced and humbled with a vengeance. It has been trimmed to *her* knowledge and *her* need of it; yet is there any ground for doubting that in her "triumph" she is already firmly planted on the moral path, the path of an immitigable human selfishness, blazed for her by her elders but also made safe for her by their victimization? She "falls" into the world, yes—but in James's essentially fantastic scheme it is the world that will pay all the price.

With the other books of the prolific 1896–1901 interval, critical disagreements are acute. Is Fleda Vetch of *The Spoils of Poynton* a heroine of the "free spirit" who alone in a company of "fixed fools" not only "feels" but "sees," on the plane of true values—so James's "Preface" describes her—or is she a self-approving prig whose arduously manufactured choice to be faithful to an ethical standard represented by a collection of house furnishings (the "spoils") brings her to a deservedly bleak prospect of life? The concentration upon fineness of consciousness here produces a certain forcing of natural emotion and natural probability, beyond the reach of irony. (Our instinct is to congratulate the story's dim young man, who is not worthy of Fleda's fineness, on his great good luck in getting instead her heartily vulgar rival, Mona Brigstock, who will at least rescue him from his domineering mother, the formidable Mrs. Gereth.) Similar ambiguity confronts us on a larger scale in the amplest novel of this period, *The Awkward Age*. This is the book that more than any other has left James open to the charge of having been morally seduced by English country-house society, or by some romantic idealization of it; for the scheme of the novel does seem to endorse, if not the whole self-approving little

circle of Mrs. Brook and her friends, then at least the taste
and wit, the "sincerity" and "decent leisure," the rare beauty
"of our effort to live together," that are her circle's declared
standards. Or *does* it endorse all this? The characters put
forward extraordinary claims to possession of a whole galaxy
of Jamesian virtues—fine moral consciousness above all—
which exist through their fulfillment of barely statable obliga-
tions to each other and to their little world as a whole. The
curious cult of "personal relationships" that came to figure
so prominently in English writing for more than a generation
after James was never so purely embodied as in *The Awkward Age,* which, appropriately, is built up entirely through
passages of dialogue, arranged as if by slide rule to bring
forward two or three or four of the ten or twelve notable
characters in new combinations for each new scene. Yet the
more they analyze the rules of their game, the more vivid is
our sense of their actual decadence or worse. Mitchy, one of
the most attractive, puts it this way: "We've supposed we've
had it all, have squeezed the last impression out of the last
disappointment, penetrated to the last familiarity in the last
surprise; then some fine day we find that we haven't done
justice to life." Is their game a model of the moral life or is it
some grotesque and horrible substitute? And is the main
dramatic action—what Yvor Winters described as "the obscure, slow, and ugly withdrawal of Vanderbank," who is
supposed to marry Mrs. Brook's daughter Nanda but refuses
—an act of moral treachery, in the high Jamesian way, or is it
a rare act of life, a strike for freedom and the real world, the
execution of which is worth any amount of ugliness and moral
violence?

These questions are real, and they are troubling. But in a
sense they are not strictly material. James's moral attitude to
his little circle and its game is indeed ambiguous—as, to take
a parallel case, Proust's attitude in his magnificent analysis of
"l'esprit des Guermantes" is not. But the paradox advanced by

Yvor Winters about *The Awkward Age* is equally true: "that though most of the important actions in the story are either flatly incredible or else are rendered so subtly as to be interminable, yet the resultant attitudes and states of mind of the actors are rendered with extraordinary poignancy."[20] It is getting harder and harder, with the Henry James of 1896 and after, to know what to think. But it is even harder not to be caught up in the imaginative power with which he bodies forth the living states of feeling and consciousness that are his true subject. James idealizes personal goodness and fineness and dreams darkly of ferocious corruptions of these qualities—but what as an artist he "believes" in, and has learned to make his reader believe in, is nothing less than the substantial reality of *spirit* in the affairs of human beings. "Tell the Anglo-Americans," he seems to say, forty years before Auden's poem, "that man is a spirit." It is in this respect that he is the heir in American letters not only of Hawthorne but of Emerson—the Emerson, specifically, who was at his best as, all at once, a definer, critic, and lyrical celebrator of concentrated states of mind and whose peculiar genius, so James himself expressed it, consisted in his never having been bribed by life "to look at anything but the soul."

The most publicized case of ambiguity in James, "The Turn of the Screw," yields to this kind of recognition as perhaps to no other. Insofar as controversies over it turn on the question whether the evil ghosts that appear to the governess are actual ghosts or exist only in her disordered imagination, these controversies cannot be settled in the terms in which they have been carried on. Curiously, criticism of this story (abetted by James's own description of it to H. G. Wells as

20. But in the last scene, where we are still waiting for fundamental enlightenment, it is embarrassing to find James descended to magazine levels of evasion: "He looked at her with a complexity of communication that no words could have meddled with."

"a pot-boiler and a *jeu d'esprit*") has mostly underestimated its artistry and its special charge of truth. The ambiguity is formally perfect—and that is as James intended. His remarks about "The Turn of the Screw" in the "Preface" to Volume XII of the New York edition stress "mystification" as his tactical object and "cold artistic calculation" as the means of achieving it. Yet the story is very much more than a Poe-esque *tour de force* of equivocation. It is one of James's most boldly imagined compositions and one, moreover, in which the free play of imagination and the close exercise of technique are most securely in balance. For however the manifestations of evil and terror are to be explained, their realized presence in the story is incontestable, as irresistible to us as to the mind of the governess. This is the "meaning" we are compelled to accept if we enter into the story at all. The whole work has its force as an account of what in spiritual reality can substantially intrude upon the affairs of "ordinary human virtue" (section xxii); and in writing it James drew upon his own instinctive willingness to "believe" in spirit-presences, to accept them as natural—"as only another turn of the screw"— in the mysterious life of consciousness: an "illimitable" life, as he had written in his extraordinary letter to Grace Norton of July 28, 1883.[21] To make his reader also accept these presences as natural, however produced, was James's task: "Only make the reader's general vision of evil intense enough, I said to myself . . . make him *think* the evil, make him think it for himself, *and you are released from weak specifications*." (Emphasis added.)

The same kind of effort, to make his "meaning" so vivid

21. This willingness may be traced to his father's religious thought, as Quentin Anderson has demonstrated in *The American Henry James*. It may also be connected to the eclectic supernaturalism characteristic of the literary mind in James's lifetime and for a while after. So Yeats, too, half believed in spirit-presences and made both mystificatory nonsense and magnificent poetry out of them.

and tangible and intrinsically logical that spelling it out in so many words would be redundant, distinguishes the curious novel, *The Sacred Fount*—though here that effort does seem finally to fall into preciousness. The title of this work and much of its language suggest an allegory of the expense and renewal of life itself, in which violations of that universal process (the characters' violations of each other's being, the prying narrator's violation of them all through the horrors of sublimated sex cannibalism his imagination discerns in them) have in the telling the enormity of sins against the holiest of natural values. At the same time the book's complicated stress on the step-by-step forwarding of its narrator's inquiry makes it seem a parable of the composing of a novel, a fantasy-history of the process of fictional creation. We recall the Romantic intuition that such "secondary" creation may well imitate life only at the expense of life. Various modernist classics, like *Six Characters in Search of an Author*, *The Counterfeiters*, *Dr. Faustus*, swim into view. But unlike these works the internal system of *The Sacred Fount* perfectly resists translation. We can discover any significance in it that we please to—and lose patience with it for just that reason. The book is indeed every bit as absorbing as its author's great intelligence. Yet it fails by the measure of one of his own leading principles: in pursuing its peculiar formal ends it too fatally sacrifices the "strange irregular rhythm of life" ("The Art of Fiction") to the calculated beat of its creator's will.

If James had died in 1901, it could be demonstrated that *The Sacred Fount* was the logical, the parodistic, dead end of his practice of fiction. It was quickly followed, however, by three strong, full novels that open out as powerfully into the passions of mature life as anything he ever wrote. More and more the consensus of Jamesian criticism is that these three—*The Ambassadors*, *The Wings of the Dove*, *The Golden Bowl*—are his masterpieces. All three are dense and rich in specification; yet one aspect of the creative advance they represent at this climax of James's career is that their themes can be fairly summed up in certain simple talismanic words that resound and echo through them all and that suggest how deeply they embody his inmost "American" idealism: "life" and "live" (as a verb), "freedom," "salvation," "love," "sacred," "renunciation," "death." We notice, too, that all three elaborately resume the "international" subject of earlier successes like *The American* and *The Portrait of a Lady*. In *The Golden Bowl* this subject is taken at once to the edge of allegory, one of the four main characters being a Prince Amerigo who defines his part in the action (in an image borrowed, remarkably, from Poe's *Arthur Gordon Pym*) as a confrontation of some mysterious curtain of blankness behind which his American bride and her father, literally a New World "Adam," hide their true natures. We notice further that the affectations of James's later manner here act mostly to support rather than to obscure the themes. What now presents itself is "the style of a writer," D. W. Jefferson remarks, "who cherishes his subjects personally, and this feeling communicates itself to the reader." There is no question that James's favorite expressive devices—qualification, parenthesis, elaborate periodicity, elaborate metaphor—constantly risk excess; only an extraordinary imaginative devotion to theme and governing situation keeps them under control. But precisely under pressure of this devotion they become the local means of rendering with special intensity what James is mainly interested in—the slow natural forming of the dramatic situation through the minutely specified participation of the characters chiefly involved; the laboring forward of actual perception and feeling in these characters by which alone that larger situation can develop.

In James's "Preface" *The Ambassadors* is called, "frankly, quite the best, 'all round,' of my productions." "The thread is really stretched quite scientifically tight"—that was his boast to one of his readers. Critical reservation may as well begin here. The achieved pattern of the book, so E. M. Forster granted, is indeed "triumphant," but at this cost: "it leaves out life too much." That of course is a judgment that the most detailed formal analysis can neither prove nor disprove. (The one thing it does *not* mean is that the subject of the novel is trivial or unimportant in the scale of human history.) Yet we do have a sense with *The Ambassadors* of blank spots and misplaced emphases. Expectably we discover, reading the notebooks and the "Preface," that James himself was aware of them. We find also that in his original conception some of these blanks were filled in; the problem thus involves something deliberately taken out, not something never imagined. So, for example, one of the motives for the way in which the hero, Lambert Strether, chooses to carry out his mission to rescue Chad Newsome from the clutches of Paris and its women was to be remorse at having long ago failed in fatherly duty to his own dead son. That motive appeared to become less and less important as James built up his composition, and in the finished work it is barely mentioned. Yet do we not sense the lack of it, or of some inward force equally momentous, as we try to "believe" in what we are asked to feel about Strether's progress? "The book," James wrote, "critically viewed, is touchingly full" of such potential anomalies of form—"these disguised and repaired losses, these insidious recoveries, these intensely redemptive consistencies"—and the case can be made that James became absorbed to the point of infatuation in the technical business of disguising, repairing, and redeeming, after which, failing to see these blanks in the finished design, he thought the novel his best whereas it is, perhaps, only his most perfectly charming.

It is *one* of his best, however, and never better than when a secondary emphasis, like the dangerously melodramatic pathos of Mme. de Vionnet's betrayal and suffering, is so vividly realized that it very nearly usurps the center, which is Strether's embassy. The most compelling occasions in James are nearly always those that involve suffering, loss, deprivation, defeat. *The Wings of the Dove* is the strongest proof of this. Looser and rougher in design—James later spoke of the whole second half as "false and deformed," full of "dodges" and "makeshift" evasions—it is nevertheless his greatest novel. The fullness of life Forster missed in *The Ambassadors* comes flooding into it by way of its strong simple subject, the confrontation of death in the midst of life. At its core the novel is an elegy (classic American form), deepened in its tones by being rooted in James's memories of the life and early death of his beloved Albany cousin, Minny Temple. It thus curiously endorses, so F. O. Matthiessen pointed out, Poe's claim that the supreme poetic subject is the death of a beautiful woman.[22] But it is not death itself but the virtuousness of living bravely in the face of death that draws James on. "The process of life gives way fighting," so he explained his treatment, "and often may so shine out on the lost ground as in no other connexion." This process shines out in *The Wings of the Dove* with the greater poignancy because the beautiful woman is young and unassuming, with the more disturbing irony because she is rich and forgiving; and all the rest of the action—most of all the doomed struggle of her counterpart, the vividly imagined Kate Croy, to make a life equal to *her* admirable capacities— is powerfully dignified by it.

Or perhaps "poignant" and "dignified" are insufficient to describe the effects James achieves in these climactic books. The Biblical titles of *The Wings of the Dove* and *The Golden Bowl* suggest that something radically deeper than humanistic sentiment has entered into their conception and that the love the heroine of *The Golden Bowl* fights for as her father's

22. *The Wings of the Dove* resounds also with that other great theme James shared with Poe, the theme of personal treachery.

daughter and her husband's wife is sacramental in its valences. The ritual absorption of James's art, the invocational language, the unwinding of coil upon coil of concentric incident and image, the frequency with which words like "sacred" and "blest" are released into the exposition: all these things generate an intensity of concern that has seemed to many of his most appreciative critics like the intensity of a religious concern. Thus it is that the one great critical argument that tells absolutely against James is the one that meets him squarely on the ground of this greatest of imputed effects: Gide's argument that his treatment of character-in-action is profane, incurably profane. Existence in *The Golden Bowl* has been cut back to the frame of personal consciousness. The author's executive intelligence has, finally, not only thoroughly distilled the figures of his conception but swallowed them whole; and he must pay the price. Nineteenth-century individualism, and in art the secular idolatry of purified workmanship, can go no further. Integrity of technique has become not the means of the work's emergence into life but the whole and exclusive life allowed to the work. Philosophically considered, this novel might well be renamed—call it instead *The Golden Calf*—provided we remember that that great object of misdirected reverence (if the Bible legend is to be taken seriously) was surely the most beautifully accomplished work of art its idolaters had ever seen; well might they get down on their knees to it.

A commoner objection to *The Golden Bowl* is that it is out of touch with the probable worldly truth about its chief protagonists, particularly the millionaire Ververs, father and daughter—about their observed social behavior as well as their incestuous counteralliance against the wife and husband they have taken possession of. This is no great fault in a fable, where we do not ask foxes to behave like the animal *vulpes vulpes*, but it can be a serious one in a novel aiming at a full narrative substantiation. As if in answer to this objection, the writing in the last completed major work of this final period in James's career comes to us at every point painstakingly engaged with the real, observed, social world. *The American Scene* (1907) was written after James's last trip to the United States and derives its form—its intellectual drama of inquiry and assessment under the rhythmic assault of concrete impressions—from James's own motives for making the trip, his first return in twenty-odd years. It used to be the fashion to remark that in his later fiction Henry James was as acute a psychologist as his brother William. In *The American Scene* he enters into another kind of competition—with such observers as Tocqueville, Veblen, Henry Adams—and analyzes, in his own style, the outward civilization and the historical prospects of capitalist democracy.[23] Of all James's later work this is perhaps the book in which he is most solidly in command of his appointed materials. Certainly it is the only one—even though its large design is loose and unfinished—that goes forward without blanks, hiatuses, and evasions in the exposition. The leading ideas in *The American Scene*—concerning democratic mannerlessness, the ambiguities of freedom, the sovereignty of business, the relation of material power and civil virtue, the historical destiny of a culture so formed—recur and recur like bold Dickensian characters, giving compositional order and strong moral coloring to the shifting niceties of observation. For thirty-five years an inquiry into the consequences of the American will to freedom and to happiness had been working itself out in James's writing; here that inquiry fastens itself at last upon the whole encountered body of American social life. Can it be true, one asks, that

23. An extraordinary passage describing New York harbor (duly highlighted in F. W. Dupee's *Henry James*) underscores Adams's imaginative speculations about American development in a scientific and technological era, and precisely anticipates the logic of Hart Crane's plans for *The Bridge*.

James was once seriously accused of having lost touch with his native province?

His renewed impressions of American life and his inmost sense of allegiance to it also underlie the other writings of his last years: the sumptuously detailed recollections of the three autobiographical books, *A Small Boy and Others* (1913), *Notes of a Son and Brother* (1914), *The Middle Years* (1917); the moral ugliness of tales like "Julia Bride" (1908), "A Round of Visits" (1910), and the unfinished *Ivory Tower* (1917), an ugliness of which the data of adultery, divorce, swindling, abuse of trust, personal abasement, and plain shameless vulgarity are simply the outward forms; the terror of the confrontation of past and present and of one's conceivable other self in the ghost story, "The Jolly Corner" (1908), or the romance of this confrontation in *The Sense of the Past* (1917). What is also characteristically "American" is the pragmatic optimism—the act of life, as James might have called it—with which during 1907–1909 he reread the mass of his own work, reimagined his creation of it, and in eighteen "Prefaces" offered his findings for instruction to the future. The variousness of these undertakings and the copious authority of each in its turn are equally extraordinary. One makes no apology for giving James so much room in this piecemeal chronicle of literary history. The demands the few greatly creative writers make on our attention, and the rewards they offer, are so remarkable and so continuous that their lesser contemporaries are lucky to be commemorated at all. Indeed the most important thing we may learn from the latter is the precise nature of the achievement of the former: the special obstacles threatening their effort, the particular means and energies by which these obstacles were overcome. And one makes no apology for having, with James, borrowed rather more freely than elsewhere in this volume from the findings of other critics. The criticism a writer attracts becomes eventually a fair measure of his quality and importance;

and beginning with the contributions of Pound and Eliot (at decisive points in their own careers) to the *Little Review* memorial issue in 1918, criticism of Henry James has been provoked by its subject to an exceptional refinement of insight and argument, a refinement, moreover, not limited to considerations of technique. Critics and novelists both are still trying to come to terms with him; the master continues to teach lessons of the first importance.

Humorists and Moralists: The Heirs of Howells and James

The matter of James's increasing "difficulty" as a novelist and his loss of his public in his later years should not be misrepresented. His novels and tales remained in demand in the magazines all through the '80s and '90s; and the trouble he eventually had in getting satisfactory contracts for serialization—*The Ambassadors* was the last novel so to appear and was rejected by the lumpish Alden of *Harper's* before being taken by *The North American Review*—resulted as much from changes in the magazine market as from any incapacity to hold attention on James's part. He did not command a mass audience; he never had. But neither was he reduced to the *succès d'estime* only. *The Golden Bowl* in fact sold well, if slowly, and went into second and third printings.[24]

24. The decline both in circulation and in critical venturesomeness of the older literary monthlies like *Harper's* and *The Century* coincides with the rise, on one side, of slicks like G. H. Lorimer's *Saturday Evening Post* or *Munsey's Magazine*, where serials by such writers as Hall Caine, F. Marion Crawford, Rider Haggard, and Anthony Hope began to flourish, and, on the other, of "little" magazines like *The Chap-Book* (Chicago) and *The Yellow Book* (London: edited by the American Henry Harland). James contributed to all three kinds during the '90s.

The rise of the slicks was of considerable importance to Anglo-American writing. It produced, among other effects, the characteristic new phenomenon of the middle-brow novelist—literate, intelligent,

The Golden Bowl is a good example of two elements in James's fiction that may appear incidental to interpretive criticism but were the solid basis of the saleability he fitfully enjoyed throughout his long career. One is the modishness of his usual subject matter; the other, the humor and wit of his exposition. James had his own good reasons for choosing subjects like international marriage and divorce or country-house manners and near-scandals—in short, the lives of the rich. The fact remains, however, that vulgar curiosity about the novel data of late nineteenth-century high life was the ready-made source of his general acceptance. Nothing he wrote served him worse with his public than those books, *The Bostonians, The Princess Casamassima,* in which he tried out other kinds of material. The art of prose fiction even in its subtlest developments has not lost touch with its ruder origins in gossip and anecdote, and James, who got more than a few of his subjects by listening at dinner tables, had no prejudice against this source of inspiration. And though the formal rendering in any one work of his may indeed transfigure its occasions, invariably it begins to be interesting

---

"serious" in choice of subject, passably inventive, thoroughly parasitic with regard to his craft, and not readily distinguishable from the genuine article—and it stabilized an audience perfectly attuned to him, which enjoyed the modest excitements of being just a little ahead of general public opinion and taste on moral questions. The *Cosmopolitan, Hearst's International, The Ladies' Home Journal, McClure's,* Mitchell Kennerley's *Forum,* and the *Post* printed Sarah Jewett, Ambrose Bierce, Kipling, H. G. Wells, Arnold Bennett, Willa Cather, Ring Lardner—and also Elinor Glyn, Marie Corelli, George Fitch's Old Siwash stories, and G. R. Chester's saga of Get-Rich-Quick Wallingford—but their staple in long fiction was the sentimental problem novel, the romance of slightly unconventional manners, by such professional space-fillers and conscience-muddlers as Robert W. Chambers, Eden Phillpotts, Maurice Hewlett, John Galsworthy (British novelists sold well on the American market, *c.*1900–1920), Booth Tarkington, David Graham Phillips, and Winston Churchill.

through the lively play of humor in his observation of things and the compositional wit through which one thing is linked to the next. Such humor and wit are James's sensationalism. They are his means, formally, of keeping up the interest initially established by the glamor, more or less, of his materials.

Two novels by friends and contemporaries of Henry James draw successfully on the same two elements and remain, in consequence, as readable, as seriously entertaining, as any work of the period. In both Henry Adams's *Esther* (1884) and Howard Sturgis's *Belchamber* (1904), modishness and humor combine to produce books that for sheer civility are very nearly unique in American writing around the turn of the century. *Esther* is one of the few American novels that, with respect to what is attempted, seem informed by a sufficiency of talk, a natural matrix of appropriate conversation, and that therefore appear sure of their own settled manner of speaking (surer, certainly, than does Adams's other and earlier novel, *Democracy*). The arrangement of characters in it is as artificial as in stage comedy—a "modernist" minister, a skeptical geologist, an artist, and two free "American" girls, one of New England descent and one from the wilds of Colorado—and so is the insistently clever dialogue (which owes something to literary models, James for one, but more to the conversational style of the Adams-Hay-LaFarge-Cameron circle). *Esther* scarcely tries for the natural realism of characterization that was almost the first rule for fiction in the heyday of Howells and the earlier James. Yet it is one of the few novels of the time that does not, in its crises, deal falsely with its people. Its show of how they react to the impersonal forces of natural feeling and social expectation, and its unembarrassed acceptance of the moral complicity of the lot in the play of these forces, are a notable imaginative achievement. Howells, for all his rumination about "moral complicity," could not have written the book in a hundred years.

The action of *Esther* revolves about the two young women (who talk with a freedom and directness that seem of 1920 rather than 1880). Their choices for the future are the significant issue of the characters' debates on religion, ethics, art, science, and evolution. Adams's conception of his heroine derives in part from James's Isabel Archer—"I want to know what she can make of life," says the artist Wharton—but is backed by an analysis that provides interesting cross-references to the analysis of "American Character" in the great *History* (see below, pp. 195–198), on which he was already at work. "She gives one the idea of a lightly sparred yacht in mid-ocean," Wharton continues. "She picks up all she knows without an effort and knows nothing well, yet she seems to understand whatever is said." That the novel comes close to tragedy is not unexpected, given this emphasis, especially as we recall what Henry Adams, contrasting primitive or medieval society to the modern age, would elsewhere make of the most intensely contemporary aspect of his heroine's situation, "her feminine want of motive in life." Esther in her intelligence and her discontent is an American version of one of Ibsen's heroines, the more effective as she embodies her creator's developing inquiry into the full historical meaning of modern civilization.[25]

Particularly in the relationship between Esther and the geologist Strong, who is her cousin and a possible husband for her and whom she fairly accuses of refusing her the moral help she has a right to expect from him, the book must always be a puzzle to Henry Adams's biographers. It may tell as much as can ever be known about his marriage, and Marian

25. Adams's Lowell lecture, "Primitive Rights of Women," had been delivered in 1876, and looks forward to his later interest as a historian in the cult worship of Venus and of the Virgin.

Adams's suicide in 1885; it may tell nothing at all. We do see that it stumbles at the climax, precisely on the point of Esther's decision to break her engagement to the minister, Hazard. Here if anywhere we must be made to feel that Esther's choice is one of heart, feeling, sensual attraction or repulsion, and not simply the sum of the co-ordinates of speculative argument that converge in the last decisive interview. Adams has drawn, in Hazard, a strong portrait of modern egoism—the better for being dressed in the robes of an enlightened Church —such as would make the drama of Esther's consent and subsequent refusal wholly reasonable. But at this climax it is the abstract co-ordinates rather than the living persons that are used to specify what happens, and it happens therefore not falsely but too abruptly, too dispiritedly; Adams defers just enough to realism to insist that passion is present in the final scene, but we feel only his insistence. The kind of philosophical comedy *Esther* points toward—it would have been a valuable addition to the rather narrow practice of American realism—Adams was to master in another form than the novel.

Sturgis's *Belchamber* seems a lighter undertaking, but it is unmistakably the more accomplished work; in its own way it is very nearly faultless.[26] That Henry James, reading it in

26. Howard Sturgis (1855–1920) was born and lived most of his life in England but remained an American and a Bostonian. He wrote three novels and a number of stories, one of which, "The China Pot" (still unpublished), evidently dramatizes the episode of Henry James's reading of *Belchamber*: see Elmer Borklund, "Howard Sturgis, Henry James, and *Belchamber*," *Modern Philology*, Vol. 58, 255–69. The brief account of Sturgis in Santayana's *Persons and Places*, II, 117–21, emphasizes, among other qualities, his personal "courage and distinction." But Santayana, whose literary taste was rather official, underrates *Belchamber* as a novel. A juster appreciation of Sturgis's intelligence and literary ability is suggested in Edith Wharton's *A Backward Glance* (1934), pp. 225–39.

proof, did find such fault with it that the modest author thought of giving it up as a bad job is an exact confirmation of just how far, by 1903, James's critical sense had put itself in hostage to the peculiarities of his own practice. James felt that, if you wrote a novel about a Marquis, there were "whole masses of Marquisate things and items, a multitude of inherent detail in his existence, which it isn't open to the painter *de gaieté de coeur* not to make some picture of"; in general he protested Sturgis's way of gliding by, in a phrase or two, some climax or confrontation that might have been worked up in brilliant detail. At the same time he objected to the "breadth" of certain scenes, in particular the pathetic little hero's unhappy wedding night. The truth is that James could no longer imagine what kind of novel Sturgis meant to write. Yet the genre is recognizable. Sturgis plays a narrow game with his satirical comedy—of a shy, good-hearted boy-man, embarrassed by his rank, steadily betrayed and without ordinary powers of resistance to his betrayers, never vindictive but never slackly forgiving either—and with the moral accents developed in it, but he plays it straight; and the fine result is as if Thackeray had somehow been crossed with the later Hawthorne. The clear intelligence directing the exposition balances the powerful simplicities of feeling that rise especially at the end, when the hero, Sainty, intercedes for and then loses the child of his wife's adultery. Sainty himself is well conceived (there is an element of self-portraiture) and firmly exploited. A great deal is "lost" on him—James could not get the point of him at all—and that is one great source of interest in him. The goodness he embodies is the more luminous just because he is pathetically unable to gain credit by it.

Satirical humor of a broader sort is the main virtue of a rather more representative work of the turn-of-the-century period, Harold Frederic's *The Damnation of Theron Ware*

(1896), which achieved a notable popular success. This interesting but recently overrated novel is at once an effort of critical realism—dealing as had Frederic's first novel, *Seth's Brother's Wife* (1887), with the decadence of village life and faith—and a problem novel (the hero is a career-making minister with clay feet), full of bits and pieces of the characteristic pseudothought of the time on questions of religion, science, race, breeding, evolution, and the like. A newspaper writer and, as correspondent for *The New York Times*, a noted figure in the literary Bohemia of Nineties London, Frederic (1856–1898) is justly remembered as a forerunner in provincial satire of Sinclair Lewis. His chronicle of Theron Ware's seduction by various arty and exotic new intellectual fashions has a journalistic facility of observation, but it is for the most part merely clever and knowing, at the expense of any clear ironic focus. The up-to-date cant Theron uses to defend his misbehavior (as in justifying his coldness to his wife and his infatuation with the sophisticated city girl, Celia, by allusions to "the inevitable harsh happenings in the great tragedy of Nature") is too frequently pressed into service for the author's own explanations. *The Damnation of Theron Ware* is most successful, its humor steadiest, with the incidental figures of Sister and Brother Soulsby, amiable entrepreneurs of a new, more efficient evangelism perfectly adapted to the rites of a society hell-bent on material success. In them the "wisdom of the serpent," which Sister Soulsby assures Theron he "simply can't get along without," is as plain and comfortable as a warm bath.

Such humor cannot entirely salvage a too hastily manufactured novel, but it can go a long way toward making the novel readable, as *Theron Ware* still is. There is no humor at all and only the crudest irony in another once-celebrated novel of the period dealing with the corruption of the socially ambitious, Robert Grant's *Unleavened Bread* (1900). Painstaking in their representation of contemporary manners and morals, the problem novels of this proper-Boston judge (1852–1940) are without a trace of developed moral perception.[27] Nor is there much humor, or insight, or even, from one book to the next, intelligible point of view of any kind in the many studies of city life and corruption by the improbably prolific David Graham Phillips (1867–1911), who had some contemporary standing as a muckraker and exposer of uncomfortable social truths. The most that can be said for most popular novelists of this breed is that the atmosphere of the Progressive movement at least improved their choice of subject. Among the many who around the turn of the century wrote about the headline problems of contemporary life, Winston Churchill (1871–1947) probably survives as well as any, at least the light-handed Winston Churchill of *Mr. Crewe's Career* (1908). Alternating best-selling chronicles of the American Revolution (*Richard Carvel*, 1899; *The Crossing*, 1904) with romances of nineteenth-century social and political life (*The Crisis*, 1901; *Coniston*, 1906), Churchill was basically as formula-ridden as any other master of the popular market. He was also, in his views of the characteristic problems of modern society, equally subject to *idées fixes* and to cure-all solutions of a vaguely religious nature, particularly in later novels like *The Inside of the Cup* (1913) and *The Dwelling Place of Light* (1917). But in passages of satirical comedy lightly posing ethical issues—as with the absurd political "career" of the self-approving financier, Humphrey Crewe, and the contrasting progress of the free-spirited Victoria Flint, a vintage "American girl" and one of the few genuinely attractive characters in all this mass of work—Churchill could tell his conventional story as efficiently as could, say, James Gould Cozzens a generation later, and with a distinctly pleasanter wit.

27. Robert Grant is chiefly remembered now for the acquiescent though undoubtedly conscientious role he played in the Sacco-Vanzetti case as a member of the Governor's committee.

Humor is perhaps not a cardinal literary virtue. But its presence even in mild solution is one of the surer signs—for unlike the cardinal virtues it cannot be faked—of that "capacity for straight impressions" which James in "The Art of Fiction" placed first among the requirements for good work. The wit that can execute figures of effective comedy is at least first cousin to the intelligence required to control the most exacting subjects. Thus it is not surprising that, of the writers who after 1885 turned their attention to contemporary city life and manners, not many hold their flavor so well as certain ones who never pretended to be more than journeymen humorists and entertainers: O. Henry (1862–1910), despite his notorious rigging of plots and ironies; Finley Peter Dunne (1867–1936), creator of the unflappable Mr. Dooley; George Ade (1866–1944), like Dunne—and Eugene Field before them both—a Chicago newspaper writer, whose sharp eye for the domestic manners of the Americans and precise ear for those shady margins of speech where euphemism mates with cliché to produce more perfect nonsense prepared the ground for Ring Lardner and Scott Fitzgerald as well as for Perelman and Thurber. If only for one passage, a permanent niche in American literary history should be held for George Ade, and that is his careful summary of his own essential career as an American author during the proconsulship of Howells:

> My early stuff [he wrote] was intended to be "realistic" and I believed firmly in short words and short sentences. By a queer twist of circumstances I have been known to the general public as a writer of slang. I never wanted to be a comic or tried to be one. . . . Always I wrote for the "family trade" and I used no word or phrase which might give offense to mother and the girls or to a professor of English.

By contrast a total absence of humor is symptomatic in the interesting case of Hamlin Garland (1860–1940), who once seemed a more important figure for literary history than he does now. It is easy to make fun of Garland—as Henry Blake

Fuller did in "The Downfall of Abner Joyce" (1901) and the critic Percival Pollard in *Their Day in Court* (1909). He conducted his career with a terrible earnestness, like a marginal Senator with vice-presidential aspirations, and he was inclined to announce its incidental readjustments with manifestoes meant to revolutionize literary history, as in the essays collected in *Crumbling Idols* (1894). Here he developed the new protorealist principle of "veritism"—which in practice seems to have meant that an author's job was to tell the story of his life over and over again. For the role of literary arbiter he wanted to play, Garland simply lacked the equipment—the discriminating intelligence, the critical (and self-critical) judgment.

Otherwise, a certain viable stock of experience and emotion was not lacking. Garland's concern for the amelioration of the common lot—he thought of "veritism" as an instrument of democratization—was genuine, being based on memories of the drab, inequitable social order of the upper Middle West of his childhood; and the novels he wrote during his affiliation with the Populist and Single Tax movements, like *Jason Edwards: An Average Man* and *A Spoil of Office* (both 1892), had the merit of propagandizing for honorable causes. But confronted by a book like Frank Norris's *Mc-Teague*, Garland showed how the liberating standard of realism could relapse into nothing more than a new way of raising the old sentimental-utilitarian test of value: "What avail is this study of sad lives?" he asked, "for it does not even lead to a notion of social betterment." Possibly the popular romances of frontier adventure he himself produced during the first fifteen years of the new century were meant as his own belated tribute to "social betterment." Yet in those few books in which Garland drew directly on childhood recollection, he made a genuine contribution to the documentary record of American life. There are his first collections of stories, *Main-Travelled Roads* (1891) and *Prairie Folks*

(1893), and there is the autobiographical work of his later years, particularly *Boy Life on the Prairie* (1899) and *A Son of the Middle Border* (1917). Of writing of this kind, nearly artless but grounded in unshakable personal impressions, Henry James, again, made the essential critical point:

> There are moments when we are tempted to say that there is nothing like saturation—to pronounce it a safer thing than talent. I find myself rejoicing, for example, in Mr. Hamlin Garland, a case of saturation so precious as to have almost the value of genius.

Of the first-generation inheritors of realism the most promising were Henry Blake Fuller (1857–1929) and Robert Herrick (1868–1938), both key figures in the Chicago pre-renaissance of 1890–1910. With both, however, our main impression now is of arrested development, of miscarriage and waste in the working out of their opportunities. This impression somewhat outweighs what they have to say as novelists. Or, perhaps, it confirms what they have to say— for they appear to us finally as victims of just those conditions of life they set themselves to describe: not only the anarchic scramble for wealth and pleasure and the surly indifference of most of the new rich to decent standards in conduct or art, but also the whole spreading disorder of spirit and civil custom of which, in Chicago near the turn of the century, they not unreasonably saw themselves at the dynamic center.

In Fuller's case the quarrel with contemporary American life found expression in two different forms. He is chiefly remembered for the critical realism of his first two Chicago novels, *The Cliff-Dwellers* (1893) and *With the Procession* (1895); it was the latter that Theodore Dreiser said had given him a first glimpse of how the actual contemporary scene might be presented in fiction. But before these, Fuller, who regularly traveled to Europe and would have settled abroad if he had been free to, had embodied his dream of escape in two fantasies of the pursuit (European) of the rarer pleasures of life: *The Chevalier of Pensieri-Vani* (1890) and *The Châtelaine de la Trinité* (1892). The studied charm and the philosophic airs and graces of these pseudochronicles have not worn well, but the mode of contemplative fantasy in which they are set deserves to be noted as a serious alternative to topical realism.[28]

But even in these books the rude American circumstance rears its head. One of the principals of *The Chevalier of Pensieri-Vani* is Mr. George W. Occident of Shelbyville, Shelby County, U.S.A., a "barbarian" and "blank page" who trails about Italy "picking up ideas with the utmost readiness" but shedding them just as quickly. At the end he returns to Shelbyville where, despite the "general awfulness," he will at last feel at home again. The more direct judgments of Chicagoism that Fuller offered in *The Cliff-Dwellers*, published the year of the Columbian Exposition, were undisguised and unsparing. The city's "thousands of acres of ramshackle" and "ugly half-built prairie" are the setting for rapacities of fortune-making that overthrow the most sacred family pieties—marriages are sacrificed, sons stab fathers, funerals (the episode is used twice) are only further occasions

28. Fantasy in this vein has had a long vogue in American writing. Though it reached a perfect pitch of vulgarization in the Poictesme romances of James Branch Cabell, the first of which appeared in 1913, it continued to attract younger talents like Conrad Aiken and Thornton Wilder in the 1920s and turned up again a generation later in Steinbeck's *The Short Reign of Pippin IV*, one of that uneven writer's trimmest performances. Fuller himself, still active in the mid-'20s as a reviewer, personally encouraged the young Wilder. His own last work in this mode, *Gardens of this World*, appeared in 1929, the year of his death.

An earlier piece by Fuller worth noting, at least for historical reasons, is a burlesque written in 1884 for the new satirical weekly, *Life:* "A Transcontinental Episode, or, Metamorphoses at Muggins' Misery: a Co-operative Novel by Bret James and Henry Harte."

for real-estate bargaining. The "cliff-dwellers," occupants of a modern office building, are pictured as a tribal community caught up in the rites of an unprecedented new culture, or anticulture. But in various small ways the force of these judgments is dissipated. Side issues are interposed: the character nearest the author's point of view, a transplanted New Englander, is made to criticize Chicago for its indifference to "the graces and draperies of culture"—as if these could redeem it! The underlying fault is in the point of view itself. Fuller's attitude toward his Chicagoans is closer to mere contempt than a basically naturalistic exposition can afford. Facetiousness and condescension freeze the book's materials within the author's prejudgment, which so much the more readily passes over into a kind of high-minded irritation that is sure death to the imaginative sympathy the form of the realistic novel fundamentally builds upon. Condescension and irritation: they are the peculiar disorders of the dispossessed superior man of modern times, and they corrode Herrick's fiction too. Novels can passably survive lapses in structure, slackness in the development of themes, but a failure of sympathy, of imaginative perception, is likely to be fatal. Just here, in contrast to Fuller and Herrick, is the incomparably greater strength of Dreiser, who took Chicagoism for what it was, without reference to superior Boston-Athenian precedent, and so could see deeper into both its glamor and its essential ruinousness to all who were bound to it.

Herrick is not so attractive a figure as Fuller, but it is possible to think that he came nearer to distinction as a novelist.[29] A decade younger, he was less the partisan social

29. New England-born, Harvard-educated, Robert Herrick taught rhetoric and literature at the University of Chicago for thirty years but stiffly kept his distance in spirit from the city and the institution that gave him his best materials and provided him with his living. A certain liberal idealism never died out in him, however, and late in life he served honorably, under the New Deal, as government secretary for the Virgin Islands.

critic, more the objective analyst of contemporary manners and character. The titles of an early and a late novel, *The Gospel of Freedom* (1898) and *Waste* (1924), frame his moral concern with the new order, and disorder, of American life. Ethical dilemmas absorb his characters' attention—is the chance for worldly success, for liberation and happiness, worth paying for in the coinage of the spirit?—and their choices are dignified by being described, up to a point, with something like a naturalistic fatality. Herrick's fictional table of moneyed American types is genuinely interesting. He is especially good on the class-conditioned folkways of male egoism and on the whole overwrought psychology of the parish of rich women. Indeed in occasional passages of psychological analysis we begin to hear for almost the first time in American writing the direct inner voice of our own harried contemporary consciousness. It deserves to be noted that the following passage, from Herrick's most ambitious novel, *Together* (1908), antedates D. H. Lawrence by several years:

> She knew what marriage was to be, although she had never listened to the allusions whispered among married women and more experienced girls. Something in the sex side of the relations between men and women had always made her shrink. She was not so much pure in body and soul, as without sex, unborn. She knew the fact of nature, the eternal law of life repeating itself through desire and passion; but she realized it remotely, only in her mind, as some necessary physiological mechanism of living, like perspiration, fatigue, hunger. But it had not spoken in her body, in her soul; she did not feel that it ever could speak to her as it was speaking in the man's lighted eyes, in his lips. So now as always she was cold, tranquil beneath her lover's kisses.

This is the best of Herrick and has the virtue of rendering directly a sufficiently acute perception with a neo-Puritan seriousness of tone; like comparable passages in the earlier Lawrence it risks a certain verbal coarseness in order to set out as directly as possible significant facts of actual feeling.

What sets Herrick apart at once from Lawrence as a novelist,
however, is his inability to judge accurately the weight such
perceptions will bear in the extended framework of a story.
Somehow he thought that the self-indulgence and self-grati-
fication of the moneyed and leisured could be dressed out in
narrative as representative of the whole stuff of significant
human experience. It is a failure in imaginative assessment.
As if to compensate, his writing is full of "philosophic" catch
phrases from half the fashionable *pseudodoxia* of the day: we
hear "Anglo-Saxon" this, "male" and "female" that, how
"Brute and God lie close together," what "Nature" decrees,
what "Life" is and what the "New Life" will be, and so on—
Herrick had a significant weakness for capital letters. He had
a weakness also for furnishing vaguely transcendental solutions to the dilemmas of the characters he favored, who escape
to the north woods or to mind-cure establishments—as in
Together and also in *The Master of the Inn* (1908) and *The
Healer* (1911)—or merge into some uncomfortable suburban
version of what is alleged to be the common lot, as in *The
Common Lot* (1904) and *A Life for a Life* (1910). Such
solutions are legion in middle-brow fiction, taking the place
of imaginative inquiry. They appear, in fact, to be the characteristic vice of writers whose imaginations, underprovided,
have not been able to take firm hold of their elected materials.
These writers, as we encounter them around 1900, form a
distinct American type. They have a sharp sense of the spreading corruption, the barbarism, round about them—but we
note that they always date its rise from some odd point early
in the history of their own insulated coming of age. They
are unable to get an accurate fix on their own position in
history; at the same time they lack the simple democratic
humility, the intelligence and the compassion, to understand
their own full participation in the common fate. They cannot
free themselves from dreams of countervailing power and

control—power and control which of course are not different in kind from that exercised by the success-worshipers and fortune-builders they pretend to despise. Such ruminators on leisure-class ethical anxieties are with us yet in middle-brow fiction; Robert Penn Warren, one of the most inventive of the type, is a case to keep in view.

The most accomplished American novelist of the generation born in the 1850s and 1860s was undoubtedly Edith Wharton (1862–1937). The quality of her achievement, however, is not easy to define. Though she dealt in her most ambitious work with "society" in the large in its Newport-Fifth Avenue-international phases, and though she could fill in the appropriate material details as thickly and emblematically as could Dreiser, she seems narrower in her range than her male contemporaries, more prepossessive morally, essentially personal in conception and judgment. Yet her talent can make theirs seem amateurish. Realism in the novel for Edith Wharton meant first of all artistic thoroughness. The inward ramifications of some geometrically compact subject were to be turned over until its dramatic content was wrung dry. For this reason technical control was a first necessity. She did her work, if not, as is sometimes claimed, in imitation of Henry James, then very much as if under James's critical eye—though unlike Howard Sturgis she does not seem to have been cowed by James's resistance to her own different manner and purpose.

It is possible to decide of Edith Wharton that absorption in technique kept her from fulfilling her potential as a writer. But the opposite is equally likely. Reading her memoir, *A Backward Glance* (1934), with its recollection of the disdain of the "old New York" of merchants and lawyers for "people who write," and remembering the difficult circumstances of her early marriage to an increasingly invalided older man to

whose strict regimen of gentlemanly idleness she was bound
for more than twenty years,[30] we may wonder at her becoming a writer at all. She was as late a starter as any comparably
important figure in our literature; she was past forty before
she produced anything at all superior to the routine magazine
work of the day. It may well have been just this willed submission to the rigors of technique—more exactly, to a solemn
ideal of right technique—that enabled her to break through
as she did to a genuine release of private feeling.

For it is as a prose poet of certain bitter, obsessive themes
of private life (they are much the same as Fuller's and Herrick's themes: victimization and self-betrayal, waste, sickness,
spiritual desolation) that Edith Wharton has her undeniable
force as a writer. Following in any particular book her sharp
satirical observation of manners and noting her ability to work
across a considerable variety of social types and conditions,
we may be tempted to see her as primarily a social historian.
But in reading several novels and stories together, we see how
repetitive and monotonous her observation is and how prearranged. The detached cleverness of her comment, the brittle
clarity of her style, the mechanical ironies of comeuppance
and retribution that regularly fall upon her characters, exposing the degrading weakness and baseness beneath their
social masks: all such effects reinforce this general impression.
She tells one grim human story over and over again, and the
more varied the circumstances she surrounds it with, the more
it seems to impose itself on her imagination from within.

Characteristically Edith Wharton's stories issue in certain
intense images or metaphors that sum up the whole drift of

30. The marriage, made when she was twenty-three and Edward
Wharton thirty-six, ended in divorce in 1913, but only after her
husband had been more or less insane for several years. Not
surprisingly her stories and novels repeatedly dramatize the plight
of persons trapped in some inescapable network of moral obligation.

the action and that communicate their moral coloring even when the plot they serve is as artificial as any of O. Henry's. These metaphoric climaxes are much alike; and though they are scrupulously fitted to the character or situation in hand, any one of them might come from any one of her stories or novels over a thirty-year period. Thus, from "The Angel at the Grave" (*Crucial Instances,* 1901):

> She felt a desperate longing to escape into the outer air, where people toiled and loved, and living sympathies went hand in hand. It was the sense of wasted labor that oppressed her; of two lives consumed in that ruthless process that uses generations of effort to build a single cell.

From the short novel, *Sanctuary* (1903):

> Her son had come: her life had brimmed over; but now the tide ebbed again, and she was left gazing over a bare stretch of wasted years. Wasted!

From *The House of Mirth* (1905), her first full-scale attempt to represent the moral order of modern life:

> She had a sense of deeper impoverishment—of an inner destitution compared to which outward conditions dwindled into insignificance. It was indeed miserable to be poor. . . . But there was something more miserable still—it was the clutch of solitude at her heart, the sense of being swept like a stray uprooted growth down the heedless current of the years.

From the pastoral tragedy, *Ethan Frome* (1911):

> The inexorable facts closed in on him like prison-warders handcuffing a convict. There was no way out—none. He was a prisoner for life, and now his one ray of light was to be extinguished.

From *The Reef* (1912):

> . . . they confronted each other, no longer as enemies—so it seemed to her—but as beings of different language who had forgotten the few words they had learned of each other's speech.

From *The Age of Innocence* (1920), generally rated her best novel:

> ... she stood before him as an exposed and pitiful figure, to be saved at all costs from farther wounding herself in her mad plunges against fate.

Or from "Atrophy" (*Certain People*, 1928):

> Somehow she managed to travel the distance that separated her from them, though her bones ached with weariness, and at every step she seemed to be lifting a leaden weight.[31]

Something of Edith Wharton's force of mind and of her bitter personal apprehension of life is in nearly everything she wrote, even the potboilers and self-parodies she increasingly permitted herself after 1920. There is a core of grim conviction in her work: that life is a prison or trap or wasteland; that frustration and abasement are the universal fate; and that persons are contemptible, at best remotely pitiable, in their persistent efforts to keep up appearances. Blake Nevius has called her primary subject the situation of "a large and generous nature . . . trapped by circumstances"—but it is a question whether any such natures are to be found in her work. The superior qualities attributed to certain characters are for the reader a matter of hearsay only; what we are really shown points another way. The only real force of character or mind in Edith Wharton's work is her own. Her men are particularly disagreeable. The strongest are caricature vulgarians, like Gus Trenor, George Dorset, and the Jew Rosedale in *The House of Mirth*; while her usual male protagonist, the cultivated, moneyed gentleman diffidently following a respectable profession like law or diplomacy—Laurence Selden in *The House of Mirth*, Newland Archer

31. Several of these passages may remind us of Edith Wharton's lifelong mastery of the special form of the ghost story: see *Tales of Men and Ghosts* (1910) and *Ghosts* (1937).

in *The Age of Innocence*, George Darrow in *The Reef*—sooner or later becomes a perfect parody of leisure-class bloodlessness and deviousness, Gilbert Osmonds without the sting. She is neither generous in herself nor able to imagine generosity in others.

It is her manipulation of character that raises the gravest doubts about Edith Wharton's fiction. Again and again, at the dramatic climax, we find her shifting her ground morally, forcing her people to behave with a melodramatic weakness or baseness that is arbitrary with respect to what has previously been shown of them. The effect is like cheating in a detective novel; essential information, suppressed earlier, is brought in at the last moment. But the fault basically is not formal (though it is thrown into relief by her incidental realism and involves what Percy Lubbock acknowledged as her tendency to cut corners, "to reap her harvest before it is ripe"). We sense a positive vindictiveness in Edith Wharton, a personal relish for punishing her characters. None are spared—neither those who violate the norms of decency, nor those who rebel against the falseness of these norms, nor those others who keep aloof from either course and so from life itself; all must be brought low and made to grovel. Edmund Wilson identified something fundamental to the case of Edith Wharton when he described her as "a brilliant example of the writer who relieves an emotional strain by denouncing his generation"—though even that formulation somewhat flatters the actual case; one might rather say that she was one who, as a novelist, regularly escaped imaginative predicaments by betraying the figures of her own grudging conception.

Nevertheless she took her art seriously and worked hard to back her dramatic themes with a sufficiency of objective detail. *The House of Mirth*, her first important success, undertakes in support of the main story a panoramic survey of New

York "society" at that point in time which most interested her—when inherited forms and traditions still ruled but were already in retreat before the coarser dispositions of a new age. (She had chosen a corresponding moment in the Italian eighteenth century for her historical novel of 1902, *The Valley of Decision*.) What is most characteristic of the scheme of *The House of Mirth*, however, is that nobody comes out of it well, neither the old families nor the vulgar new rich, and certainly not third parties like the social worker, Gerty Farish. In the curiously varied books Edith Wharton wrote during the next several years, control of technique and tone remains the constant factor, sometimes sufficient, sometimes not. The short novel, *Madame de Treymes* (1907), is an essay at the Jamesian "international" theme, while *The Fruit of the Tree* (1907) is an ill-advised offering to the contemporary fashion for problem novels on important topics (factory conditions and mercy killing are leading themes); neither succeeds. Yet with *Ethan Frome* (1911), treating a subject that might again seem beyond her imaginative reach, she had her greatest popular success. About this bleak *tour de force* of circumstantial tragedy critical opinion stands divided. Those who have heard it praised too much invariably react against the mechanical ironies of the plot, while those who come back to it over this objection invariably rediscover its undeniable power and integrity of feeling.[32]

Right after *Ethan Frome* Edith Wharton published her most

32. Two subsequent studies of poverty and village desperation—"The Bunner Sisters" (1916: the "village" in this case being Manhattan) and *Summer* (1917)—show at least that *Ethan Frome* was not a fluke. *Summer* especially, with its tense images of desire and impulse, "lost years" and "wasted passion," and its strong contrast of the freedom of the degenerate "Mountain" people against the "harsh code of the village"—the pathetically rebellious heroine, Charity Royall, is caught between—is a more affecting book than the lurid melodrama of its climaxes would seem to permit.

slavishly Jamesian work, *The Reef* (1912), a polite melodrama whose strict formal concentration won from James himself an elaborate letter of congratulation that makes rather free use of the designation "Racinian." This is also, however, the novel in which the author's subjective interference is most flagrant, quite shockingly so in the open malice with which the most vital and passionate (hence least assimilable) of the main characters is disposed of in the last chapter. With *The Custom of the Country* (1913), she shifted again, to a broad satire of contemporary manners featuring, in gross caricature, the social-climbing, man-eating Undine Spragg of Apex City. Sinclair Lewis's dedication of *Babbitt* to Edith Wharton, a decade later, pays a just tribute to this precedent. But the novel as a whole is put seriously out of joint by the absoluteness of the author's hatred for her main character; it is one of several books in which we have to say that she overplays her hand. The more restrained satire of *The Age of Innocence* (1920) is considerably more effective. Edith Wharton's control of her "old New York" subject is at its most tactful in this novel, and though her development of the story (once more, of the sacrifice of persons to a standard of traditional decorum) again leans on the conveniences of melodrama, it does not wholly surrender to them. For all its occasional sharpness of tone and comment, it is more tolerant in its outlook upon human character, more acquiescent in the playing out of empty and unprofitable lives. Like Howells's *Vacation of the Kelwyns*, issued the same year, *The Age of Innocence* looks back to an earlier, simpler time—the 1870s in both instances —and sees clearly enough its strange human inadequacy, but does not judge it harshly; looks back to it, rather, with a touching degree of personal forgiveness.

Susceptibility to the highest forces is the highest genius.
—Henry Adams, *The Education of Henry Adams*

3. LITERATURE OF ARGUMENT

𝒯HE BOOKS that belong to literary history are above all the books that have "changed our minds"—if only, at first, the minds of a few other writers. These books are not all novels, poetry, drama, what is zoned off in libraries and college catalogues as the domain of "literature." Particularly for the late nineteenth century, the empire-building age of modern learning, the line of demarcation between works of creative imagination and works of constructive argument cannot be drawn distinctly; indeed the classic qualities, for the arts, of original perception, compositional intelligence, and concordant style were if anything rather more frequent and more compelling in certain works of disciplined scientific inquiry than in any other department of letters. If we do not admit such works into our conception of the literature of the period, it is surely our conception of literature that is at fault. It will not only be too narrow by half but confused and incomplete about the actual nature of what it does embrace, about the "meaning" of novels, poetry, drama. Let our standard of classification be at least as generous as the one matter-of-factly set out in the letter William James wrote to Howells in August of 1890, as from one secure virtuoso to another: "The year which shall have witnessed the apparition of your 'Hazard of New Fortunes,' of Harry's 'Tragic Muse,' and of *my* 'Psychology' will indeed be a memorable one in American literature."

The prose writing discussed in this chapter is not to be thought of merely as "background." In terms of creative originality, of conscious experience put in order in language which is itself a prime agent and correspondent of that ordering, *The Principles of Psychology* and a dozen other prose treatises of the succeeding twenty years represent a literary achievement of the first importance. Nowhere did the literary potentiality, so to speak, of this period express itself more characteristically than in these thorough, detailed works of systematic description or inductive synthesis, particularly in fields of thought—history, sociology, psychology, anthropology—the very submission of which to disciplined empirical inquiry was at the heart of the period's essential effort of mind. It is really in this body of writing (for which our critical custom lacks convenient designations) that the great questions which play through all the literature of the period were identified as statable questions: what kind of creature the creature man is and bound to what kind of history; whether creaturely life and its "evolutionary" patterns of growth and change are morally intelligible and whether intelligence can affect them to the point of exerting control over them, substituting "mastery" for "drift"; whether the present disorder of society and the accelerating multiplication of the general capacity for creating disorder constitute a decisive turning point in mankind's long tenure of earth; and whether, in all such speculation, what is meant by terms like "God" or "consciousness" or "reason" or "evolution" or "the world" or any other referential absolute can be said actually to "exist."

Literary history has not generally avoided such work without good reason. The problems of rating it are difficult enough within the separate fields of thought, the professional disciplines, involved, to say nothing of making comparisons. The present chapter is not put forward as constituting any sort of breakthrough in critical procedure. It is not intended as even a preliminary survey of the intellectual history of the period. Specialists may find the emphasis peculiar and may well question the selection of names and titles. But that some such account belongs at the center of this volume and that the kind of writing discussed in it has a place on the full spectrum of literary creativity are points to be insisted on. Poetry, philosophy, science, history, narration are all, in the hands of their major practitioners, ways of clarification and explanation. In each case, success is a function less of the will to make a significant impression than of the sustained imaginative effort to take fair and full account of some troubling complex of actual experience; the motives and capacities required for high achievement are not fundamentally different. Also, the more we recognize the symbolic and absorptive nature of all the languages used by men (perhaps even those expressly created to be otherwise—philosophers of language disagree on this point), the more we sense the singleness of the directing imagination that exercises and renews itself in them.

Sociology and Anthropology:
William Graham Sumner

The main relevance to imaginative literature of the characteristic new "life sciences" coming into prominence in the late nineteenth century is in the inherent realism of their approach to human conduct and human history. The relation is not one of intellectual cause and effect—though direct borrowings from scientific argument can be found in abundance and though (to take an important case) the immense self-assurance of the English polyhistor, Herbert Spencer (1820–1903), in setting out laws to explain everything all at once and in one way, has much to answer for as a practical influence on the minds of writers. The situation is rather that a common shift in outlook, responding to all the tendencies of the age, underlies the conscious emergence of an element of empirical realism, or of outright positivism, in, at one and the same time, fiction, journalism, social theory, and social science.[1] Modern sociology, psychology, and anthropology, as they developed, were according to their nature empirical and relativistic in outlook, though individual practitioners could be perfect dogmatists. Sired by ambitious curiosity out of disillusionment, and reared to serve the western world's widening consciousness of ways of behavior not included in its received books of rules, these disciplines inevitably took a

1. The sense of undertakings in common must be kept centrally in mind, although our description of them proceeds piecemeal. If somehow it was not known that Stephen Crane's *Maggie*, Jacob Riis's *The Children of the Poor*, Henry Demarest Lloyd's *Wealth Against Commonwealth*, Richard T. Ely's *Socialism and Social Problems*, Lyman Abbott's *The Evolution of Christianity*, and G. Stanley Hall's *The Contents of Children's Minds on Entering School* were products of a single two-year period in the '90s, might it not reasonably be guessed?

central place in the extraordinary reconstitution of philosophy and learning that has characterized the past century.

There is little fineness of mind and less grace of expression in the writings of the two leading American sociologists of the period, the redoubtable William Graham Sumner (1840–1910) and Lester F. Ward (1841–1913). Jargon and tautology may be unavoidable in such work, and when a writer of social analysis (or historian or critic) is praised for style, what we usually find is only the gross fluency of second-hand journalism or classroom lecturing. Nevertheless a continual insensitivity in expression to both the observed particularity of things and to the effective idiom of common discourse—resulting in lapses of tone and imaginative reference more damaging than any thinness of evidence or even faulty reasoning—must force us to ask not whether the line of argument is true but whether it seriously touches the phenomena of experience it presumes to address. The professional importance, however, of Sumner's and Ward's writing is beyond question. Moreover, precisely as the opposing hypotheses they are remembered for—the Darwinistic fatalism of the first in describing the competitive relations of men, the evolutionary meliorism of the second in looking toward some rational transformation of this system of relations—no longer require us to choose sides, the qualities of mind common to both come to the fore and increasingly hold our attention. These qualities are the representative Victorian intellectual virtues: energy, abundance, organization. The whole progressive argument of Ward's *The Psychic Factors in Civilization* (1893) especially bears witness to them. That they also correspond to the leading virtues of the school of naturalism in fiction, emerging with Zola and entering American literature in the 1890s, is a notable fact of modern literary history.

Sumner's writing, in the lecture-essays that made him for a

generation a figure of consequence among Yale under-
graduates and truth-seeking magazine subscribers, is generally
brisk and fluent, in that style of oratorical hectoring that
passed and still passes for responsible public discussion in our
society. He had a special flair for phrasemaking and slo-
ganeering—"History is only a tiresome repetition of one
story," he launches out, or (in a sentence which, except for its
entire earnestness, could plausibly be attributed to Mark
Twain), "The maxim, or injunction, to which a study of
capital leads us is, Get capital." The harsher the better, is the
rule here. In fairness it must be said that the notorious
Gradgrindism of the tract on social obligation from which
both these sentences are taken, *What Social Classes Owe to
Each Other* (1883), derives in part from Sumner's insistence
on the right of the social scientist to study the laws of actual
behavior objectively and dispassionately, a right that had to
be fought for in American universities of the 1880s. Sociology,
like literary realism, had to make its way forward against the
high-minded suspicion that it was morally destructive. Nevertheless it rather serves Sumner right that his tract's key
epithet, "the Forgotten Man"—by which he meant that
curious petty-bourgeois folk hero, the man who has "behaved
himself, fulfilled his contracts, and asked for nothing"—
should have been rehabilitated by the rhetoric of the welfare-
minded New Deal in the 1930s to describe all those victims
of poverty and disadvantage whom Sumner coolly wrote off
(though granting them "good will" and "mutual respect") as
evolutionary misfits. Sumner was at least consistent in expressing his views. In a more attractive cause, yet still in defense
of traditional American morality as he conceived it, he issued
an equally uncompromising attack upon American imperialism
in 1898, the ironic title of which, "The Conquest of the
United States by Spain," suggests his ordinary competence

in fixing attention verbally upon the issues that concerned him.[2]

In the nature of the task set, Sumner's chief work, *Folkways* (1907), is more descriptive compendium than organized treatise. But a first measure of its actual impressiveness is that in the classic way of truly original work its key terms, "folkways" and "mores," became household words. The encyclopedic method and mass of the work made Sumner's coinages something more than mere catchwords. *Folkways* never became any such source of metaphor for poets and novelists as *The Golden Bough* (1890–1915); compared to Frazer, Sumner is an assiduous and perceptive compiler of data but no restorer of forgotten myth. But if it is not a book that changed the literary mind, it is a monument to a change of mind of the utmost importance. (So, too, is Franz Boas's influential essay of 1911, *The Mind of Primitive Man*, one of the sacred books of contemporary American anthropology.) Beginning with the table of contents—with chapter headings like "Kinship, Blood Revenge, Primitive Justice, Peace Unions," or "Sacral Harlotry, Child Sacrifice," or "The Mores Can Make Anything Right and Prevent Condemnation of Anything"—the drift of Sumner's book, as John Chamberlain said of it, "is perfectly plain: the one great idea that you take away from 'Folkways' is the idea of the relativity of cultures." Documented backwards and forwards, how could this idea fail to make common cause with literary realism,

2. An ideological partisan of Sumner's views called this, forty years later, "one of the noblest pieces of polemical writing in the language." More recently Sumner has been reclaimed as a minor prophet of radical, or Pyrrhonistic, "conservatism," and *What Social Classes Owe to Each Other* has been reissued by a publishing house specializing in tracts against the welfare state, the "Yalta betrayal," "Communism's Stronghold—THE INCOME TAX," and similar windmills.

reinforcing the spreading revolt against the rule of defunct illusion and inherited prejudice?

Thorstein Veblen (1855–1929)

With Thorstein Veblen, distinctions of intellectual background and creative foreground give way altogether. "The keenest social thinker of his time," in the judgment of the English sociologist, J. A. Hobson, Veblen was also a master of prose explanation and argument and, in his most widely read book, one of the few satirists, or caricaturists, of adult stature and strength in American letters. More than that, he was a mythmaker; it is difficult to think what our conception of the culture of industrialism (or our practice of cultural analysis) would be without the element of Veblenism. Much of the intellectual history of the era being examined may be characterized as an inquiry into the meaning of the evolutionary point of view, that is, of the definition of phenomena according to their observed capacity for growth, change, and deterioration; and it is first of all by the inventive thoroughness of Veblen's application of this point of view that his work secures its authority. The idea of an evolutionary dimension in phenomenal existence meant, to Veblen, not only that new theories and value-standards would have to be devised for the proper consideration of data. It meant that the data itself would have to be reimagined, including the very language for dealing with it. Veblen's service to economic theory was to graft upon it, through a Darwinian "institutionalism" which focused on the living totality of the economic process in the whole life process of its agents, a fresh stock of concepts from sociology, anthropology, and psychology, thus setting a standard for serious work which academic successors have found difficult to live with but impossible to discard. His coincidental service to letters is scarcely less important. It is to have done his work with a specifically literary authority, a self-fulfilling responsiveness (conceptual, formal, stylistic) to the problem of statement and definition; and in the peculiar nature of the history of thought—where what is done can never be exactly predicted, yet, once done, cannot be undone—it is possibly the more permanently valuable service.

The case for Veblen as a writer does not rest merely on those mock-solemn satirical passages on the fashions of the "pecuniary culture" in dress or church-going or educational ritual which brought his first book, *The Theory of the Leisure Class* (1899), immediately into general notice; these passages have, in fact, dated faster than nearly anything else in his work. It rests rather with his power of concentrated prose argument, in a style which may appear idiosyncratic but which, as it goes forward, shows itself equal to the ends in view and creates a thoroughgoing imaginative acceptance. This judgment may be put at once to the test. Here is the opening paragraph of Chapter VIII of *The Theory of the Leisure Class* (a title which is itself the stroke of a natural stylist):

> The life of man in society, just like the life of other species, is a struggle for existence, and therefore it is a process of selective adaptation. The evolution of social structure has been a process of natural selection of institutions. The progress which has been and is being made in human institutions and in human character may be set down, broadly, to a natural selection of the fittest habits of thought and to a process of enforced adaptation of individuals to an environment which has progressively changed with the growth of the community and with the changing institutions under which men have lived. Institutions are not only themselves the result of a selective and adaptive process which shapes the prevailing or dominant types of spiritual attitude and aptitudes; they are at the same time special methods of life and of human relations, and are therefore in their turn efficient factors of selection. So that the changing institutions in their turn make for a further selection of individuals

endowed with the fittest temperament, and a further adaptation of individual temperament and habits to the changing
environment through the formation of new institutions.

This is not, at first glance, a style that charms hearing. The
passage lacks even that heavy rhetorical irony—with allegedly
neutral and scientific terminology pounding home in sentence
upon loaded sentence the severest moral accusations it can
manage—which has made Veblen a folk hero of twentieth-
century dissidence and noncompliance. It only does its job
irresistibly. Not only is the burden of the argument clear and
definite, including the Darwinian vocabulary that carries its
major accents; the composition of the whole—built up
through the precise joining of its mostly compound sentence-
equations, and rounding back in the last of these to the firm
point of departure secured in the first—is an instrument that
itself positively compels assent. If we can speak of architecture in prose argument we can speak of it with Veblen.
Functional, compact, undecorated (though making use of
various wry flourishes of wit and humor), above all unpre-
tentious, a passage of Veblenian argument is like a Louis
Sullivan office building: an original feat of appropriate engineering that only gradually reveals itself as simultaneously
a feat of imagination, of harmonious form.

Veblen's first admirers recognized his specifically literary
competence. Howells, discussing *The Theory of the Leisure
Class* in two successive numbers of the short-lived New York
journal, *Literature*, especially praised "the clear method, the
graphic and easy style, and the delightful accuracy of char-
acterisation"—all qualities indispensable to effective satire.
At the same time questions were promptly raised by Veblen's
peers concerning the propriety of his chief stylistic device,
his reliance on a set of terms—"conspicuous consumption,"
"conspicuous waste," "pecuniary emulation," "predatory temperament," and the like—obviously bulging with moral judgment. Reviewing the book in the *American Journal of*

Sociology, Lester Ward simply denied that such terms were anything more than aids toward more accurate definition. But the economist John Cummings, in a review for Veblen's own Chicago-based *Journal of Political Economy*, expressed the more common professional view in observing that the "consummately clever" language in which the theory is developed consistently damns the phenomena it describes and is consistently meant to, and that the author's pose of scientific objectivity is sophistical in the extreme: "disregard of the ordinary significance of words used is carried so far as to suggest a lack of frankness." "The reader," Cummings went on, "cannot easily correct the pervading psychic influence of common ethical terms and reconstruct a 'morally colorless' definition of them."

We must recognize, of course, that the issue raised here is not limited to judgment of Veblen's work. The most perplexing questions of language and intelligibility, of the "meaning of meaning," are involved. Veblen's reply to Cummings is, or ought to be, a landmark in modern thought, and we may note first of all that it is *not* pitched, as was Cummings's criticism, on the irrelevant premise of "the reader's" illiteracy. All terminologies, Veblen suggested, even those intended not to, contain a psychic or a moral dimension; all convey in some part "an attitude of approval or disapproval toward the institutional facts of which they speak" and a disposition to uphold or to alter those facts. Specially designed terminologies are no exception. The special virtue, for a cultural theorist, of using "everyday words in their everyday meaning," and of appealing through them to the "categories of popular thought, with all the moral force with which they are charged," is that better than any others these words and categories designate what the theorist is ultimately concerned with, "the motive force of cultural development." "To forego their use in a genetic handling of this development means avoidance of the substantial facts with which the discussion is concerned." Thus, particularly for the open-ended concerns of social science, impurity of address is not a factor to be eliminated; it is a factor to be contained and put to use. It is a basic condition of serious work. In fact, Veblen argues, "a scientist inquiring into cultural growth, and an evolutionist particularly, must take account of this dynamic content of the categories of popular thought as the most important material with which he has to work." An inability to do so without falling into confusion, Veblen adds with characteristically intimidating irony, "may reflect credit upon the state of such a person's sentiments, but it detracts from his scientific competence." There are traps in all this for the unwary, but they are in the nature of the enterprise. What is at stake is simply the proper advancement of serious learning, and that cannot stop for second-rate minds. For:

> If the free use of unsophisticated vulgar concepts, with whatever content of prejudice and sentiment they may carry, is proscribed, the alternative is a resort to analogies and other figures of speech, such as have long afflicted economics and have given that science its reputed character of sterility. In extenuation of my fault, therefore, if such it must be, it should be said that, if one would avoid paralogistic figures of speech in the analysis of institutions [that is, false analogies, euphemisms], one must resort to words and concepts that express the thoughts of the men whose habits of thought constitute the institutions in question.[3]

3. The last sentence in this passage may recall some singsong lines that were to haunt a later, more despairing generation: "I gotta use words when I talk to you. . . ." Veblen, as a stylist, may well be paired with those word magicians of the Symbolist era who, acknowledging the disappearance of a stable *sermo communis* for serious discourse, reacted by devising autonomous styles the relation of which to conventional speech would be fundamentally parodistic and which would gain thereby a special invulnerability to debasement—though not of course to misconstruction. Vulgar misconstruction indeed would be a first sign of success.

This lecture on the problem of style—ironic, faintly defiant, more than faintly remonstrative—is characteristic of Veblen. There is the shadow of a suggestion that no other solution but this one is conceivable but that probably nobody else can make it work. A fundamental pessimism regarding human enterprise coexists in Veblen with a reserve of intellectual tenacity and courage that could not have emerged to function creatively without the breathing space provided by deliberate irony. In a series of magistral papers and treatises—*The Theory of Business Enterprise* (1904), the essays collected in *The Place of Science in Modern Civilization* (1919), and *The Instinct of Workmanship and the State of the Industrial Arts* (1914), which Veblen himself considered his most important work—he filled out the theoretical structure of his analysis of modern society, supporting it with studies of the inadequacies of modern social theory and of modern education in general (a notable early essay is called, "Why Is Economics Not an Evolutionary Science?"). After 1914 the nature of his work changes somewhat. The outbreak of world war brought on a spate of practical pamphleteering—though the speculative amplitude and solidity of his three wartime books require some redefinition of that term: *Imperial Germany and the Industrial Revolution* (1915), *An Inquiry into the Nature of Peace and the Terms of Its Perpetuation* (1917), and *The Higher Learning in America: A Memorandum on the Conduct of Universities by Business Men* (1918). The very existence of these closely reasoned treatises, addressing great current problems from the standpoint of root causes, argues a kind of rational hopefulness about human evolution. Yet none of them flatters the future. Each bears out the glum estimate of historical probabilities set down in the opening chapter of *The Instinct of Workmanship*. Just occasionally, Veblen there remarked, the "life-interests" of communities, all that makes for actual welfare, *have* succeeded in prevailing over the destructive inertia of the ruling institutions:

... the bonds of custom, prescription, principles, precedent, have been broken—or loosened or shifted so as to let the current of life and cultural growth go on, with or without substantial retardation. But history records more frequent and more spectacular instances of the triumph of imbecile institutions over life and culture than of peoples who have by force of instinctive insight saved themselves alive out of a desperately precarious institutional situation, such, for instance, as now faces the peoples of Christendom.[4]

It is against this considered historical pessimism (not untimely in 1914, or in 1965) that Veblen's idealization of certain cultural prototypes gains the mythopoeic force which commended it to the novelists of the 1920s and 1930s. Above all the figure of the "engineer" is celebrated, the man who labors for no merely selfish ends, but with disciplined intelligence, to create something useful and original, perhaps even beautiful, where no such thing existed before. By thus joining an anthropological conception of *homo faber* to the alluring post-Christian ideal of ethical disinterestedness, Veblen created within his survey of the circumstance of modern life a model of rational virtue that has not yet lost its hold on the moral imagination of disaffected contemporaries, a model not less compelling for its very considerable ambiguity.

William James (1842–1910)

The differences between Veblen's prose—quarried and blocklike in its heavy sentence-units, deliberately unaccommodating, securing its effects by a kind of relentless massing

4. What exactly Veblen meant by "instinct" and "instinctive" is a complicated matter. Here it is only necessary to say that the term, in his usage, does not mean a biological sixth sense but rather a certain long-term complex of conditioned responses, culturally transmitted, which imposes itself (in or out of conditions of stress) on the participating human agent. The bearers of "instinct," in this sense, are the true avatars of historical culture.

—and the pungent, quick, familiar grace of William James's seem so nearly absolute that certain major correspondences are worth pointing out. In both, style is suffused with personal presence; the intellectual signature is unmistakable. In both, too, the idealized behavioral types through which the writer projects his thought—the categories of producer and parasite, or of tough-minded and tender-minded—seem more than a little autobiographical in provenance. But where Veblen's stylistic presence, even in his humor, was reserved and forbidding (though capable of winning converts and disciples in cadres), James's was all vibrant charm. It was one with his conversation, which, his oldest son recalled, "was full of earnest, humorous and tender cadences" delivered in "an unforgettably agreeable voice." Veblen's mastery of expressive argument reveals itself only slowly and, as it seems, grudgingly.[5] William James, in contrast, could not draw breath without displaying his.

From the appearance of his monumental *Principles of Psychology* (1890) this extraordinary natural eloquence in William James had a double effect. It could "suspend disbelief" beyond the power of any American poet, or preacher, between Whitman and T. S. Eliot—and it could simultaneously provoke the most emphatic objections concerning method and fundamental intellectual responsibility in just those fields of science and philosophy which James sought to occupy. The issue of style was, in fact, promptly joined, in the long review of the *Principles* contributed to *The Nation* by Charles Saunders Peirce (1839–1914), James's friend, mentor, and (to a point) fellow pragmatist, and probably the most original intelligence, certainly the most exacting logician, in the history of American philosophy. Interestingly, Peirce's

5. Joseph Dorfman reported that when Veblen was writing for the revived *Dial* in 1918–19—the "Veblen *Dial*"—he was asked "to limit his articles to 1000 words, but Veblen said that it took him that much space to get started."

criticism of James's writing reverses the criticism Veblen commonly met, of having relied too exclusively on an untranslatable technical jargon, ambiguously deployed. James's fault was rather that he was all too easily translatable. He was ambiguous by an excess of idiomatic clarity; he was colloquial, familiar, and personal precisely where strictness of terminology was most desired. "With an extraordinary racy and forcible style," Peirce wrote, after granting the high importance of James's whole treatise, "Prof. James is continually wresting words and phrases of exact import to unauthorized and unsuitable uses. He indulges himself with idiosyncrasies of diction and tricks of language"—and here the comment becomes a little malicious, in an ostensibly objective review—"such as usually spring up in households of great talent." As James turned to philosophy, in books like *The Will to Believe and Other Essays* (1897) and *Pragmatism* (1907), Peirce's disapproval grew more severe and more comprehensive. Eventually a private exchange of views over the language of James's paper, "Does 'Consciousness' Exist?" (which became the pivotal first chapter of the posthumous volume, *Essays in Radical Empiricism*), led to this culminating outburst, in Peirce's letter of October 3, 1904:

> What you call "pure experience" is not experience at all, and certainly ought to have a name. It is downright bad morals so to misuse words, for it prevents philosophy from becoming a science. One of the things I urge in my forthcoming *Monist* paper ["What Pragmatism Is"] is that it is an indispensable requisite of science that it should have a recognized technical vocabulary, composed of words so unattractive that loose thinkers are not tempted to use them; and a recognized and legitimated way of making up new words freely when a new conception is introduced; and that it is vital for science that he who introduces a new conception should be held to have a *duty* imposed upon him to invent a sufficiently disagreeable series of words to express it. I wish you would reflect seriously upon the moral aspect of terminology.

William James was in fact as continuously alert as perhaps only a gifted prose stylist is likely to be to the moral aspect of words—the moral aspect of all discourse, one must say, and not simply of terminology. His defense of his own style against Peirce's argument for scientific propriety of expression might well have followed Veblen's against Cummings: one *must* resort to words that express the whole thought of the beings whose habits of thought constitute the subject under discussion. It would not at all be a foolproof defense, but it would be a serious and intelligible one; and backed by the richly sympathetic penetration and sheer figurative abundance of James's explanations of psychological phenomena—the famous chapter on "Habit" early in the *Principles* is a fair example—it would carry enormous authority. James himself was characteristically articulate about this aspect of his work. The great moral danger in philosophic or even scientific writing of a descriptive nature was not that it might fall into error but that in concentrating upon absolute and unassailable verification it might cut itself off from its own sources and goals in the observation of living experience. In eliminating error it could lose the chance of finding truth: that was the burden of James's critique of rationalism.

James's own early training in science, R. B. Perry has suggested, helped to deliver him from the mesmerizing ideal of an absolute scientific authority. Passionately opposed to absolutism in any form, he was not likely to countenance it simply because it put on the up-to-date mask of positive science. But beneath that native skepticism lay a deeper concern, which James made superbly explicit in a letter to L. T. Hobhouse (August 12, 1904), who had attacked the argument of "The Will to Believe":

> . . . in these matters each man writes from out of a field of consciousness of which the bogey in the background is the chief object. Your bogey is superstition; my bogey is desiccation; and each, for his contrast-effect, clutches at any text

that can be used to represent the enemy, regardless of exegetical proprieties. In my essay the evil shape was a vision of "Science" in the form of abstraction, priggishness and sawdust, lording it over all.

The passage is immensely revealing, historically as well as personally. Nothing perhaps so forcibly displays the continuity of James's thought with that of Emerson and the transcendentalist era (and of Henry James, Senior) as the complex of motive and tactical solution here defined: the radically empirical critique of human intellect developed in vivid colloquial language to serve the goal of a life-renewing encounter with the actual body of experience.[6] In the manner of Emerson, what James chiefly feared was the triumph of nonlife, the waste or the disintegration of natural capacities through underdevelopment. Yet as of Emerson so of William James it may be said that instead of evolving a style to serve his philosophy, he created a philosophy to serve his style, which from the first was a vitally responsive mode of moral and cognitive action. "The whole originality of pragmatism," he eventually wrote, "the whole point in it, is its use of the concrete way of seeing." The strength of James's prose corresponds to this formulation. It rests in his ability to find concrete terms for those actually experienced states of mind in which the problems of life—and of philosophic argument— are faced most intensely. Again and again he fixes some critical issue into a compact verbal equation and then confirms that equation by going on to suggest the appropriate dramatic response that follows from it, bringing the formu-

6. This historical continuity is still insufficiently explored, though William James, as he turned from psychology to philosophy, grew more and more conscious of it. So, too, the dedication of *Pragmatism* to the memory of John Stuart Mill—"from whom I first learned the pragmatic openness of mind"—indicates another aspect of his general indebtedness to that earlier generation.

lated idea itself back into the condition of phenomenal experience:

> If the passing thought be the directly verifiable existent which no school has hitherto doubted it to be, then that thought is itself the thinker, *and psychology need not look beyond*. (*Principles*, I, 401; emphasis added)

—a simple instance, but characteristic of James's reliance on verbal gesture and cadence to round off his formulations. It is impossible with William James ever to forget the presence in reasoned discourse of very much more than merely reasoning beings. The remarkable concreteness of his analysis of mental states—in *The Varieties of Religious Experience* (1902) as well as in the *Principles*—and the psychological realism of his speculative essays on being and consciousness, faith and morals, continually serve this end of vital engagement with actual existence. That is why his philosophic papers, for all their irregularity of form and method (including their shameless concessions to the inspirational occasion of the public lecture), persistently touch the root of the whole matter of thought and experience which they address. We are brought to recognize the human subject's logic of action in, so to speak, his own words. The *will* to believe, the *sentiment* of rationality, does consciousness *exist?*—the very titles are definitions and claim priority over other issues.

Undeniably, James—drawing as need arose on that long-established American tradition of practical eloquence which Emerson, in particular, had perfected—used his style to protect his argument where it was vulnerable, if not actually untenable. And, undeniably, trouble results from this freedom of usage. If the terms "tough-minded" and "tender-minded," even further reduced, have entered into the corrupting vocabulary of modern political comment and gossip, finding a natural home in the *mensonges raisonnés* of the red-jacketed

American newsmagazine, some responsibility conceivably attaches to James (some, too, for this abominable style, to Henry Adams, who improvised a comparable shorthand for historical events). The man "born afresh every morning," as Alice James said of her effervescent brother, cannot deny kinship with those men without memory or any sense of actual history who have been agents and spokesmen for the grosser forms of American willfulness and know-nothingism. James himself, let it be said, would not have denied this kinship. His willingness to admit the weirdest of aberrations onto the spectrum of normal, hence expectable, behavior, though it is involved perhaps with a certain ingenuousness of personal outlook, can nevertheless stiffen with the courage of common realism the most deeply tragic or ironic apprehension of human probabilities. His hospitality to *all* the varieties of psychological experience had, after all, a solid enough philosophic basis. He saw that the human mind, in its vivid fits of will and faith, was "successfully" acting out a real attachment to real existence, whether or not speculative philosophy had given its blessing and logical sanction. So in general it is James's unceasing critique of a purely cognitive understanding—his recognition of consciousness as, in very essence, *willful, sentimental,* and *performative*—that secures him that place among the makers of modern thought and literature for which his native eloquence is only a first, though indispensable, recommendation.

Peirce, Royce, Dewey, Santayana

William James taught at Harvard (with frequent leaves and absences) for nearly forty years; brought Josiah Royce from California and tried to find a place for Charles Peirce; and "grunted with delight at [the] thickening up of our Harvard atmosphere" which the young Santayana's presence in the philosophy department effected—though privately he railed at Santayana's "pessimistic platonism" as "the perfection of rottenness." Veblen on the other hand bears the stamp—insofar as a stamp can be discerned on that tough hide—of Johns Hopkins, a university perhaps less devoted to belletristic accomplishment than Harvard but rather more systematically responsive to the new currents of post-Darwinian thought.[7] At Johns Hopkins—where in the '80s the Hegelianism in which Royce had been trained was finally giving way to the new-model social science of Herbert B. Adams in history and Richard Ely in economics and sociology —the pioneer sociologists E. A. Ross, Albion Small, and John R. Commons all were trained, and John Dewey (in 1884), Woodrow Wilson (in 1886), and Frederick Jackson Turner (in 1890) took graduate degrees. There, too, William James had come to lecture in 1878, and there for the five years ending in 1884 Peirce held his one academic post. Columbia; Chicago after its founding in 1892; Wisconsin, after 1900, among the several ambitious state universities of the Middle West: these also were centers of the new learning. The creative renaissance in American thought of the late nineteenth century was largely a university affair. Peirce himself, though never acceptable at Harvard, was born, literally, to the academic purple and to the scientific bias of the new era; his father taught mathematics and astronomy at Harvard for half a century. In the nature of his interests and cast of mind, both formidably technical, Peirce's philosophic writings can find only an oblique entrance into the most generously conceived literary history. It is worth noting, however, that his seminal papers, "The Fixation of Belief" and "How to Make Our Ideas Clear," were published in *Popular Science*, the monthly journal founded in 1872 by the Spencerian publicist

7. At Yale, where he went to finish his degree, Veblen heard Sumner lecture—with what immediate reaction one would dearly like to know.

E. L. Youmans, which for its first three or four decades served as a forum for the new thought and drew heavily for articles and reviews upon American university faculties; it is, in fact, a mother lode of the intellectual history of the period and deserves prospecting.

A full chronicle of this span of American intellectual life would have to take account of the fact that only a handful of its leading figures survive as writers—that is, as minds of original energy not to know whose thought, in their own words, is to remain in a fundamental way semiliterate. Neither Josiah Royce (1855–1916) nor John Dewey (1859–1952) quite belongs to this handful. Their work suggests among other things how difficult it was to find, between the oracular colloquy of an Emerson, James's nearest model, and the ponderous jargon of a Herbert Spencer, depressingly contagious among the rank and file of treatise writers, an effective middle style for prose argument. Royce's gift for sustained philosophic demonstration was genuine and formidable. He was particularly effective as a lecturer and as a reflective interpreter—as in *The Religious Aspect of Philosophy* (1885), *The World and the Individual* (1900–1901), or *The Philosophy of Loyalty* (1908)—of some great standing issue of traditional speculation. And he remained for years an ideal interlocutor, and whetstone, for James's quick-flashing mind. It is worth remarking, too, that Royce introduced a course in the philosophy of science into the Harvard curriculum and that his work in mathematical logic (see, for convenience, the Supplementary Essay to *The World and the Individual*, Volume I) has survived to interest contemporary students. But one does not have the sense in reading Royce that his style, his actual effort of discursive intelligence, is seriously involved in testing out the quality of truth in the propositions it expertly frames. His forte, so Santayana put the matter, is the common "parliamentary jargon" of academic philosophy, and its effect is a kind of special pleading, though invariably high-minded and well conducted. (His curious California novel, *The Feud of Oakfield Creek*, 1887, is surely one of the most bodiless and juiceless narratives in the history of fiction, besides being written in McGuffey Reader English.) Nevertheless Royce remains historically interesting as an index to the latter descent of the old Calvinist moral imagination and of the dialectical and oratorical traditions supporting it. As with the original Puritans, so with Royce: metaphysical absolutism, ethical rigor, and millennial hopefulness go side by side. Thus in no part of his career does he present so attractive a figure as in sponsoring, toward the end of his life, a visionary scheme for promoting world harmony through a universal system of voluntary insurance—see *War and Insurance* (1914) and *The Hope of the Great Community* (1916)—his passion for which interestingly resembles the evangelism of the composer Charles Ives's transcendentalizing pamphlet of 1912 on insurance selling, written for the Ives & Myrick agency and entitled (in language that would have been appreciated in Concord seventy years before) *The Amount to Carry— Measuring the Prospect.*

The case of John Dewey is a more puzzling one. His enormous influence on several decades of American thought and public consciousness cannot be doubted. With books like *The School and Society* (1899) and *Democracy and Education* (1916), he affected the context of American schooling as no one since Horace Mann; and it may be urged in passing that Dewey's educational thinking, grounded in a pragmatic conception of the mind's actual growth, remains a richer source of practical experiment than its tarnished present reputation might lead one to suspect. His *Reconstruction in Philosophy* (1920) compactly sums up the whole epoch of socially conscious, science-minded, liberal and pragmatic hu-

manism of which he himself was the foremost American
representative. And we may well ask, reviewing the main
directions of his thought—his insistence that philosophy serve
the end of social betterment, his valuation of ideas according
to their capacity as instruments to that end, above all his
unflagging awareness of the element of *interest* in philosophic
argument and his passion for maintaining a certain standard
of honesty in the conduct of such argument—who would not
now willingly call himself a Deweyite? John Dewey, moreover, not only survives the cynical detraction of certain
recent depreciators of his outlook ("new conservatives," last-
ditch partisans of natural law and an arbitrarily imposed
moral order) but also retains power to strike back at them.
Who recently has so pungently called the turn on those who,
from positions of already secured and protected privilege,
justify resistance to every new effort to correct social wrongs
by appeals to tranquillity and a Platonic "public interest,"
and who clearly prefer the institutionalized violence of settled
injustice, so long as it "keeps order," to the irregular counter-
violence of a fight for chartered rights? These are the men,
Dewey wrote in *Human Nature and Conduct* (1922), who,
lying in the face of history,

> say, peace, peace, when there is no peace, who refuse to
> recognize facts as they are, who proclaim a natural harmony
> of wealth and merit, of capital and labor, and the natural
> justice, in the main, of existing conditions. There is something
> horrible, something that makes one fear for civilization, in
> denunciations of class-differences and class struggles which
> proceed from a class in power, one that is seizing every means,
> even to a monopoly of moral ideals, to carry on its struggle
> for class-power. This class adds hypocrisy to conflict and
> brings all idealism into disrepute.

But the unhappy truth is that passages as clear and solid as
this are hard to find in Dewey's books. An inspiring teacher,
he was also a remarkably careless writer; one whose instinct

for right-minded catch phrases was stronger than his feeling for precise usage; a critic and publicist who too often carried out his attack on unexamined assumptions with unexamined verbal equipment. The chapter section from which the above passage is taken opens with this sentence—"Since morals is concerned with conduct, it grows out of specific empirical facts"—of which one is compelled in charity to think that it simply does not say what the writer must have meant to say. Joseph Warren Beach once drew attention to an even more disturbing example of Deweyism in prose—"The opaqueness of human nature to reason is equivalent to a belief in its irregularity"—which he could not explain without assuming, in its author, a certain positive "pride of carelessness." One longer example may be given, from the ambitious later treatise, *Art as Experience* (1934)—

> An experience has pattern and structure, because it is not just doing and undergoing in alternation, but consists of them in relationship. . . . The action and its consequence must be joined in perception. This relationship is what gives meaning; to grasp it is the object of all intelligence.

—since it suggests that in this manner of writing nothing more, but nothing less, than the basic selection and arrangement of nouns, verbs, and connectives is at fault. Edmund Wilson has recalled, from his work as literary editor of *The New Republic*, the "peculiarly exasperating way" in which Dewey's contributions "both called for and resisted revision": "It was not only a question of clarifying the author's statements but of finding out what he meant; and when you did get the sense of his meaning, there was no way of straightening out the language: you would have had to try to give his meaning in a language of a different kind."

The work of George Santayana (1863–1952)—Spanish-born, Boston-bred and Harvard-tutored, Catholic by "sympathy and traditional allegiance" and, by his own account, a

Platonic materialist in philosophy[8]—presents so many points of contrast with that of John Dewey, and nearly all (it seems now) so much in his favor, that by a kind of nervous reaction one is tempted into a certain suspicion of just those qualities in his writing which immediately recommend it: the breadth, ease, and unassailable tact of his cultivation, the perfect adequacy and fitness of his style. In the intellectual history of this period, dominated by scientific models of inquiry, he stands apart not only from Dewey but from everyone else so far mentioned. "Santayana," Professor Henry D. Aiken has remarked, "probably had less command of mathematics and natural science than any other first-rank philosopher since Hume. His education was overwhelmingly humanistic and literary." What is unique, Professor Aiken continues, is that this relative incompetence became a basis of insight and mastery: "it freed him once and for all from that fatal worship of science and mathematics as models of perfect communication, which until very recently has impaired the philosophical study of other dimensions of human discourse"—and coincidentally from the characteristic modern temptation "to regard ordinary language as merely an unconscious repository of outmoded metaphysics ... an adolescent progenitor of some ideal language of science."[9]

Santayana's own elegant command of discursive English is conspicuous to the point of giving offense. What keeps it from cloying is, first, his sharp and always slightly malicious wit and, second, his extraordinarily precise tactical sense of the right use of philosophic names, the necessary abstractions of reflective discourse, and of the weight they will bear in any given argumentative context. He is a master of tone,

8. See "A Brief History of My Opinions," *Contemporary American Philosophy*, edited by G. P. Adams and W. P. Montague, New York, 1930.
9. "George Santayana, Natural Historian of Symbolic Forms," *Kenyon Review*, Summer, 1953, pp. 338–56.

indicating through the idiom of statements how his point is to be taken and how understood. For prose at least as much as for poetry, there is a sense in which it is always a first consideration that (in Keats's phrase) English be "kept up"; and one can think that Santayana's disciplined, shapely, undistractible prose style performed a service as valuable in this regard as the more picturesque, and idiosyncratic, vernacular of William James. Whatever place he holds in the creative history of philosophy, his place in the literature of critical reflection and argument is secure. He became, perhaps remains, one of the few indispensable ministers to a rounded American education—and not only for his remarkable divergences from the long-dominant Protestant and Anglo-Scottish norm. It seems evident that Santayana played this part for the young T. S. Eliot, who heard him lecture at Harvard and whose influential early criticism pays him—in the authoritative clarity and appositeness of its formulations—the best sort of tribute a master can receive from an attentive pupil.

But it is hard to read Santayana at length without beginning to wonder whether as a writer he did not sacrifice too much to mastery of tone. If his style is the style of cultivated, unastonishable wisdom, its special risk is a too perfect knowingness. His sensitivity to nuance and contingency can modulate almost imperceptibly into a corrupting unwillingness ever to be caught out. The primitive question of *seriousness* rises, and the specter of a flaw, deep in temperament, that keeps his mind at a numbing distance from the vital core of motive in what he addresses; a fear of appearing foolish or indiscreet which, because its expression is always dignified and reasonable, makes for the subtlest and worst sort of equivocation. In any event, in his earlier treatises, *The Sense of Beauty* (1896) and the magistral *Life of Reason* (5 volumes, 1905–1906), it is the detail of argument, the incidental definition, that is compelling, rather than the whole. The virtues of his major philosophical work are those of an impeccably mannered encyclopedism that accepts all phenomena as natural and interesting and positively deprecates only those transcendentalizing ideologies which make men fanatics of some partial truth. That the true natural history of intellect may be a succession of commitments of this latter sort, more or less sublimated, is not his affair.

We are likely to think now that Santayana's manner serves him best in his fine *critical* essays: *Interpretations of Poetry and Religion* (1900), with the important chapter on "The Poetry of Barbarism"; the studies of Lucretius, Dante, and Goethe in *Three Philosophical Poets* of 1910 (who can make sense of Wallace Stevens without knowing the Santayana represented here?); and those collected in *Winds of Doctrine* (1913), which includes his much-borrowed definition of "The Genteel Tradition in American Philosophy," and in *Character and Opinion in the United States* (1920), the most incisive of his many inquiries into that peculiar "Protestant combination of earnestness with waywardness" which distinguished, in his view, American intellectual life. But even about this work reservations may be suggested. Always a perceptive critic of the contexts of thought and art, Santayana nevertheless seems curiously passive before certain ideas —ideas, for example, of race, national ethos, historical moment —in the fixed and pre-established frame of which, and nowhere else, his fine perceptions harden into shape. On the other hand, coming to grips, as now and then he must, with the concrete particulars of the work under discussion, he often seems to grow impatient with them, if not actually embarrassed. It must be granted that his effort to see Dante, Goethe, even Shakespeare whole is very nearly unique in the history of modern Anglo-American criticism. But Professor Aiken's commentary is again to the point: "What he most delighted to contemplate were the ideal stages of human progress, removed from their accidental historical embodiments." To this end individual works of art, even the grandest, were never finally satisfactory: "They tied him down to the perspectives and emphases of the particular artist." Just here Eliot's criticism, at its best in fitting general proposition to specific text, notably surpasses Santayana's, and has had as a result the wider practical influence, and the healthier, in contemporary letters.

John Fiske, Henry Brewster

To turn from Santayana to nearly any of his American contemporaries in philosophy is to be reminded of the degree to which speculative argument in the United States was still in hostage to the intellectual habituations of traditional Protestantism: in method, to the old theological exercise of searching for "evidences"; in language, to the rhetorical fervency of the conversion-seeking sermon. Two lesser figures of the period (one almost forgotten, the other hardly known at all) suggest in their very different ways the residual weight of this tradition. John Fiske (1842–1901), who was the first of the generation of Sumner and William James to make his name in letters, is one of those interesting products of the Protestant dispersion who, combining a Quaker and a Calvinist inheritance, tended, whatever the field of inquiry, to give hopeful Quakerish answers to ominous Calvinistic questions. With articles and lectures on evolution, Spencerianism, and the "Positive Philosophy," Fiske was well established by the end of the 1860s as an authority on the post-Darwinian controversies in science and morals. His two-volume *Outlines of Cosmic Philosophy* (1874) and later collections like *Darwinism and Other Essays* (1879) and *Excursions of an Evolutionist* (1884) were widely circulated; and when he turned to the writing of history, tracing the providential development of New World institutions in a long series of *chroniques à thèse* of which *The Critical Period in American History*

(1888) is the most notable, he merely broadened his hold on the high Victorian audience for serious popularization.

Writing and lecturing until he wore out his energies, Fiske did as well in the literary marketplace as a serious American author ever has, and lived long enough to enjoy a reassuring round of honorary degrees and ceremonial lectureships. Not in any way original, he was nevertheless a serious and responsible synthesizer. His respect for such facts as he had and his effort to combine these facts into useful hypotheses put a respectable face on his claim to be considered philosophic, and scientific, in method. Yet the fundamental loyalty of Fiske's mind to the rhetorical forms of his ancestral faith, though no longer to the letter of it, is transparently evident, especially in the argumentative climaxes of his books. So in this chapter-ending late in his popular monograph of 1884, *The Destiny of Man, Viewed in the Light of His Origin*, though the evidence cited is sufficiently "scientific," the language of presentation can turn without breaking step into cadences once delivered to the saints:

> Man is slowly passing from a primitive social state in which he was little better than a brute, toward an ultimate social state in which his character shall have become so transformed that nothing of the brute can be detected in it. The ape and the tiger in human nature will become extinct. Theology has had much to say about original sin. This original sin is neither more nor less than the brute-inheritance which every man carries with him, and the process of evolution is an advance toward true salvation. Fresh value is thus added to human life. The modern prophet, employing the methods of science, may again proclaim that the kingdom of heaven is at hand. Work ye, therefore, early and late, to prepare its coming.

Again, in the same monograph's closing pages:

> The dream of poets, the lesson of priest and prophet, the inspiration of the great musician, is confirmed in the light of modern knowledge [that is, evolutionary science]; and as

we gird ourselves up for the work of life, we may look forward to the time when in the truest sense the kingdoms of this world shall become the kingdom of Christ, and he shall reign for ever and ever, king of kings and lord of lords.

The sense of the meeting, after a lecture by Fiske, may well be imagined.

Beside these perorations let another be placed, a dramatic soliloquy climaxing a philosophic dialogue, *The Prison*, published in London in 1891:

> Now my struggle is over; the time is come and my choice is made. I abandon to destruction the unity of which I am conscious; I take refuge in the lastingness of its elements. . . . My hopes have become an heirloom of the centuries which it is my turn to take care of; my thoughts are here on deposit for a little while; they have been passed around since the dawn of time and someone else will have charge of them tomorrow; the laughter I have laughed rose in the bulrushes of yore and mingled with the sound of the syrinx; the kisses that have wandered to my lips will never grow cold; no heart but mine shall ever ache and leap. My passions are the tingling blood of mankind. Now someone says to me: It is well so far; taste also the death. Then let there be banners and music; this is no leave-taking; I am not even going home. I thank you, days of hope and pride; I thank you, lamentable solitude, and you, shades of those that loved me. I sorrow with you, grieving ones, and melt with you, O fond ones. I triumph with those who vanquish and I rest with those who are dead. I descend to my father and return again for ever. I have nothing that is mine but a name, and I bow down in my dream of a day to the life eternal. I am the joy and the sorrow, the mirth and the pride; the love, the silence, and the song. I am the thought. I am the soul. I am the home.

The fervor here is familiar enough, but the voice itself seems drawn from distinctly different sources from those Fiske tapped—almost, despite the Whitmanesque rhythm of certain sentences, from another language. Indeed, if the passage is put into French, the logic of its style, vitrified nouns and predi-

cates arranged around mostly inert verbs, emerges clear. So
does its latent distinction. *The Prison* was in fact written in
France and Italy, and its author was Henry Brewster (1851–
1908), a philosopher-by-avocation so removed from the
America of his day (though he retained citizenship) that he
can scarcely even be considered an expatriate. Son of a New
Englander who made a modest fortune at St. Petersburg and
Paris through his American skill at dental surgery, Henry
Brewster was reared and educated in France, and was as much
at home in the French language as in English. The last of his
four short philosophic books is written in French, as are two
surviving verse plays, *Les Naufrageurs* and *Buondelmonte*,
and a small corpus of lyric poetry. To have imposed French
prose values upon the idiom of nineteenth-century philosophic
English was no insignificant experiment, though accidental;
and a part of the continuing interest of Brewster's work is
just in the discursive style that results, a style which is perhaps
a little forced and awkward in idiom yet at the edge of an
exceptional originality.

Brewster's work represents a clarifying fusion of the nineteenth-century French literary intelligence with the doctrinal
inheritance of Anglo-American Puritanism. He was one of
the first Anglo-American writers to have absorbed the influence of Renan—not so much the *Vie de Jésus* (1863) as the
Souvenirs d'enfance et de jeunesse (1883) and its celebrated
"Prayer on the Acropolis"—and, co-ordinately, something of
the underlying philosophic rationale of French symbolism.
The titles of Brewster's books provide further guidelines.
The Theories of Anarchy and of Law (1887) indicates an
involvement in nineteenth-century speculation about social
evolution and the psychic factors in culture; *The Statuette
and The Background* (1896) attaches to the aestheticism of
the period, specifically its partiality toward self-contained
objects of art as evidence for propositions in ethics and
epistemology; while *L'Âme païenne* (1902) develops a pre-

occupation with the essentially "fictive" and "dramatic" nature of the soul over against its abstract unreality in conventional religious doctrines. Cardinal references to the Brahma, the Buddha, and the Tao, and in general a casual assumption of familiarity with eastern and classical literature and with European philosophic history, bring us closer to a definition of Brewster's type—for it is as one fulfillment of a type that he remains notable; the authority that comes from a fully rounded achievement, or from the sheer mass accruing to an exertion of intellectual power sufficiently persisted in, simply does not obtain in his case.

The ethos Brewster's writing gives expression to is a hybrid one. It is the ethos of that international bourgeoisie of cultivated leisure which created a significant if minor chapter in early modern literature in general, and which seems most at home in the expatriate colonies of Florence and Rome.[10] Its absorbing concerns are ethical freedom, the purifying of personal relationships, and the maintaining—in the face of historical chaos and the pervasive unreality of this world's names—of a certain countervailing grace and beauty in the spirit's necessary acquiescences. Conversion to esoteric cults, or cults of cults, such as those of the Virgin or the Magna

10. A French admirer, Edouard Rod, remarked of Brewster that he had neither a country nor a career nor even a language of his own. A comment by the English writer, Maurice Baring, adds an interesting emphasis: "The most refreshing thing about Brewster was that he was altogether without that exaggerated reverence for culture in general and books in particular that sometimes hampers his countrymen . . . when they have been transplanted early into Europe and brought up in France, Italy, or England, and saturated with art and literature." See *The Puppet Show of Memory* (1922), pp. 249–53.

Among the leading American writers of the period, it was Henry James and Henry Adams who were most affected by this ethos, to a considerable extent refining certain of their characteristic insights against its actual social presence. But clearly Henry Brewster himself is not—as has been suggested—the model for Gilbert Osmond in *The Portrait of a Lady*.

Mater, is characteristic of this ethos, which provides a natural way station for consciences sprung loose from the Puritan creed but unable to rid themselves of nostalgia for the Puritan intensity. But characteristically, too, it tends to find in the mundane labor of art or thought, as distinct from the refinements of connoisseurship, a threat to freedom and personal integrity. As a consequence it always puts itself to work with a positive inward diffidence; so indeed we may find Henry Brewster as a writer hardly more interesting in his published books than in his private correspondence, which deserves to be collected. For all its limitations, however, one is reasonably tempted to see in the outlook of this class an anticipation of the astringent ethics of mid-twentieth-century existentialism—an outrageous existentialism, of course, that could not conceive of its engagement with life without the expensive accompaniment (see the passage quoted above) of "banners and music." Brewster's special accomplishment, historically, is to have registered that outlook with a certain controlled unity of style and apprehension and, incidentally, to have preempted for it, in his principal book, *The Prison,* one of the master metaphors (as in Kafka, or Camus) of modern existentialist writing.

History and Some Historians

In the middle '80s, Santayana—his bias toward a dialectical skepticism having been ratified at Harvard by the experience of listening alternately to Royce and William James—made the customary scholar's pilgrimage to Germany, to have confirmed a second and weightier intellectual influence, one that had already reached him, he wrote later, out of "the general temper of the age." This influence was "the historical spirit of the nineteenth century," and all the "splendid panorama of nations and religions, literatures and arts, which it unrolled before the imagination." Historicism, with the methods of analysis based upon it, is beyond doubt a central force in nineteenth-century thought, but it emerged slowly and unevenly, against considerable resistance; and the curious truth is that it made its way into the actual writing of history not a bit faster than into other disciplines. As Santayana himself remarked, the historical imagination, particularly in the United States, was still chiefly addressed to the Romanticist values of picturesqueness and dramatic grandeur. To the older New England generation of Prescott, Motley, Bancroft, and Parkman, the graphic narration of ideally significant events—heroes and nations exemplifying sovereign moral and political truths—was the worthiest of literary undertakings; the writing of history, sacred to earlier New England generations as a record of Divine Providence, was scarcely less so to these nineteenth-century heirs. Much of what passed for serious history after 1880 (in bulk of production it remained perhaps the leading genre in American letters) continued in their tradition, though mostly without their occasional literary distinction.[11] Yet in the very nature of the effort involved, the study of history was bound to submit sooner or later to the new temper of thought, specifically to the standards of documentary realism (or "positivism") and of "scientific" method. Formally, Gibbon and Macaulay gave way to Ranke, indirectly, and to Buckle and Taine, as master influences. After 1880 more and more historical scholarship was carried out in imitation of the German methods of inquiry and verification introduced the previous decade at Harvard (by Henry Adams), at Michigan and Johns Hopkins, and soon at most of the important eastern and midwestern universities, as well as in the historical division of the Carnegie Institution at Washington.

The mass of American historiography in the late nineteenth century remains interesting mostly for the insight it gives into

11. Bancroft and Parkman were still at work at the beginning of this period, publishing their last books in 1882 and 1892 respectively.

contemporary opinion and the sociology of knowledge (the
durable work of Henry Charles Lea on the Inquisition is a
notable exception). The history of the United States was the
pre-eminent concern. Of the many who set out in these years
to compose multivolumed chronicles of the near or far
American past—Fiske, H. E. Von Holst, H. H. Bancroft,
Moses Coit Tyler (whose still valuable *Literary History of
the American Revolution* appeared in 1897), James Schouler,
John T. Morse, John B. McMaster, Henry Adams, Theodore
Roosevelt, James Ford Rhodes, Edward Eggleston, John
Burgess, Woodrow Wilson—the majority were self-trained,
coming into history by way of the law, civil engineering,
journalism, popular authorship, or public affairs and also, in
most cases, out of some romantic personal commitment to their
chosen subject. Several had fallen under the influence of
Buckle's evolutionistic *History of Civilization in England*
(1857–1861) or of Lecky's *History of the Rise and Influence
of the Spirit of Rationalism in Europe* (1865), and conceived
of their work as a search for laws of social and political development analogous to Darwin's laws for natural history or
Lyell's for geology. Inevitably the interpretations thus imposed on the past reflect the pressure of contemporary issues
and tensions—and inevitably, for this generation of political
historians born between 1830 and 1860, the long crisis of the
Civil War (in which only Schouler saw active service) and
of postwar Reconstruction was the formative experience.
Inevitably, too, nationalism and progress became first premises.
The Civil War appeared all the nobler, the passions and
energies it had aroused the more self-justifying, when it could
be seen as the last great ordeal in the providential evolution
of a united continental nation: not only northern partisans
like Rhodes but those born to a southern bias, like Burgess
and Wilson, were attracted to this dignifying conception.

By contrast the issues of civil and political rights in a
democratic state, opening out into the larger context of demo-

cratic freedom, were very much more hesitantly addressed, except as in the rigid frame of Von Holst's rather melodramatic constitutionalism. The war Whitman recorded in *Drum Taps* and *Specimen Days* and Melville in *Battle-Pieces*, conceived as the definitive American-democratic tragedy, very nearly drops out of sight in these histories. Where a democratic consciousness does continue to find direct expression, it is in the work and very choice of subject of certain social historians who set themselves the task of compiling (more or less optimistically) the life records of the general population—McMaster for one, who called his series *A History of the People of the United States;* Eggleston, for another, who had started out as a local-color realist.[12] Political biography also flourished: democracy may show little enough respect for persons, but it is infinitely curious about them. Not many large-scale undertakings of the time have worn as well as Morse's *American Statesmen* series (1882–1900), to which Henry and Charles Francis Adams, Von Holst, Henry Cabot Lodge, Theodore Roosevelt, Moses Tyler, and Carl Schurz contributed notable volumes. Some of the most original work of this period carried the inquiry into the logic of democratic history onto new ground. Implicitly in Roosevelt's four Parkmanizing volumes on *The Winning of the West* (1889–1896), more directly in Captain Alfred Thayer Mahan's *The Influence of Sea Power upon History* (1890), a kind of new-model democratic nationalism, with a pronounced geopolitical and imperialist accent, shows its face and brings us forward to the peculiar fervors of 1898 and after.

12. A remark of Eggleston's, in an interview upon publication of the first volume of his projected "History of Life in the United States," points up the linkage between the newer methods in social history and the methods of realistic fiction. Describing his field trips in search of authenticity, he said, "There is really no other way of writing [history] vividly and familiarly except by *saturating* one's self." The word, we note, was Henry James's, too.

Yet in a sense all these themes and causes—Union, the nation, constitutional liberty, popular democracy, manifest destiny (even under geopolitical metaphors)—belong to an earlier phase of national life. The post-1870 America of coal, steel, and railroads, industrial complication, trusts, and labor riots, mass immigration, metropolitan slums, agricultural depression and back-country decay, and all the coincidental symptoms of civil anxiety and rancor deriving from an accelerating rate of social displacement, seem to have made less of an impression on the minds of professional historians than upon novelists and journalists. Until the work of proponents of a "new" history like Frederick Jackson Turner (1861–1932), beginning with his frontier paper of 1893, and Charles Beard (1874–1948), whose *Economic Interpretation of the Constitution* (1913) seemed to efface generations of ancestor worship, the critical intelligence of American historians lagged behind their capacity for hard work. The blatant facts of civil life in a society more thoroughly given over to the norms of exploitative capitalism than any other in the history of the world did not significantly interfere with a simple, generalized sense (now thoroughly secular) of rhythmic progress and providential destiny. Facts were assembled, in some cases new kinds of facts, but standards of interpretation remained primitive and sentimental. For the most part the writing of American history in the '80s and '90s was only a kind of superior newsgathering, a retrospective journalism. It merely substantiated conventional opinion and left undisturbed the simplifying accretions of popular memory.[13]

13. If it had done more than this, if there had not been among American historians a real vacuum of disciplined inquiry and conjecture and of critical reflection. the theses of Turner and Beard, arbitrarily constructed and highly vulnerable to empirical objection, could scarcely have been so enormously influential or gone so long without serious challenge.

Brooks Adams, Henry Adams

To this general rating there were important exceptions, which require closer attention. Coming upon this provocative paragraph in the preface to the expanded American edition of a work of 1895, Brooks Adams's *The Law of Civilization and Decay: An Essay on History*, we move as if into a different intellectual sphere, where the work going forward commends itself first of all by an element of critical self-discipline, of conceptual control:

> The value of history lies not in the multitude of facts collected, but in their relation to each other, and in this respect an author can have no larger responsibility than any other scientific observer. If the sequence of events seems to indicate the existence of a law governing social development, such a law may be suggested, but to approve or disapprove of it would be as futile as to discuss the moral bearings of gravitation.

Alongside may be put a paragraph from the last chapter of Henry Adams's stately *History of the United States During the Administrations of Jefferson and Madison* (9 volumes, 1889–1891)—although isolating these dry sentences sacrifices much of the force and interest they carry within the whole tightly reasoned interpretive argument upon which this long methodical work rests its case:

> Whether the scientific or the heroic view [of the past] were taken, in either case the starting-point was the same, and the chief object of interest was to define national character. Whether the figures of history were treated as heroes or as types, they must be taken to represent the people. American types were especially worth study if they were to represent the greatest democratic evolution the world could know. Readers might judge for themselves what share the individual possessed in creating or shaping the nation; but whether it was small or great, the nation could be understood only

by studying the individual. For that reason, in the story of Jefferson and Madison individuals retained their old interest as types of character, if not as sources of power.

For Henry and Brooks Adams, born into a family in which the discipline of speculative inquiry was as customary as the habit of eloquence among the Jameses, history was valueless if it was not a form of experimental learning, and its success was to be measured not by popularity and the sale of multi-volume sets but, like the work of scientists, by its usefulness to the evolutionary intelligence of the race. Prediction is *not* the chief measure of such usefulness, though both Adamses were later acclaimed for having predicted a world crisis in 1938, world domination by Russia and the United States, and the like. Rather it is a matter of relevance to the conscious human effort to gain a degree of imaginative control over the drift (or slide) of the present, and to hold up against the unpredictable opening out of future possibility a model of rational, and realistic, understanding. The work of the Adamses as historians, of Henry Adams in particular, remains exemplary for the same reason that it remains absorbingly readable: because it is consistently intelligent, not least about its own purposes and procedures; because its rendering of past events is ordered by a critical interest in both the phenomena examined and in itself as an instrument of examination; because it is always a study *of* "history," of the very possibility of a significant knowledge of events, as well as a stylish chronicle of what, on the basis of existing records, is thought to have happened.

Criticism and literary history alike have fallen into no little confusion over this matter. Both Adamses (who talked out their ideas and corresponded about them for two or three decades) made free in their writing with words like "law," "scientific," "force," "energy," "acceleration," "entropy," "unity," "inertia," "types," "variants," and the like; and both enjoyed alluding to great scientific theorems (the Second Law of Thermodynamics is the well-known case) as if these provided analogies directly applicable to the control of historical knowledge. What did they think they were doing? If they meant that the data of history and the data of natural science were identical as objects of knowledge, and the job of the historian was to find a formula or law covering all his discovered evidence, then two damaging objections can be raised against them. First, history is not nature; the progressive affairs of men do not in fact correspond to the dance of atoms or the life cycles of biological organisms. Second, they did not in any case understand the character and use of scientific "laws." Beyond question their work lies open to these objections: especially that of Brooks Adams, who invoked scientific analogies with a kind of hammer-and-tongs assertiveness of which the crankery of his later years seems a natural extension. What must also be said is that their starting point was a critical concern for method and for fundamental relevance and truthfulness which the common practice of Anglo-American historiography mostly prefers to do without. This concern weighs greatly in their favor. It is precisely the Adamses' sense that written history is not simply a communication of knowledge but a form of discourse aiming to establish knowledge that sets them apart from their contemporaries, and from most of their successors as well.

The Adamses' first premise was the bankruptcy of nineteenth-century historicism in general. We may note at once that this premise is interestingly borne out in the careers of two of the most respected historians of the period, the Englishman Acton (1834–1902) and the American Turner (1861–1932). The deeper each got into the complications of his pursuit of truth, the more hesitant and uncertain he became, and the more unencompassable the historian's great traditional task of explaining what actually had happened during some momentous span of the past. So both are known as much for the masterworks they were unable to write—Acton's history of liberty, Turner's sectional history of the United States— as for the impressive fragments they did get into print. (In Turner's case the one book he managed to finish in his life-time, his *Rise of the New West: 1819–1829* [1906], was proposed to him, and had to be dragged out of him, by the general editor of the series for which it was commissioned.) The difficulties of Acton and Turner and the record of Anglo-American historiography since their time (not in the main a field of inquiry in which the modern mind has greatly distinguished itself, in the English-speaking provinces) might reasonably temper the usual judgment of Henry Adams's work in history and the philosophy of history, which is that it "failed." Neither the major intellectual history of his times nor his own numerous explanations of what he was attempting to do have been sufficiently taken into account. His references to scientific models of formulation are, in a word, experimental. They are the rhetorical form of his effort to "return to first principles"—in case any can be found. The test of their value is pragmatic. Thus, when confronted with such formulations, "the student or professor who is properly trained, or who is naturally fit for study," so Henry Adams wrote in 1909, with legitimate irony, "will not be concerned with the question whether it is true, which has no meaning to him; but he will be curious to test its convenience or its scope." So long as it works to extend understanding, above all to break out of the trap of positivism, there can be life and health in it.

The Adamses' conception of the writing of history is set out compactly in the defense Brooks Adams made to Lodge of his first book, *The Emancipation of Massachusetts* (1887), which had been received in Boston (not altogether unreasonably) as a scandalous piece of ancestor defamation. "It is not really a history of Mass. but a metaphysical and philosophical inquiry as to the actions of the human mind in the progress of civilization; illustrated by the history of a small community isolated and allowed to work itself free."[14] With Brooks Adams (1848–1927), however, we are less likely to be satisfied that scientific analogies have not become fixed in his mind as axiomatic truths. A splendidly forthright debunker when the chance fell his way, he had an erratic critical intelligence. Dogmatic oversimplification tempted him beyond his means and is the pervasive fault of those later books, written during the period of the Spanish-American War and the ascendancy of Theodore Roosevelt, in which he attempted to fit America's momentous emergence as a world power into a general scheme of universal history. These books are *America's Economic Supremacy* (1900), a collection of more or less prophetic magazine articles; *The New Empire* (1902), a survey of the rise and fall of imperial states, from dynastic Egypt to the Sino-Japanese and Boer Wars of the '90s; and *The Theory of Social Revolutions* (1913), a rather scrambled inquiry into the interaction of political institutions and economic power. By 1913 Brooks Adams appears to be saying whatever comes into his head, in the order in which it comes. Invariably he writes his thought down with point and rhetorical cogency—but we increasingly suspect that what we are referred to is the tortured history not so much of actual empires and nations as of his own intellectual travail in contemplating them. We are likely to think this, for example, of the question eloquently posed at the beginning of Chapter V of *Social Revolutions*, concerning the excesses that overtake

14. Readers of Henry Adams's nine-volume *History* will note how this defense corresponds to Henry Adams's choice to concentrate on a span of sixteen years in the life of the American democracy.

even successful assailants of the always deteriorating received order of things:

> Why should a type of mind which has developed the highest prescience when advancing along the curve which has led it to ascendancy, be stricken with fatuity when the summit of the curve is passed, and when a miscalculation touching the velocity of the descent must be destruction?

With Henry Adams, failure to impose his mind's prescience upon history is a pose, however tiresome, a means of dramatizing his broader theme. With Brooks Adams, it becomes something more substantial, and self-defeating, a private obsession that warps his later books out of the line of truth.

Brooks Adams's best book is unquestionably *The Law of Civilization and Decay* (1895). And it is superior, as a work of history, in conventional ways: in concreteness of exposition and argument, in harmony of narrative design. Solidly based on contemporary researches in economic history and on published sources, it is a full-bodied exercise in historical thesis-making, in which a Tocquevillean concern for the process of political centralization furnishes the binding thread. But it is something more than that, too. In recreating the great economic crises of European development through the agency of their characteristic participants (the "new men" of each new era), it is also richly dramatic, and in no spurious way, combining panoramic overviews and microscopic detail with an artist's sureness of execution. The great virtue of *Civilization and Decay* is its imaginative adequacy to its ambitious subject, its concrete grasp upon historical succession as the formative dimension of collective human experience. Perhaps the writing of history has not yet got out of thrall (can it ever?) to the method of Herodotus, in which myth-making is no less an instrument of truth than documentary reconstruction. Perhaps it will always at its best draw upon the visionary and prophetic imagination as well as tabulation and measurement. Such freedom of method has its obvious risks of misuse and debasement; nevertheless, though not much in favor at present, it remains to haunt an era of quantitative scholarship with an alternative model of truthfulness; and Brooks Adams's major "essay on history" is among other things a strong argument for its continuing practicability.[15]

It has been suggested more than once—for example, by Charles Beard in a valuable introduction to a reprinting of *Civilization and Decay* (1943)—that Brooks Adams had the more original mind of the two brothers and that in their informal collaboration the novel ideas were largely his. The matter does not seem to be one that can be decided positively (it cannot even be intelligently discussed if the measure of "ideas" is merely descriptive, or nomenclative). The fact is simply that from the first evidences we have of it the character of Henry Adams's thought—the acute consciousness of the special quality of his own age and of the special discipline of mind required to comprehend it; the immediate recognition

15. An interesting critical essay on the novels of Scott and Dickens and the historical mores embodied in their characters (reprinted in *America's Economic Supremacy*) shows off in a marginal quarter the general virtues of Brooks Adams's interpretive scheme. A complementary example of the historical criticism of literature, a method common enough in the period of Taine though slow to enter Anglo-American writing, is Henry Adams's account of Homeric epic as "a running commentary on the Greek law of marriage," in his Lowell lecture, "Primitive Rights of Women" (1876).

It was this imaginative combination of interests, and not only their sophisticated pessimism, which made the Adamses significant figures in the modernist renaissance of 1912 and after. The much-remarked influence of Henry Adams upon Eliot's poems of 1920 and 1922 is matched by Brooks Adams's influence upon Ezra Pound, for whom he figures as a kind of Yankee Confucius—lawgiver for civil and economic affairs, historical critic of good and bad rulers, prophetic keeper of the public conscience.

of the right intellectual masters and the consistently superior argumentative tact (as compared to Brooks) in expressing his concerns; even the distinctive style of the *Education* and of his remarkable private letters—is clear and definite and shows itself continuous with his final preoccupations. In 1862, as news of the ironclads at Hampton Roads reached him in London, he wrote home: "I tell you these are great times. Man has mounted science and is now run away with." A year later he was studying, in the context of a Civil War that had become a national war against slavery, "the philosophic standing of our republic" and reflecting upon the complementary "advance of the democratic principle in European civilization." "I have learned to think De Tocqueville my model," he added, "and I study his life and works as the gospel of my private religion." His papers and reviews for the *North American* during the late '6os and '7os—several are reprinted in *Historical Essays* (1891)—are increasingly full of his double concern, at once practical and speculative, to see whether the historian's method could indeed make the events of past and present intelligible, and what exactly America had come to represent in the continuing cycles of universal history.[16]

16. As editor of the *North American* from 1870 to 1876, Henry Adams seized the chance to review works by Freeman, Henry Maine, Fustel de Coulanges (*The Ancient City*), Stubbs (*The Constitutional History of England*), Parkman (*The Old Regime in Canada*), Von Holst, Bancroft, J. G. Palfrey, and J. R. Green (*Short History of the English People*). In nearly every case his emphasis falls somewhere on questions of rationale and method.

The *North American* was never closer to being a national forum of educated opinion than during Adams's editorship. A partial list of contributors between 1870 and 1876 includes Charles Francis Adams, Jr., James Russell Lowell, Chauncey Wright, Howells, Boyesen, Parkman, William and Henry James, Charles Kendall Adams, Simon Newcomb, Daniel Coit Gilman, Sumner, Lewis Morgan, Nathaniel Shaler, Palfrey, Peirce, Lodge, and Brooks Adams.

When he settled down in the '80s to the long project of his *History*, his very choice of subject—the United States during the decade and a half in which it could be shown how the course was finally set for unified and committed nationhood— was directed by this double concern. Though he withheld his explanation of this choice until his closing pages, it was bold and forthright—almost, one might say, chauvinistic—when it came: "Should history ever become a true science, it must expect to establish its laws, not from the complicated story of rival European nationalities, but from the methodical evolution of a great democracy." (By "science," it bears repeating, Adams meant self-critical knowledge, as distinct from gossip and opinion-mongering.) As a historian Brooks Adams belongs essentially with figures like Carlyle or Spengler, prophetic writers who collate the evidence in search of a higher and preconceived truth. But Henry Adams's place is in a different company, with his master Tocqueville (whose *Recollections* set an artful precedent for the combination of autobiography and generalized inquiry in the *Education*), and with Burckhardt, Veblen, Ortega, Toynbee, Karl Jaspers, Malraux, all writers who have reinforced a philosophic concern for the character of historical knowledge and historical statement with an imaginative perception of the revolutionary nature of modern democratic and technological society.[17] If, comparing Henry Adams with these peers, we sense that his practical opportunities for testing and refining his insights were somehow fewer and narrower, and his capacities so much the less thoroughly trained, we may also find in his work a compensating freedom of association and hypothesis. If his point of departure in argument often appears

17. Some of the most striking and original passages in the *History* are those demonstrating in specific detail the inventiveness of inexperienced American military forces in mastering not the strategy but the technique, and technology, of contemporary warfare.

more abstract, and his line of advance more tenuous and problematical, that indeed is one measure of his essential Americanness; it is the kind of difference that strikes our attention also in placing Emerson beside Carlyle and Arnold, or Ezra Pound beside Valéry and Rilke.

There is a clear logic to the progression of Henry Adams's work. Out of his teaching in the Revolutionary and Federal periods of American history he produced, soon after resigning from Harvard and the *North American* in 1876, two bulky works of scholarship, which still stand as models of their kind: a collection of public papers, *Documents Relating to New England Federalism, 1800–1815* (1877), designed to clarify what seemed to Adams a critical phase in the momentous drift of provincial American society toward national unity; then a thoughtfully proportioned biography, the *Life of Albert Gallatin* (1879), of that one early American statesman toward whom—for his qualities of disinterested patriotism, humane (and trans-atlantic) cultivation, and efficient political intelligence—Adams was most sympathetic personally. (Adams's Gallatin may be described as the one American figure in the whole body of his writing who would have made a suitable husband for the attractively idealized heroines of his novels: see pp. 128–130). On the way toward his *History* he produced a short biography of John Randolph (1882) for the *American Statesmen* series, a book, however, in which irritation at the private character of his subject opens the door to fundamental errors of tact (Randolph's eccentricities hardly required exaggeration) and, worse, to a fundamental distortion. If the man was indeed a "lunatic monkey" who should not be taken seriously, as Adams wrote to John Hay, his actual pre-eminence in Congressional debate becomes unintelligible. It is of interest that Adams corrected this lapse in the finished *History*. There Randolph is treated fairly, even respectfully, his exceptional prescience about the broad political drift of his era making him, in fact, a key figure in the interpretive design.

The *History* itself is a masterpiece of reasoned exposition and analytic conjecture. The dry, pungent chapters on the general condition of American society and culture that open and close this richly detailed work are models of economical generalization, the more so in being steadily responsive to Adams's main narrative theme: that double revolution in material development and in popular "ideas" which in one short war-crossed generation transformed a loose chain of divided coastal provinces into a secure and immune national society whose extraordinary progress could be read—"with almost the certainty of a mathematical formula"—for a century to come. As an account of this span of political history, Adams's work, or rather his interpretive scheme, has inevitably been superseded. As a work of historical imagination, however, it retains its integrity, its synthesizing power; and it suggests by the way that, although history may well be primarily an "empirical science" (the dreary phrase recently revived by H. R. Trevor-Roper), it may nevertheless still be written, as morally it must be, in the grand manner.[18]

"With almost the certainty of a mathematical formula": Henry Adams's *History* is spotted with such locutions, red herring to the unwary. "The laws of physics might easily be applied to politics," another passage risks saying. But the use of qualifying adverbs and the auxiliary expressing possibility is to be noted. In proposing that historical learning consider

18. The solid competence of Henry Adams's ordinary scholarship may be illustrated by the fact that when, in 1944, *The Infantry Journal* wished to bring out a satisfactory military history of the War of 1812, the editors simply extracted the relevant chapters from Adams's *History*. Since they wisely retained the passages on the political and economic management of the war and on the diplomatic negotiations that ended it, the result was as if a new minor classic had been added to our historical literature.

the example of experimental science Henry Adams stopped short of Brooks's dogmatism. Indeed an ironic demonstration of the peculiar difficulties in the way of discovering causes and laws in history lies close to the surface of this long work. It may be that the philosophic doubts that stir in the reader's mind are deliberately stimulated. For beneath the conscientious particulars of the exposition an intellectual comedy is already beginning to be played out in the *History*, a comedy that would increasingly absorb Adams's attention. Can the most scrupulous historian organize his materials into an intelligible design? can he define essential causes and motives, and show why one thing happened and another did not? The inquiry, the examination of evidence—not only presidential decrees, battles, acts of Congress, but also population figures, financial data, ordnance estimates, postal statistics, religious controversies and literary achievements—goes steadily forward, closing in again and again on a causal field which, however, the more completely it is surrounded, grows the more perfectly mysterious. It is, specifically, the field of national character, historically considered ("American Character" is the title of the *History*'s closing chapter); of that which by its nature lies outside any conclusive codification, yet inspires the writer to attempt codification as nothing else does; and thus also of the whole radical indeterminacy of human history, in contemplating which even the questions asked as well as the topics addressed have their inextricable complement of subjective contingency. This inquiry, we also note, has the further interest of showing us Henry Adams grasping at that special problem of apprehension—the problem of the peculiar condition, among all other conceivable forms of being, of being "American"—which preoccupied Henry James in the novel, and, what is more, bringing to his treatment of it a comparable sophistication of method.

It was under the burden of desolation after his wife's suicide in 1885, though also as a relief from it, that Henry Adams completed his *History*, seeing the last volumes into print during the summer of 1890. Then, with a conscious effort of cutting loose, he turned his back on the sufficiently conventional career and profession he had so far pursued. There followed a year-long voyage through the South Seas (which produced, in 1893, a privately printed curiosity entitled *Memoirs of Marau Taaroa, Last Queen of Tahiti*), further travels to Europe, to the Chicago World's Fair, to Central America and the Rockies, and an excited tour of the cathedral towns of northern France (whose great monuments to medieval energy and concentration had already deeply affected Brooks Adams's thinking); and all these episodes mark a division in Henry Adams's work as consequential as the disastrous campaign to conquer the theater in Henry James's. In 1894, in an essay, "The Tendency of History," sent as a letter to the American Historical Association in place of the presidential address he had not even considered giving, Adams predicted the end of conventional historiography, or at the least a crisis so grave that it could only be got through by some nearly inconceivable change of direction. The study of history had come in sight of the norms of scientific exactness and could not dodge the consequences— "A science cannot be played with." But neither could history now avoid giving offense to the superego of modern capitalism; to the life interests, that is, of an order of society that did not wish and would not allow systematic estimates to be made of its actual course of development and that, in its present state of organization, was supremely well equipped "for the suppression of influences hostile to its safety." Adams himself pretended in this essay to have abandoned the intellectual battle. "Beyond a doubt, silence is best," and his remarks, he cautioned, were to be taken as "only casual and offered in the paradoxical spirit of private conversation." Having thus, to his own satisfaction, covered his tracks and escaped from public view, he settled upon new lines of historical inquiry that were closer to his heart than any he had yet followed and that resulted, by 1907, in the two masterly works of narrative synthesis for which he is chiefly remembered, *Mont-Saint-Michel and Chartres* and *The Education of Henry Adams.*[19]

It has become somewhat the fashion—inevitably, perhaps, in view of the popularity of these books in the 1920s and '30s —to depreciate Adams's later writings; to see them as idiosyncratic private undertakings, privately motivated, full of a certain nostalgic poetry and a rather overinsistent irony, but, with regard to their objective intention, possessing no durable intellectual value. The *Mont-Saint-Michel* in particular lies open to professional disparagement, its central hypothesis of the cultural unity of the high Middle Ages proving, of course, as vulnerable as most such hypotheses to empirical objection; while the *Education,* in pretending that a "dynamic" or any other "theory of history" is a reasonable and important goal, is held to compound the sin of being unreliable as autobiography with a display of overreaching unworthy of a mature professional intelligence.

Judgments of this sort are not such as can be argued against in a summary way, by casual counterassertion. All that really needs to be established here in defense of these two remarkable books is their right to occupy the ground, formally, of their author's choosing. As essays in research and definition aiming above all at "the air of reality"—that key Jamesian phrase figures decisively in the "Preface" to the *Education*— they have an originality and intellectual distinction nearly

19. The first was privately printed in 1905 and published in 1913; the second was privately printed in 1907 and published after Adams's death in 1918.

unique in our period. They are executed with style, energy, and compositional integrity; they exist as books, and as books of an unusual maturity of interest, as do few others in our literature. They belong, moreover, to a literary type that exists and must be acknowledged even though we have no proper name for it: the descriptive analysis of some great collective phenomenon (consider *The Anatomy of Melancholy, The Stones of Venice, The American Scene, The Psychoanalysis of Fire, The Voices of Silence*) in the writing of which the imaginative effort and excitement of the writer himself, or it may be of some fictive protagonist, appear as more or less of a major countertheme. *Mont-Saint-Michel* is an eloquent book really. It happens also to be about the exceptionally interesting subject (especially from the point of view of a democratic and technological culture) *of* eloquence—specifically, the eloquence common to all the great creations of the medieval consciousness, in architecture, in theology and systematic philosophy, in court and folk poetry and folk religion. It is also an exploratory study in the materials of history and in the truth of historical knowledge; in the process it becomes one of the first works of modern historiography to make use of the peculiar stability of art objects as determining items of historical interpretation. Even considered as a contribution to conventional learning, *Mont-Saint-Michel* is extraordinary. For all its lyric celebrations of medieval homogeneity, it recognizes violent, rapid change as no less a factor in the twelfth century than in the chaos of the nineteenth, and it finds clear ways of describing such change; it finds ways, also, of including the factors of art and religious passion and the factors of money and trade on the same presentational spectrum. Moreover, it is in execution, one may finally say, a modest book, with a submissive tact and proportion in the management of all its magnificent materials—Chartres cathedral, the worship of the Virgin, the *Summa*

Theologica, the "Cantico del Sole," and the "Chanson de Roland"—that win for its argument the kind of imaginative assent that no writer can secure who has not found and mastered the forms appropriate to his work.

The Education of Henry Adams was also conceived as a work of history. Like *Mont-Saint-Michel* it is an inquiry into the distinctive character of an age (1850–1900), but more particularly into the field of forces, the pattern of "motion" and "relation," determining that character. For Henry Adams, now well past sixty, this had become the one kind of history worth a major effort of mind. Having discovered in the course of publishing a dozen volumes of American history (so he wrote) that historical "truth," what had actually happened, was quite unknowable, he now proceeded to write a chronicle of the mind's experience of a span of history: his own informed and meditated experience of his own times. The vision of the book that resulted, Ernest Samuels has remarked, is "romantic and grandiose" and casts a "cosmic glare." What keeps this vision in sharp focus is an ingenious compositional scheme that Robert Morss Lovett in his *Dial* review of 1918 was first to recognize: the scheme of a Quixotic pilgrimage after the ancient New England idol, education. Within this scheme the figure of "Henry Adams" is given to us as a historical type being acted upon in his time and reacting, a single random unit of force operating among a vast play of forces which can be named and studied but subjected (it increasingly appears) to no other control. Consciousness alone can be known in the round and used as a basis for historical induction; therefore his own consciousness must be starting point and denominator in any effort to calculate directions. At the same time every such unit of consciousness has its own history and goes down to defeat in its own way, so that the life story of one such consciousness becomes at once the most suggestive means of charting an intelligible course through the chaos of the historical and also a first measure of that effort's inevitable failure.

The basic metaphor of this severely pessimistic book is Darwinian. "Education" as Adams imagines it signifies, first of all, adaptation, the organism's struggle to adjust to the influences conditioning its progress through life; and the rhythm of the narrative is one of stimulus (always astonishing) and response (always insufficient), of historical drift and human travail. The great forcing events of the era—the American Civil War; the economic eruption of steam power, railroads, and electricity, and the social revolution resulting; the tremendous revolution in thought of which Darwinism, Marxism, and modern physics were crystallizing agents; the ominous new diplomacy of great-power imperialism—are simultaneously instruments of change (and of change in the rate of change) and symbolic antagonists of the civilized mind's selective ordeal of involvement and repulsion. This wide array of materials is a source of high interest in itself; and what more than anything else distinguishes the *Education* is the consistent clarity and intelligence (backed by an artist's flair for the organizing symbol) with which all parts of the presentational scheme are developed. What other American book takes firmer hold on the whole outward, public, historical circumstance of common life? Fault can be found with the structure of the book. The narrative rhythm breeds repetition, as new shapes of force appear and the mind rocks yet once more with ironic disappointment; the strict refusal to include the years of Adams's marriage and, even more, of his obviously successful professional career as teacher and writer produces a breach in the sequence of chapters that is not covered over in argument; and the effort, toward the end, to articulate a workable theory of history, though it is hardly unprepared for, comes somewhat arbitrarily into what is fundamentally a work of narrative exposition. (The author's scheme, Adams wrote in an "Editor's Preface" signed by Henry Cabot Lodge, "became unmanageable as he approached his end.") But to say all this is to say nothing very damaging. There is no end of books that abdicate their own best chances by a cheating deference to compositional propriety—and there are a few others about which our only real disappointment is that they do not go on indefinitely. Henry Adams's *Education* is of this second class.

The same intelligence and diverse consistency of interest characterize Adams's letters, of which three volumes are in print; he was, as Marcus Cunliffe has said, "one of the best letter-writers in the language."[20] The very freedom with which he could address himself, in private correspondence, to a chosen audience, sure of being read in the right spirit, give the mannerisms of his later style their most effective setting. Adams's letters are his Journal—classic New England literary form—conducted in this case without the disadvantage of having only himself, on earth, to talk to. Of the two odd speculative essays written in 1908–1909 on the future of the historical discipline, the longer takes naturally the form of "A Letter to American Teachers of History." Even the *Education* Adams described at this time as no more than "a letter; garrulous, intimate, confidential, [such] as is permitted in order to serve a social purpose, but would sound a false note for the public ear." In this form more easily than in any other he could both develop extravagant hypotheses and dismiss them as mere casual private suggestions. Thus he carried forward one of the great traditional enterprises of the New England mind in literature: that radical-subjective critique of experience, including the mind's experience, which Santayana understood to be at the core of New England

20. See *Letters of Henry Adams*, edited by W. C. Ford, 2 volumes, 1930, 1938; *Henry Adams and his Friends*, edited by H. D. Cater, 1947.

Transcendentalism and which Henry Adams brought back into the dimension not only of the national and racial, as had the admirable Emerson of *English Traits*, but also of the specifically historical. The method involved may well have been, in Adams's case as in Emerson's and William James's, what Santayana called it, "a personal, arduous, and futile art, which requires to be renewed at every moment"; but not until comment on Adams's effort as a writer becomes established on a corresponding plane of critical relevance can his pose of failure and ironic apology, in the practice of that art, be considered a formal mistake, a misconceiving of the tactical occasion.

The Critique of Society:
Prophecies and Field Reports

The richness of late nineteenth-century American writing in the description and analysis of essential society is a leading symptom of the ascendancy of realism. Here, too, more often than not, practical criticism and evangelical prophecy go hand in glove. That union—infusing even moderate ideas of reform with a crusading intensity—is the forensic element common to three of the most influential social critics of the period, Henry George (1839–1897), Edward Bellamy (1850–1898), and Henry Demarest Lloyd (1847–1903), all forerunners and patron saints of turn-of-the-century progressivism.[21] Their common cause was social justice. The standard of economic equality, the attack on monopoly, George's Single Tax or Bellamy's scheme for universal industrial conscription were the temporal means to this essentially spiritual end. Their thinking, especially George's and Bellamy's, was

21. This element sets their work apart from that of the Danish-born Laurence Gronlund, author of *The Co-operative Commonwealth* (1884), the one thoroughgoing socialist among these liberally hopeful antagonists of the capitalist ethos.

suffused with millennial optimism and looked toward a condition of society in which the Golden Rule would be embodied in the common institutional order of life. For all three, political economy was fundamentally a moral science. So their critique of industrial civilization turns on a set of moral distinctions (essentially Veblenesque) between the productive and the parasitic, those who do real work and add real wealth and those who corner markets and collect rent. None of these writers, however, visualized returning to an Arcadia of handicrafts and village community in the manner of William Morris; all were excited by a sense of the extraordinary material well-being possible to all men through the advance of industrialism and the machine process. Thus they were concerned as much with the inefficiency of *laissez-faire* capitalism as with its injustices; and both concerns come together in the Veblenesque hatred of waste—the waste of productive capacity, the waste of human and natural resources —that is one of their steadiest practical motives.

Henry George's *Progress and Poverty* (1879) is one of the prophetic books of modern social reform. Its influence upon the early development of Fabian Socialism is well known, and it still has organized disciples in the Scandinavian democracies. An "intensely personal and sincere" work, as Daniel Aaron has remarked, it possessed to an extraordinary degree the power to convert, and also the steadiness of purpose and argument required to sustain the faith of those converted. Less a finished theoretical treatise than a hortatory primer of fundamental problems and issues, it fixed a generous sympathy for human aspiration and human suffering into a panoramic overview of the rise and fall of civilizations (see Book X, "The Law of Human Progress") that gives its proposals the gravity of universal truths. The same general tactics were used no less effectively in the essays composing its sequel, *Social Problems* (1883), where in fact the personal urgency of George's concern is felt rather more directly than in *Prog-*

ress and Poverty, free of the apparatus of proofs and close reasoning he thought necessary for his first book. A comparable imaginative logic underlies Edward Bellamy's immensely popular Utopian novel, *Looking Backward* (1888), in which mouth-watering anticipations of the world of A.D. 2000, a very paradise of middle-class comfort and leisure, plus the dramatic machinery of mesmeric rebirth by which the hero crosses over from the brutally anarchic world of 1887, override the general vagueness of social and political detail. Bellamy's futuristic romance, however—along with its sequel, *Equality* (1897)—owes more perhaps to Jules Verne than to nineteenth-century socialism, though Gronlund's *Co-operative Commonwealth* was an immediate influence. It owes something, too, to nineteenth-century transcendentalism and panpsychism—the hero of *Looking Backward* falls in love in the year 2000 with a reincarnation of his sweetheart of 1887, and the conception of a radical change in the whole spiritual temper of human life is central to the conception of reform in social institutions. One consequence of this element in the book's appeal was the curious rallying to the Bellamyite movement in the early '90s of Madame Blavatsky and her Theosophists.

A fundamental reform of the human spirit as well as of the institutions of capitalist society is a premise also of Lloyd's otherwise more down-to-earth and matter-of-fact exposé, *Wealth Against Commonwealth* (1894), the first great "muckraking" work of the period and probably the most influential. The book's solidly detailed chronicle of corporation piracy and the systematic corruption of popular government by great wealth loses nothing by being joined to what one reviewer called the "noble argument on behalf of industrial Christianity" to which it rises at its close. Lloyd, a Chicago-based journalist and political reformer, was a devoted Emersonian (see the essay, "Emerson's Wit and Humor," in *Mazzini and Other Essays*, 1910). Unhappily, he carried discipleship to the point of attempting to imitate the master's style. As much as any one writer it was Lloyd who seems to have invented the caption-making, cartoon-reductive manner of modern American journalism in dealing with public affairs and current history, the result of which, now, is to insinuate the kind of doubts about his seriousness and sincerity that the plainer style of Henry George precludes. Nevertheless *Wealth Against Commonwealth*—which frightened off every publisher it was sent to and finally got into print largely through the support of Howells, who had published Lloyd's original exposure of the Standard Oil Company in the *Atlantic* in 1881—is an absorbing book: "as interesting and disagreeable," one reviewer commented, "as a realistic novel." And it is an important book historically. Not only the politics of the Progressive movement but also the closely documented business novels of Frank Norris, Dreiser, and Upton Sinclair owe much to its pioneering description of the actual workings of trusts and monopolies and their destructive disregard of the general welfare.

The grounding of these books in economic fact is a first measure of their superiority to those written by several eminent Protestant clergymen of the period, books all more or less social-welfarist in outlook and evolutionary in their conception of social change.[22] On the other hand, the generous imaginative sense, in George, Bellamy, and Lloyd, of the human cost of corrupted institutions gives their writing a vital human truthfulness lacking in such works of reasoned analysis as Woodrow Wilson's *Congressional Government* (1885) or even Herbert Croly's influential *The Promise of American Life* (1909). The same combination of fieldwork and imaginative sympathy, inspired by an instinctive late-

22. See, for example, Washington Gladden's *Applied Christianity* (1886), Lyman Abbott's *Christianity and Social Problems* (1897), and Walter Rauschenbusch's *Christianity and the Social Crisis* (1907).

Protestant humanitarianism, also distinguishes G. W. Cable's writings in the '80s and '90s on the Negro question and the "silent south" (see p. 86). Cable in this phase of his work was but one of a crowd of pamphleteers and journalists concerned to alert the public conscience to particular faults and wrongs in the rapidly materializing new order of American life. A society now recognized on all sides as being in the throes of a vast continuing crisis of inward evolution suddenly had become as great an object of common curiosity as had the extraordinary structures of physical nature being revealed by contemporary science.

The new culture of cities, and of cyclical capitalism, was the main focus of attention in such writing. "The amount of literary labor," *The Times* of London remarked in the '90s, "which is now being expended in America upon economical and industrial problems is something prodigious." And certain books of this kind, based on field trips and frontline observation, were as original in conception as any realist novel of the period. Two in particular which deal with the notorious "tramp" problem deserve mention, for this was one of the most publicized social symptoms of the time and, to the middle-class imagination, one of the most frightening: they are *Tramping With Tramps* (1899) by "Josiah Flynt" (1869–1907), renegade nephew of the bluestocking feminist Frances Willard, and Jack London's *The Road* (1907), which in turn was dedicated to Flynt.[23] But among books of this class a special place of honor must be held for two by the Danish-born newspaperman and reformer Jacob Riis (1849–1914), *How the Other Half Lives* (1890) and *The Children of the*

23. London's book is the more vivid and readable of the two, but Flynt's is of special interest for indicating, with its chapters on hoboism in Great Britain and Europe, that the tramp problem was in some way a universal consequence of the modern industrial order of life and not due simply, as was assumed by polite opinion, to the moral delinquency of certain undesirable Americans.

Poor (1892). Typically, Riis's writing is shot through with moralistic assumptions. The social disorders multiplying in the tenement districts of New York City are caused, he wrote in the "Introduction" to the first of these books, by the "greed and reckless selfishness" of general society; and the life of crime and immorality into which the "other half" is inexorably driven comes "but as a just punishment upon the community that gave it no other choice." Riis's essential concern, however, was practical and not at all prophetic or revolutionary; he asked only that these outcasts be given a fair chance to take their places freely in modern society's necessary work force. Yet a radical commitment to an ideal of social justice is implied throughout his work. And though his books lack the sustained argumentative authority of George's and Lloyd's, their very matter-of-factness (backed by documentary photographs) made a strong public impression. In its cruder way, the story of "Kid McDuff's Girl" in *The Children of the Poor* stands close to the shocking novelty of Stephen Crane's *Maggie*, published a year later, and is based on the same kind of sympathetic personal observation.

The one masterpiece in the genre of sociological reporting written during this period is of course *The American Scene* (see pp. 18–19, 124). All that needs to be said at this point is that James's extraordinary book, the record of a few months' impressions, endorses in its own intuitive way nearly every charge except perhaps that of productive inefficiency brought by these critics and reformers against civilization in the United States.

Literary Criticism

A lively moral concern for the progress of American civilization and the general health of the national culture is also the leading common motive in literary criticism during this period. The historical Puritanism of high American thought—if not in abeyance while realism was gaining acceptance, then concentrated upon the simple propositions of truthfulness and plain-speaking—re-emerged imperious and resilient as ever, holding works of art and letters strictly accountable for their service to the common spiritual estate and finding them directly symptomatic of prevailing conditions. The more doctrinaire of these critical moralists were usually academic men—"new humanists" defending classical standards, such as Irving Babbitt and P. E. More—and they were also, not surprisingly, the least hospitable to the really interesting new work of their time. But even the strongest partisans of the new, after 1900, used the same ultimately moralistic standard of valuation, defending their very different allegiances in art by reference to comparably abstract conceptions of the general spiritual welfare.

Even for newspaper critics like James Gibbons Huneker (1860–1921) and Percival Pollard (1869–1911) the great cause was national maturity. Would American writers continue to produce a literature for children and maiden aunts, or would they begin to seek a place as a matter of course in the company of the accomplished masters and free spirits of contemporary Europe? To Huneker the business of spreading the news about the new "supermen" in all the seven arts— Chopin, Wagner, Richard Strauss, and even Schoenberg; Whistler, Cézanne, and Matisse; Nietzsche and Strindberg, Huysmans and Jules Laforgue—was a civic duty as well as a private enthusiasm, a means of supporting the younger New York artists and writers whose work promised a renaissance in America, too.[24] To Pollard, praising Ambrose Bierce and Henry James was a way of pointing out what Americans were really capable of, giving the few best of them "their day in

24. The same proselyting motive characterizes the emergence of a lively cluster of *avant-garde* magazines in the '90s: Vance Thompson's *M'lle New York*, Thomas Bird Mosher's *The Bibelot*, the Chicago *Chap-Book* and the San Francisco *Lark*.

court" (title of the collection of articles he published in 1909) and flogging meanwhile the Philistinism that had made such nobler spirits outcasts or exiles from their own land. Both Huneker and Pollard functioned as popularizers of existing trends and reputations rather than formative influences on new work. Yet the point of view implicit in their writing closely anticipates that of the younger critical captains of the post-1910 resurgence. To Van Wyck Brooks and Randolph Bourne—and also to Ezra Pound, for all his stricter service to "Beauty alone"—literature was ultimately significant as the quintessential test of whether or not the civilization producing it had "come of age." Maturity in art and maturity in nationhood were aspects of the same historical development; reform in society and reform in standards of craftsmanship were one cause. Thus it was that in the creative bull market of 1910–1920 social revolutionaries and Symbolist poets, partisans of unflinching realism and apostles of the transcendent mystique of pure art could join forces with barely a second thought and might be published interchangeably in *The Masses* and *The Little Review,* if not in both at once.

Of the academic humanists Irving Babbitt (1865–1933) and Paul Elmer More (1864–1937), a remark by Ellen Glasgow suggests a final judgment at least for *literary* history: "It isn't what they think, but the way they think it—the iron armour they wear over ideas." Babbitt in particular was an influential teacher during his forty years at Harvard; the fact, for example, that both Van Wyck Brooks and T. S. Eliot had his ideas to listen to and his personal authority to react against early in their careers must be taken into account in any proper reckoning of literary thought after 1900. But the ambitious series of critical manifestoes in which Babbitt attacked Romantic naturalism and humanitarianism and advanced against them a doctrine he incautiously labeled "ethical positivism"—*Literature and the American College* (1908), *The New Laokoön* (1910), *The Masters of Modern French Criticism* (1912), *Rousseau and Romanticism* (1919)—have not stood up well in modern criticism's prolonged wars of truth. Babbitt's thought never quite seems relevant to the actual circumstance of the making of works of literature. Moreover, it is rarely possible to tell what his formulated ideas mean, objectively applied. They hardly seem, introduced into his writings, more than coarse polemical names, catchwords by which the children of light may be more quickly divided off from the children of darkness. (The famous and wholly elusive doctrine of the "inner check" testifies to nothing in actual experience so much as to the dangers of lecturing to audiences of boys year after year after year.)

Babbitt is a formidably advanced case of the academic nominalist, satisfied if he can find, for any given complex of evidences and tendencies, a label that will make a good course title or notebook slogan. In the practice of criticism More seems now much the more sensitive and discriminating writer —at least during the period of the earlier *Shelburne Essays* (14 volumes, 1904–1936) and his literary editorship of, successively, *The Independent*, the New York *Evening Post*, and *The Nation* between 1901 and 1914. Even more satisfactory, perhaps, than either Babbitt or More and correspondingly less doctrinaire in his conservative-humanist outlook is the New Yorker W. C. Brownell (1851–1929), whose *French Traits* (1889) and *American Prose Masters* (1909) are still valuable.[25] None of this work, however, belongs to major

25. With these men differences of working environment appear to have made a difference intellectually. To set Brownell's writing, and judgment, against Babbitt's, or the earlier More against the later More, is in a way to set New York against Cambridge and Princeton as forcing beds of talent, to the advantage of New York. The same conclusion materializes in matching lesser figures like Brander Matthews (1852–1929) of Columbia, an attractive gentleman-

literary history. None of it contributed much to the effort of the significant artists and writers of the period, who took their critical cues, when they took any, from more challenging sources: from Taine and Georg Brandes, from Emerson and Matthew Arnold, from Remy de Gourmont and John Addington Symonds, from Whitman, Tolstoy, Flaubert, and Henry James.

The most original of these humanists, the nearest to becoming a creative force in American letters, was John Jay Chapman (1862–1933). Chapman's concern for art and letters was as deeply moral as Babbitt's, but he had a clearer understanding of works of art as created phenomena subject to their own laws of being. So in a passage in an article on Kipling—rescued by Edmund Wilson in his fine appreciation of Chapman in *The Triple Thinkers*—we see how the case for humanism's moral-therapeutic valuation of literature is greatly strengthened in being rejoined to a firm Emersonian notion of natural, or organic, form:

> Permanent interest cannot attach to anything which does not consist, from rind to seeds, of instructive truth. A thing must be interesting from every point of view, as history, as poetry, as philosophy; good for a sick man, just the thing for Sunday morning. It must be true if read backwards, true literally and true as a parable, true in fragments and true as a whole. It must be valuable as a campaign document, and it must make you laugh or cry at any time, day or night. Lasting literature has got to be so very good as to fulfill all these conditions.

Chapman's own writing, however, though always pungent and alive, rarely steadies down to the standard of performance

---

enthusiast specializing in the drama, and Barrett Wendell (1855–1921), a provincial schoolmaster whose *Literary History of America* (1900) is mostly remembered for the alternative title proposed, not unfairly, by an outlander: "An Intellectual History of Harvard College."

here defined. A birthright inheritor of both the Old New York worldliness and the New England pride of conscience, as occupied with politics and religion as with literature, passionately independent and iconoclastic, he seems at too many cruxes to give his judgment wholly away to personal bias, with the unfortunate effect of obscuring its essential soundness. At the same time he withholds the inward, intensely personal logic that determines his judgment's allegiances and that would have given their expression an imaginative authority. A memorable temperament, strong, generous, willful, Chapman was an erratic thinker and writer. His work is mostly eloquent fragments; he was constitutionally incapable of the performative "insincerity" of art, though he approved the idea of it in principle. His book on the abolitionist Garrison (1913) is biography in the partisan-prophetic manner of Carlyle, with a starker element of ego projection. His social criticism, as in *Causes and Consequences* (1898) and *Practical Agitation* (1900), is radical and comprehensive, but marred in expression by overstatement and by that curious strain of patrician bloodymindedness that troubles one also in the out-of-court speeches and pronouncements of his older contemporary, Justice Holmes. Chapman's literary criticism is at its best in *Emerson and Other Essays* (1898); later collections like *Memories and Milestones* and *Greek Genius and Other Essays* (both 1915) concede too much to attitudinizing and opinionatedness. And even the remarkable essay on Emerson gives the curious impression, even in its praise, of condescending to its subject. Perhaps only in the freedom of private correspondence could Chapman express himself without distortion; his vehemently epigrammatic letters may indeed make up his most enduring legacy as a writer.[26]

The best critic of the period—the one American man of

26. See M. A. DeWolfe Howe, *John Jay Chapman and His Letters,* Boston and New York, 1937.

letters, in fact, capable of meeting the need, recognized pre-eminently by Henry James, for a critical standard which might be appealed to over the heads of "the great common-schooled and newspapered democracy"—was surely James himself. Howells, the more regular observer of the American literary scene, remained the more diligent in the job of calling attention to merit and interest in the steady run of new work; he was the most useful of literary journalists and hardly pre-tended to be more than that. James was incomparably the shrewder and wiser critic, the more exactly discriminating in judgment, the more steadily perceptive in defining the virtue and limitation of individual cases. Once past the young man's witty superciliousness that had produced, at twenty-two, his notorious review of *Drum Taps*, James always read other men's books, and wrote about them, with the utmost generos-ity. Short of empty flattery, he invariably made the best case possible for the work in hand. At the same time he never with-held reservation and disapproval when he felt them, though he usually fell back, in doing that part of his job, on an in-exhaustible talent for circumlocution. Praise with qualifica-tions from Henry James could be more devastating than open abuse from anybody else, as Edith Wharton amusingly testi-fied.

This dread of giving offense was saved from priggish affectation by his steady concern to clarify the general prin-ciples governing his judgments. And James's judgment, how-ever muffled in extenuation and forgiveness, and in generous recognition of limiting circumstances, went unfailingly to the root of the matter. (Even the callow review of *Drum Taps* anticipates by half a century T. S. Eliot's formulaic half-truth of 1917, that the creation of durable art requires a suppression of individual personality.) The one considerable objection that can be made to James's critical writing is to his style. Edwin Muir once accused him (in *The Structure of the Novel*) of having infected modern criticism with a whole set of "question-begging terms," like "pattern," "rhythm," "surface," and "point of view," and with a mannered general vocabulary of "hints" and "nods" expressing essentially sentimental shifts of approval or disapproval. Muir's description of James's criticism as the work of "an incurable impressionist" is not easy to refute, if faced squarely; and it has since proved true enough that imitations of the highly contagious Jamesian manner are more often than not "ridiculously inadequate" (Muir's phrase) to literature of the first rank. In James's own case, however, the governing impressions are gathered and distributed by a strong, precise intelligence which seldom fails to define the special point that was naturally of greatest interest to a fellow practitioner: the point where the personal presence of the writer met and merged with the generic requirements of his art. To read through James's critical essays —on the leading French and English novelists of the nineteenth century; on classic American figures like Emerson and Hawthorne; on Howells and on Whitman's prose; on Bret Harte, Constance Fenimore Woolson, John Jay Chapman, Henry Harland, Gertrude Atherton, Winston S. Churchill, Theodore Roosevelt, E. L. Godkin, Arnold Bennett, H. G. Wells; on the "art of fiction" or "the future of the novel" or "the question of the opportunities" or the "scenic art" of the drama—is to realize how little has been added to our understanding of these diverse topics by any English or American critic since.

Each generation has something different at which they are all looking.

—Gertrude Stein, *Composition as Explanation*

4. LIVES OF THE
AMERICANS:
THE CLASS OF THE '70s

*T*HE perpetually novel conditions and requirements of life which one generation struggles to discover and
bear witness to may in the end be all that the next generation
really knows—such, in literature as in other spheres of action,
appears to be the natural chemistry of historical succession.
The lapse of time need not be great. And the work of successive generations will overlap: Stephen Crane's *Maggie* is very
nearly contemporary with *A Hazard of New Fortunes*;
Gertrude Stein's *Three Lives* antedates *Ethan Frome*. For
Howells and James the conscientiously realistic novel was

still a matter of choice and had still to be defended critically. For their nearer successors, Fuller, Herrick, Edith Wharton, other choices remained equally compelling—the problem novel, the philosophic fantasy, the insulated comedy or romance of manners—though the business of holding up to inspection and judgment "the way we live now" had intensified its claims. But with the next distinct generation in American writing we sense a different, in some ways a narrower, commitment. It is not only that realistic conventions have become matter of course. The difference appears rather in the manner of individual writers' involvement with their work, above all in the impression gradually forced on us that they have not so much chosen their characteristic themes and occasions as been chosen by them. With this new generation, born in the decade after 1869 and coming to maturity around 1900, the whole rapid and disruptive emergence of the modern cultural order has become a condition of life as inexorable as the order of the seasons or the division of the sexes and as strictly determining. Moreover, what this new order of common life might mean and count for was best known, so far as it could be subdued to ordered knowledge, through the lives that were actually being lived within it, lives devoted willy-nilly to learning its indifferent discipline and, in one case after another, discovering themselves victimized by it. And for the younger writers after 1900 the whole damning story of such lives was just what the accessory conventions of the older realism—dramatic framing, the well-constructed plot, the deductive geometry of the prearranged—were most likely to falsify, however authentic the observed detail. All at once it seemed, as if by common consent, that a new effort of honesty and plain speaking had to be made, and that the surest way of making it was to trace out *seriatim* the known facts about characteristic individual cases.

The new manner of American realism shows at once in the titles and tables of contents of new work. Crane's *Maggie*,

Norris's *McTeague*, Robinson's *The Children of the Night* and *Captain Craig*, Dreiser's *Sister Carrie* and *Jennie Gerhardt* or his admirable *Twelve Men*, the stories of "The Good Anna," "Melanctha," and "The Gentle Lena" in Gertrude Stein's *Three Lives* and of "The Dehnings and the Herslands" in *The Making of Americans*, London's *Martin Eden*, Ellen Glasgow's *Virginia* and *Life and Gabriella*, Abraham Cahan's *The Rise of David Levinsky*, Willa Cather's *My Ántonia*, Zona Gale's *Miss Lulu Bett*, the epitaph-soliloquies of Masters' *Spoon River Anthology*, "The Tales and Persons" of Anderson's *Winesburg, Ohio*—or of Frost's *North of Boston* ("this book of people," its dedication reads): all take form as particular life stories and private histories, not finished until we know, or cannot really mistake, the full course and latter end of them. With nearly all these writers we discover, too, that their own American lives have directly prepared them for their common undertaking as private historians of disruptive public change. For the first time the children of the mass continental migrations of the middle nineteenth century begin to find voice in our literature—Dreiser, Sandburg, Gertrude Stein—along, also, with the children of our endless internal uprootings and displacements, like Willa Cather and Robert Frost, and with the displaced spirits, endlessly seeking compensation, thrown up by our fluid, unformed social order, such as Jack London and Sherwood Anderson. An element at once documentary and confessional is the common denominator of all their best work.

They carry us, one might say, out of the picture gallery, the scenes and portraits, of the earlier American realism into the somehow more earnest and deliberate enterprise of a dictionary of national biography. It is distinctly a period enterprise, collective in its nature and fairly hypnotizing in its repetitive patterns of demonstration. What it has to say about the main directions of American life is hardly flattering. We know that free individualism, our secular faith, can have various effects, not all benign. We know in particular that it furnishes no guarantees of virtue or of happiness, its great moral objects; that it can dehumanize as well as liberate; and that paradoxically it can breed—not least among those who have profited most from its special advantages—a consciousness that is ungenerous and illiberal in the extreme and positively insolent in its indifference to actual history, its disregard of the enabling circumstances it lives and thrives among. To the novelists and poets of the talented class of 1869–1879 in our literature, the whole drift of their times was in just these troubling directions, and their work developed largely in response to this drift, in protest and opposition. Like that of the historians and sociologists among them (Charles Beard was one) their effort as spokesmen for the life of their times was fundamentally corrective and revisionist; their realism, as V. L. Parrington (b. 1871) understood, was a "critical" realism. Daydreams and fantasies of wholly different alternatives sometimes supported this effort, and found direct expression; but at their best the writers of this generation were not to be distracted from their essential task, from bearing witness to fundamental conditions. Their common aim was to get down the full composite truth about the casual progression of American lives, and their great achievement was to create a vivid contemporary mythology, rich in local habitations and authentic names and directly implicated in the main currents of popular feeling.

Their limitations as writers must also be acknowledged. These, too, are collective as well as individual. By the measure of their greater European contemporaries—Gide, Proust, Valéry, Mann, Rilke, Pirandello: the makers of modern literature—the literary accomplishment of this American generation appears provincial and, so to speak, incomplete (though not more so than that of English writers of the same period). Their work represents a kind of holding operation, the fundamentally defensive gestures of a set of displaced persons; one misses in it the resourceful amplitude and self-assurance of—to cite American precedents—a James's or a Whitman's sustained effort to create within the imaginative consciousness of his times the very terms and reasons of his art's eventual acceptance. But their own incontestable resource as novelists or poets is the vital honesty of this common concern of theirs, to get at the truth of their singular experience. They kept American writing in saving contact both with the actual circumstance of American lives and with that passion for interior truthfulness which since Emerson and Poe has remained the central formal motive in all our practice of the arts.

Frank Norris, Stephen Crane

The first members of this rising generation to come into prominence did not live past the turn of the century and stand somewhat apart from its distinctive effort. Frank Norris (1870–1902) and Stephen Crane (1871–1900) are Nineties writers in character as well as chronology. An element of willfulness and affectation hangs about their work (in the case of Crane, by far the finer talent, this element is not easily distinguishable from an extraordinary originality). It seems to be the price each paid for precociousness.

With Norris in particular the impression is strong of a writer who never got beyond the synthetic ambitions of his apprenticeship. His continuing reputation as a serious figure in American literature is hard to understand. University-trained (at California and Harvard) and widely read, though scarcely "educated" in any serious sense of the word,[1] he

1. At Harvard, encouraged by his teacher, Lewis Gates, Norris worked on *McTeague* and drafted *Vandover and the Brute* (published posthumously in 1914). He is the first of our writing-course novelists and not the least typical.

worked hard at the role of the Important Writer, the explorer of new tendencies, and published a succession of essay-manifestoes on topics like "The Novel with a 'Purpose,'" "The 'Nature' Revival in Fiction," "The Great American Novelist," and "A Plea for Romantic Fiction" (collected in *The Responsibilities of the Novelist*), the first characteristic of which is their emptiness of genuine critical intelligence. Norris's fatal weakness as a writer is that he is never able to suggest that there is any real pressure of necessity, even idiosyncratic private necessity, in what he chooses to say. His panoramic California novel, *The Octopus* (1901), in which he aimed at what he called "the big, epic, dramatic thing"—it is centered in the conflict between wheat ranchers and the railroad oligarchy—may well be in a publicity sense what Professor Robert Spiller has called it, "the most ambitious novel of its generation," but it is also very nearly the most preposterous. Norris's hectoring style can rarely deliver the simplest, tritest observation without repeating it three times over and in the process blurring it beyond credibility. "He was dizzied, stunned, stupefied. . . . Terrible, formless shapes, vague figures, gigantic, monstrous, distorted, whirled at a gallop." So, too, a "sense of melancholy" is something "lugubrious, lamentable, infinitely sad." When a certain charismatic name is dropped into a tense debate, it is "abrupt, grave, sombre, big with suggestion, pregnant with huge associations." The grossest effects of this kind are produced when the book's mystical Earth-theme is brought forward:

> It was the long stroking caress, vigorous, male, powerful, for which the Earth seemed panting. The heroic embrace of a multitude of iron hands, gripping deep into the brown, warm flesh of the land that quivered responsive and passionate under this rude advance, so robust as to be almost an assault, so violent as to be veritably brutal. There, under the sun and under the speckless sheen of the sky, the wooing of the Titan began, the

vast primal passion, the two world-forces, the elemental Male
and Female, locked in a colossal embrace, at grapples in the
throes of an infinite desire, at once terrible and divine, knowing no law, untamed, savage, natural, and sublime.

It is as if Cole Porter had written novels. "Veritably" is the
giveaway. The word is a favorite with Norris—"It was no
longer a supper. It was a veritable barbecue," or, "Around
Caraher's was a veritable throng"—a precise admission of his
own helpless sense of incurable fuzziness.

Frank Norris may be the writer this history will be most
unjust to. But his incapacities are worth specifying. He can
not write credible dialogue (or dialect, which he unwisely
attempts); he can not describe appearances convincingly; the
whole tendency of his conveyor-belt sentences, pieced together like exercises in a grammar workbook, is to obscure
rather than substantiate the matter at hand. His development
of plot and incident is always arbitrary, fantastic without
being interesting. Human character appears to baffle him
totally; his own characters, distinguished principally by the
presence or absence of "virility," act out the parts assigned
them with comic-strip predictability. All in all, composition in
Norris's novels seems to be reckoned exclusively in calculations
of decibels and gross tonnage. He is a fair example of the
writer who proceeds by echoing other writers—Kipling for
one, and poorly, as in the Three Black Crows stories collected
in *A Deal in Wheat* (1903)—and by exaggerating currently
fashionable effects; who aims at "something big" and then
can only aim at something bigger. Norris's reputation as a
novelist seems an accident of publicity. Word was abroad
that "realism" was giving way to "naturalism," and Norris was
pressed—pressed himself, after taking note of Zola—into
service. Of *The Octopus* something may be said for a few
relatively efficient passages of California scene-painting and
for set pieces like the ambush of the ranchers or the death of

the mortgage-taker, S. Behrman, under an avalanche of wheat in the hold of a grain ship; something even for the large melodramatic design of the book as a whole. The lame effort in its sequel, *The Pit* (1903), to "do" modern Chicago in a comparable way is merely noisy and makes it hard to think of Norris's failure to complete his "Trilogy of the Epic of the Wheat" (the final volume was to have a European setting) as a loss to literature.

McTeague (1899) is surely his best book.[2] Most effective in passages of preliminary description, like the opening paragraphs of Chapter I, it suggests now and then that Norris's real talent might have been for a kind of laconic satirical comedy delivering (in the manner, roughly, of Eliot's early "observations" of Sweeney and others) simple cartoon images of certain debased and unregarded figures characteristic of contemporary life. The overriding weakness of the book appears to be its formulaic devotion to a rather crude species of "naturalism," and to the crude apparatus of dominant passions, environmental determinism, and garish symbol-brandishing that typifies rudimentary examples of that curious school of prose fiction. Literary naturalism, we know, evolved as both a "philosophy" of life and a strategy of expression. Human behavior is understood as being determined by absolute biological and social forces and is therefore most truthfully characterized through a set of fixed symbols or leitmotifs signifying the domination of such forces. But it is a question whether the method of naturalism is really compatible with the genre of the novel. For drama or for opera this question does not arise. The formal abstractions char-

2. Maxwell Geismar, however, in *Rebels and Ancestors,* has made an interesting case for *Vandover and the Brute,* particularly its sketch-portraits of the new American breed of "society" lummoxes and flappers, and suggests that the book may have influenced Scott Fitzgerald's earliest work.

acteristic of naturalism are in fact standard and generic in the theater, where the real presence of human voice and gesture, of actors in company, secures a relation to familiar human experience that the most thoroughgoing artificiality can hardly break. So the greater masters of literary naturalism have been dramatists: Wagner, Hauptmann, Strindberg, Brecht, Eugene O'Neill. But as the novel works first of all through the illusion of free individual character or personality capable of an answering participation in the actions it is contracted into, a strictly naturalist novel may be a logical contradiction. In any case, however, the question cannot be decided on the basis of Norris's fiction, which is too clumsily contrived to provide a fair test. But it is worth noting that what is weakest in *McTeague*—the crudely deterministic psychology, the Gothic exaggerations of landscape and of physical violence— become elements of positive strength in the film, *Greed*, which Erich von Stroheim abstracted from it. In this mutation the bad writing matters not a bit, and we are left with a workable scenario for an impressive *silent* movie. The California that would have served Norris's ambitions did not come into existence until twenty years after his death.

In Stephen Crane's fiction, too, where the violences of war or of slum life and the dumb suffering of the insulted and injured provide the main occasions, the formulas of naturalism are called into service; they do not, however, determine what is presented. Crane's motive was not to diagram conditions or assert universal truths but to produce a certain kind of composition, a vivid showbox of serial impressions in an appropriate style. A passage late in one of his best-known stories, "The Blue Hotel," is in fact as compact a statement of the naturalist point of view as can be imagined, but its effectiveness is all in its placing and timing; what is impressive is not the point of view but the ironic poise and discretion with which the essential commonplaceness of the point of view is overcome and perhaps transfigured. With the narrative sentences framing it, this passage offers a fine instance of the expressive tact and virtuosity which are at the center of Crane's achievement and which led first Garland and Howells and then Joseph Conrad and Henry James to accept him at once into the company of the elect. In it the doomed Swede of the story—the swaggering, quick-eyed outsider who will soon, in ironic fulfillment of his own gratuitous prediction, be haphazardly murdered—is seen struggling across town at night through a prairie blizzard:

> He found a street and made travel along it, leaning heavily upon the wind whenever, at a corner, a terrific blast caught him.
>
> He might have been in a deserted village. We picture the world as thick with conquering and elate humanity, but here, with the bugles of the tempest pealing, it was hard to imagine a peopled earth. One viewed the existence of man then as a marvel, and conceded a glamor of wonder to these lice who were caused to cling to a whirling, fire-smitten, ice-locked, disease-stricken, space-lost bulb. The conceit of man was explained by this storm to be the very engine of life. One was a coxcomb not to die in it. However, the Swede found a saloon.
>
> In front of it an indomitable red light was burning, and the snowflakes were made blood-color as they flew through the circumscribed territory of the lamp's shining. . . .

Coming as it does just before the story's theatrical climax, the passage serves like a chorus or a reflective soliloquy; it brings the whole rising occasion into a more brilliant focus. But within this focus the naturalist view of life is applied not differently from the rays of the red lamp: not to explain or interpret but to spotlight and transfigure.

The passage is not faultless. The quick changes and contrasts in perspective and in grammatical voice, though achieving the ironies they aim at, only just miss being disagreeably affected; and "coxcomb" does seem a lapse into the kind of Kiplingesque smartness of diction that Willa Cather later identified as the period mannerism Crane had chiefly to over-come.[3] A certain susceptibility to lapses of this kind and in general a continuous brittleness of improvisation are char-acteristic of the best of Crane's work. They have become less obtrusive in *The Red Badge of Courage* (1895), the Civil War fantasia of frontline terrors and sublimities that estab-lished his reputation overnight, and in the psychologically acute novella of city life, *George's Mother* (1896), than in the journalistic ironies of his first novel, *Maggie, A Girl of the Streets* (1893); and they are most steadily under control in certain stories of the later '90s. But nothing Crane wrote is entirely free of the quality of the *tour de force*. On the other hand there is something of his virtuoso inventiveness in his slightest and most perfunctory work; nothing he wrote is altogether unrewarding. The shortness of his career and that ripeness of individual sensibility evident in his style from the first—the basis of Howells's remark that Crane had sprung into life "fully armed"—make chronology and questions of development nearly immaterial in his case. Toward the end of his hurried life we do note an increase of potboilers: *The Third Violet* (1897), *Active Service* (1898), the local-color collection *Whilomville Stories* (1900), the unfinished parody-romance *The O'Ruddy* (1903, completed by Robert Barr). Surer now of a market for his work and needing income, Crane was writing too much and too fast, to the point of becoming, like one of the young artists in *The Third Violet*, "a trained bear of the magazines." But between 1896 and

3. Crane himself was aware of the general danger in this quarter. In a letter of 1894 he speaks of having "renounced the clever school in literature," along with the "clever Rudyard-Kipling style" he had begun with.

1899 there is also the assured narrative mastery of his admirable longer stories, "The Little Regiment," "The Blue Hotel," "The Open Boat," "The Monster," "The Price of the Harness," and (even if we grant H. G. Wells's reasonable objection that it overinsists upon its message) "Death and the Child."

Flaws in Crane's work are easy enough to spot; it is the peculiar integrity of his art, at its best, that has escaped definition. Criticism has been clearer about what he did without, among the traditional procedures of English fiction, than about what exactly took their place. There is, in short, a Crane problem, and it is as well stated as it has ever been in the puzzled excursus Joseph Conrad wrote into a letter to Edward Garnett in 1897. "His eye is very individual and his expression satisfies me artistically," Conrad remarked of Crane, but then asked:

> Why is he not immensely popular? With his strength, with his rapidity of action, with that amazing faculty of vision—why is he not? He has outline, he has colour, he has movement, with that he ought to go very far. But—will he? I sometimes think he won't. It is not an opinion—it is a feeling. I could not explain why he disappoints me—why my enthusiasm withers as soon as I close the book. While one reads, of course, he is not to be questioned. He is the master of his reader to the very last line—then—apparently for no reason at all—he seems to let go his hold.

Can the broad truth of this be disputed? Crane's work is artful, original, concentrated, indistractible sometimes to the point of a mesmerizing intensity. Nevertheless it lacks mass, moment, tenacity; it has no power of imposing itself beyond reversion on our fully extended consciousness of experience. The themes it appears to carry—in *The Red Badge*, for example, the young soldier's encounter with the gods of battle and, so it has been claimed, his "growth into manhood"—dissolve to fantasy as we try to trace out their actual progression. It is understandable why most recent commentary on Crane has

got diverted into biographical and psychoanalytic speculation. So it has been argued that Crane lacked "culture," that
he had no training besides yellow journalism to guide his
highly individual talent, that in any event the principal co-
ordinates of his understanding of life were drawn from the
conventional ethos of his parents' Methodism or else from
the Oedipal dilemmas inflicted on him as the youngest of
their ten children. These probabilities are all relevant. But
they do not confront the specific problem Conrad defines,
which is that Crane possesses as a writer an irresistible authority that is nevertheless transient, provisional, uncompel-
ling.

Conceivably it is in Crane's very artfulness, what he does
at his best, that we must look for explanations. To explain
the frailness of his hold on our attention as resulting from that
"impressionism" of style and of notation by which his work
has been identified from the first—"He is *the only* impressionist, and *only* an impressionist," Conrad declared—is still
not enough, however. For Crane's work presents itself not
as a record of impressions and observations drawn from life
but as a barrage of self-generating images and inward conceits
whose essential function is to rival life, perhaps supplant it.
He is, at his best, a visionary writer (Conrad is at the edge
of saying so), and his authority is a visionary authority. It is
visionary in a peculiar way, however, in that the images it
presents refer to nothing equally authoritative beyond themselves, no clear pattern of understanding, no really coherent
structure of imaginative experience. Except by a kind of
parodic mimicry, they scarcely even refer to each other or to
the narrative events they coexist with. *The Red Badge of
Courage* is the fullest demonstration of Crane's special power;
again and again particular gestures or moments of consciousness are given a dream-like autonomy. But these visionary
flashes are as fleeting as they are brilliant. The emotions, the
dramatic convergences, that contribute to their making some-

how do not survive their crystallization in words. As they thus form no proper succession, neither can they be made to yield up a coherent narrative theme or argument. There is a gap between the story and the concrete demonstration that would be disastrous to the work as a whole if the story was anything more than a moving screen for the author's vision-generating eye to project its inventions upon. Much the same view may be taken of Crane's abrupt, laconic little poems, despite his claiming to have written them, in contrast to his stories, in order "to give my ideas of life as a whole." If anything about them persuades, it is not their epigrammatic parable-arguments, and certainly not their "philosophy," which is mostly the second-hand agnosticism and ironic fatalism of the period, but rather the absoluteness of certain free-floating images now and then projected in them. Nothing quite like this naked magic-lantern work exists elsewhere in our literature. Even Poe's inventions carry a more consistent reference to common experience or to some stable conception of it. The nearest parallels to Crane's best manner are to be found, rather, in the work of certain graphic artists—in Daumier, perhaps, or above all in Goya, the rapt, strict master of the *Tauromaquia* and the *Disasters of the War*—work of a kind, moreover, that for all its transcendent purity of composition is like Crane's in being continuous with the documentary concerns of nineteenth-century journalism.[4]

The test of seriousness in visionary expression, which is always radically simplifying, is a peculiar one: purity of specification, undivided attentiveness to the real presence of the projected subject. Representations of divinity do not have to be theologically accurate or complete; they only have to eliminate everything that is not numinous. We would not think of asking whether Goya's record of the Peninsular War

4. It is of interest that one important influence on *The Red Badge* appears to have been the richly illustrated series, *Battles and Leaders of the Civil War* (4 volumes, 1884–1888).

is, as a record, comprehensive or symbolically coherent or universally valid with respect to the order of experience contemplated. We only notice its terrifyingly consistent apprehension of actual terror and outrage, its reduction of all contingencies to that one overmastering perception. Yet we do not hold the whole of it in mind as we can the formal order of dramatic tragedy. There is a passivity of observation about it; in each new instance it seeks only to dissolve itself into the occurrence that calls it forth. It tells us simply, "I saw this—and this, too." Crane had some such consciousness of his own essential effort as a writer. "I go ahead," he writes in a letter of 1898, "for I understand that a man is born into this world with his own pair of eyes, and that he is not at all responsible for his vision—he is merely responsible for his quality of personal honesty. To keep close to this personal honesty is my supreme ambition." And it may be said that everything convincing in Crane's work turns on visionary images which have, as they succeed one another, the hallucinatory serenity and intactness of dream images. So the conventional village ironies in "The Monster" about the practice of charity and common decency draw what force they have from the strange, self-animating flame-blossoms and chemical serpents in the burning laboratory where the Negro stableman saves his employer's son and is himself deformed; without these actual terrors we are left with a sentimental parable more outlined (though it is brilliantly outlined) than told.

Crane's poems offer even purer instances of his puzzlingly inconclusive power. They come to life as they manage to convey the sense of some self-contained and irreversible apprehension; otherwise they offer remarks. The opening lines of *The Black Riders* (1895), Crane's first collection, are characteristic:

> Black riders came from the sea.
> There was clang and clang of spear and shield,
> And clash and clash of hoof and heel. . . .

—a setting out of autonomous images which the inert closing line of this first poem ("Thus the ride of sin") simply has no necessary contact with. These transfiguring lines from the volume, *War Is Kind* (1899), are less spectacular but have the same visionary autonomy:

> In the morning
> A noise of men at work came the clear blue miles
> And the little black cities were apparent.

Even the many poems about God and faith divide according to the same general measure. There are those that make assertions, and there are those (or passages in them) that compose incontrovertible images. The significant difference between, on the one hand,

> God lay dead in heaven,

or,

> Well, then, I hate Thee, unrighteous picture;
> Wicked image, I hate Thee,

and, on the other,

> Withal there is One whom I fear;
> I fear to see grief upon that face,

is a difference not primarily of argument or emotion but of imaginative realization.

Crane's is not in any case a religious sensibility, the subject of these poems notwithstanding. He himself is not possessed in consciousness by the images his poems articulate. The visionary is rather his way of reporting, of proving his presence on the scene of this world. He seems unable to verify his awareness of phenomena except by turning them into something rich and strange, forcibly removing them from the familiar continuum of life and consciousness, imputing to them the fixity of the legendary, the already translated. What results is of course a kind of idealization. The real itself is not real until it has been glazed into purity. "One feels," V. S. Pritchett remarks, "that Crane stands apart from his scene and that a great skill has taken the place of an innured contemplation of the subject." It is hardly literature that he is involved in. It is rather a way of living by means of words and phrases; Crane is our first Action Writer, our New Jersey, Protestant, newspaper-office Rimbaud. Though his writing frequently reproduces certain general patterns of subjective experience—violation, abandonment, the defensive effort to survive, the overwrought sequences of deprivation, yearning, and despair—what it regularly lacks is the inward organization that gives the structures of developed art their power to coerce, and hold, attention, and that comes into them dialectically, by way of some renewed encounter with the material occasion or with other possibilities of statement or simply with their own formal advance. That is why in the general development of modern Anglo-American writing Crane's remarkable achievement is marginal and diversionary, but at the same time—a little like that of Hemingway, and for like reasons—disproportionately influential. At certain moments achievement of this kind can be a liberation. For whatever else one may decide about Crane's work, the best of it must be granted that minimal integrity of voice and registered perception the securing of which, in the general slackness of the '90s, was bound to be a precedent of genuine value.

Theodore Dreiser

If we were to choose one writer to tell in what way the mass of Americans lived in the years between 1870 and 1920, Dreiser's claims to priority could hardly be overturned. One scarcely thinks of him as a writer; he has too much to say, he can barely compress it into words. From the first, with his novel *Sister Carrie* (1900) and stories like "Nigger Jeff" and "Butcher Rogaum's Door" (1901), Theodore Dreiser (1871–1945) introduced a new seriousness and authenticity into American realism. It is not only that conventions of subject matter were stretched a little further, nor that the documentation of city life, in *Sister Carrie*, was more massive and thorough than ever before. It is rather that the reality of common existence, reality of feeling and aspiration as well as of visible behavior, had somehow been captured from within —captured, moreover, by a spokesman, a witness, whose emotions were interchangeable with those of his characters and to whom it simply did not occur *not* to be, in their presence, uniformly sympathetic and considerate though at the same time self-protectively detached and objective in his curiosity about them. Dreiser's manners as a novelist are perfectly common, and that is his peculiar strength. What takes shape in his imagination justifies itself simply by its presence there. He takes his characters and their histories as seriously as he takes himself; no other novelist of this era, not even Henry James, is as free of the cardinal sin, in storytelling, of condescension.

By his own account Dreiser hardly knew what he was about when he began writing fiction. Challenged by a newspaper friend to put his vague literary ambition to the test, he wrote the name, "Sister Carrie," at the top of a page but had "no idea who or what she was to be"; years later he recalled composing the book by fits and starts, as if under dictation. When Doubleday, Page accepted the novel that resulted (on the recommendation of Frank Norris) and then in effect suppressed its own edition, Dreiser lost heart. Work on a second novel, for which he had received an advance, ground to a halt. After a period of severe depression he drifted back into journalism and eventually into a surprisingly successful career as a popular-magazine executive. A few admirers of

Sister Carrie (reissued in 1907) urged him to continue in its vein, but his return to serious fiction after 1910 was more or less accidental, coming about only after he had lost his job and a salary of $10,000 when an affair with a business colleague's adolescent daughter was exposed. Yet in *Sister Carrie* and even more in *Jennie Gerhardt* (1911), the book he now resumed writing, Dreiser strikes us as knowing instinctively the right way to deal with the materials he had at hand.

These first two novels are less ambitious, less purposefully calculated, than their successors—*The Financier* (1912) and *The Titan* (1914), *The 'Genius'* (1915), *An American Tragedy* (1925)— but it is possible to think that they are his best books. The stories told in them, based in good part on the drifting, compromised lives of members of his own family, are relatively unobscured by what is most tedious and unrewarding in Dreiser: those heavy-handed explanations of the single great meaning or unmeaning of life which he always thought it was the chief business of reflective minds to search for and articulate, and also that melodramatic forcing of big scenes which so nearly wrecks even *An American Tragedy*. It is part of Dreiser's extraordinary accomplishment, especially in *Jennie Gerhardt,* and a first mark of his superiority to the more expert craftsmanship of an Edith Wharton, to have understood how *un*melodramatic, how commonplace and familiar, the slow long tragedy (if it is that) of such lives would be. Dreiser's erratic command of narrative is at its surest in *Jennie Gerhardt* and, on a smaller scale, in the fascinating personal histories of *Twelve Men* (1919) and several stories in the collections *Free* (1918) and *Chains* (1927). For he was essentially a teller of life stories and private histories, of which it is fair to say that the more directly these stories came out of his own direct, bemused observation of life, the better.

What Dreiser knows casually about the common slovenly

custom of American life is always redoubtable; it is the
foundation of his authority as a story-teller. The sheer massing of naturalistic detail contributes to this authority but is
not the whole cause of it. The truthfulness of Dreiser's best
work is more particularly in its internal sequences and associations (curiously, the effect produced is one of *formal*
originality, which is always shocking). The general liberty
that the novel as a form takes with life involves first of all the
ways in which human feeling, impulse, motive, along with
the significances imputed to them, are translated into particular fictive events and relationships; the ways (in E. M.
Forster's formula) "by which thought develops into action."
The shock of Dreiser's early work was in great part that it
had sharply narrowed this conventional gap between the
fictive and the actual. It is as if nothing was clearer to him
than the essential fictitiousness, to our understanding, of
everyday events and of the self-excusing interpretations we
make of them in order to keep our balance among them. No
other twentieth-century American novelist has caught so well,
so matter-of-factly, the inner logic of our personal alienation
from the behavior we find ourselves committed to; the whole
dreamlike way we pass through our lives and doings, secretly
disclaiming responsibility for them, looking on as we act.
What was most shocking was not that the country girl, Carrie
Meeber, city-bound, let herself drift into being the mistress
of one man and then another and into dropping them when
they ceased to be of use to her; nor that she was not punished
for her misconduct; nor even that she never learned to think
of it as misconduct and was not required to, as if she were
immune to those processes of psychic retribution assumed to
be essential to the right ordering of respectable society. It
was rather that Dreiser had somehow completely excluded
the possibility of her following any other course, and had
made her behavior seem in fact a natural and even healthy

response to a social order that was as little to be questioned (however unjust it seemed) as the caprices of the weather.

The American way of life in which Dreiser's characters find themselves wears the standard features that have been attributed to it since *Democracy in America*. The extraordinary looseness of social relationships, the mobility of position and status, the corresponding insecurity of personal existence, above all the indefinite opportunities offered by a free society and the general conspiracy of aimlessness and repression that all but cancels these opportunities out—all this is second nature to Dreiser's characters.[5] The author himself may talk about his people, intermittently, in the jargon of naturalism, speaking of "affinities," "instincts," "magnetisms," "chemisms," and so on, and he may, at the same time, unload upon them no small amount of his own chronic tension of fear and desire. But the truth he reaches derives primarily from his objective grasp of an actual social type. It is the type, in brief, of those middle-placed persons neither above nor below the common possibilities of life, neither wholly committed to them nor capable of detachment from them, who make up the mass of our free-floating population; who are the most reliable gauge of our society's characteristic tendencies; and who breathe with least dilution "that pervading atmosphere of liberty in our national life which"—in the mass, if not in each individual case—"is productive of almost uncounted freedom of thought and action" (*Jennie Gerhardt*, Chapter xvii). Dreiser himself was one such, as he understood well enough—a self-recognition that helps to make the auto-

5. Small wonder then that among the younger novelists of the 1920s it was Scott Fitzgerald who particularly admired Dreiser and who remarked in 1924 (before *An American Tragedy*, incidentally) that he considered Dreiser—and H. L. Mencken—"the greatest men living in the country today."

biography of his early years, *A Book About Myself* (1922), a social document of the highest interest.

For such persons, as Dreiser understands them, nothing in life is "proved," nothing is settled, except what immediate experience has brought home to them. "In all other things," he writes of the remarkable Lester Kane in *Jennie Gerhardt*, "he wavered, questioned, procrastinated, leaving to time and to the powers back of the universe the solution of the problems that vexed him." Dreiser's characters' pursuit of fortune is passionate enough, but it is also casual, dissociated, fatalistic. It is of a piece with their curiously passive and uninvidious envy of those who somehow "are so much more fortunate." The major distinction that is made among his characters assumes this inward dissociation; it is hardly a moral distinction at all. It is simply between those who, like Jennie, possess some inner "heart and faith" for life and those who do not. All drift, whatever their worldly circumstance; all vacillate; all are ultimately determined by "time and the powers back of the universe"; and the second type is not to blame for being less resilient and life-embracing than the first. Nevertheless the show of determining fate counts most in Dreiser's fiction when it descends upon a character of the first rather than the second type, upon Jennie Gerhardt, for example, as against Clyde Griffiths in *An American Tragedy* or even the grimly inert Hurstwood of *Sister Carrie*.

The special poise of truthfulness in *Carrie* and *Jennie Gerhardt*, among Dreiser's novels, owes much to the pairing, in each, of two leading characters, in contrast to the relative concentration upon one only in his later books. Hurstwood's fall balances Carrie's rise—too geometrically, one might say, if it was not for the sympathetic thoroughness of detail with which both actions are presented. In *Jennie Gerhardt* the pairing is more complex. We are given the story of two families; and the unforced correspondences between the Gerhardts' struggle for a minimal security and the Kanes' wrestling with the affairs of industrial wealth and position create for the whole novel an exceptional balance and unity of presentation. The formal proportions are hardly perfect. For much of the second half of the book Lester Kane pre-empts the stage; indeed the whole business of getting him married to a modish society widow—thus breaking his relationship with Jennie—shows Dreiser at his most laborious. What is incidental is ground out in as thick detail as what is important. The account given of Lester Kane's gradual physical deterioration is equally cumbersome and overdrawn. We hear that a "plethora of substance was clogging every essential function" of his body and that "his liver, kidneys, spleen, pancreas—every organ, in fact—had been overtaxed for some time to keep up the process of digestion and elimination," and it is as if we were overhearing the incessant bowel gossip of twenty million middle-class parlors and breakfast tables, the vital daily concern for regular functioning. Yet out of just these explanations we are brought directly on to the novel's poignant conclusion, with Jennie, always loyal to the life she has made, returned briefly to Lester's side and then seen looking on as an outsider at his elaborate family funeral—a termination that begins quite beautifully in a passage describing her dream of a boat coming to her in her isolation, out of fog and still waters, bearing "her mother, and Vesta [her dead child], and some one whom she could not make out."

In *The Financier* and *The Titan* Dreiser worked closer to the documentary method and "scientific" outlook of naturalism proper. The long chronicle unfolded in these books of business aggrandizement and of the private life of a Gilded Age adventurer is impressively detailed; it competes successfully, we can say, with the monumental exposés of the more serious muckrakers. As a novel, however, a chronicle of imaginable persons and events, it is something less than convincing.[6] The central fault is in the matching of the story on the grand scale of Dreiser's intention to the hero his imagination actually produced in the figure of Frank Cowperwood. (The leading secondary characters are more persuasive, particularly the women, Cowperwood's wife and his mistress; Dreiser rarely fails in rendering the force and wretchedness of unfulfilled desire under unmanageable constraint.) Modeled on the traction magnate Charles Yerkes, Cowperwood is (in F. O. Matthiessen's summary) "Dreiser's version of the 'survival of the fittest,' intermingled with traits of Nietzsche's 'Superman,' and possessing also what Dreiser calls a 'Machiavellian' brain." That at any rate was the intention. But in what is actually shown of his behavior Cowperwood scarcely measures up to this titanic design. Even at the peak of success his "immoralism" seems little more than the ordinary everyday immoralism of the middle ranks of the anarchic scramble of business society. (There is indeed more social truth in the actual Cowperwood than in the epic hero Dreiser had in mind.) Cowperwood is simply one more of Dreiser's middle-placed floaters, though the scale of his operations has been artificially inflated. He is most credible when shown as a petty opportunist working his way up to the point where he can begin to gratify an in fact not particularly heroic appetite for sensual pleasure. As for the sex magnetism and the sensitivity to beauty and art that are attributed to him, a verdict of "not proved" has to be returned. We recognize in these details the same sort of ungoverned ego projection that operates at more embarrassing length in the presentation of Eugene Witla, the "genius" of Dreiser's next novel. When Dreiser wrote about what he wanted in life, or what he wished to

6. This is quite apart from what the academic critic Stuart Sherman, no admirer of either Dreiser or naturalism, promptly labeled its "club-sandwich" organization: "slices of business alternating with erotic episodes" in mechanical series.

believe, as opposed to what he could not escape knowing and remembering, his imagination failed him. Dorothy Dudley remarked of him that "if he has sentimentality," it appears not when he expends his brooding sympathy upon figures like Hurstwood or the Gerhardts but "when he idealizes the rich and worldly" and "accepts their standards as desirable." Sentimental misrepresentation of this kind figures also in *An American Tragedy*, in his treatment of the affluent Finchleys, although there it is more appropriate to the pitiful yearnings of the weak and corruptible hero, Clyde Griffiths.

There remains, with Dreiser, the problem of style; the stumbling block it presents has not been exaggerated. In many respects Dreiser's working style is a remarkably effective instrument of exposition—inclusive, adaptable, open to intensifying accents, capable of strong concentration and complex emphasis, distinctly novelistic. But there is no denying that the idiom he writes in is often labored and toneless. Solecisms, blunders of diction, grotesque lapses into "fine" writing abound; and they rather increase in frequency as his career advances.[7] The norm of statement in Dreiser was well summed up by the admirable Dorothy Dudley: "moments of precision and passages of approximation." Yet as she recognized, this

7. How much this incapacity has to do with his origins is arguable. But it is a fact that idiomatic American English had not really taken hold in Dreiser's family during his childhood; he is the first important American writer who had to work in what was very nearly an acquired language. His father was a German immigrant; his mother came from a Mennonite settlement in Ohio, of Pennsylvania Dutch origin; some of his early schooling was with German-speaking priests. Particularly in his earliest stories there is a noticeable incidence of Germanic locutions: "little progress was making," or, "the budding Theresa (eighteen just turning)." This is quite apart from his ability to mimic immigrant English—"Muss ich all my time spenden calling, mit you on de streeds oudt?" says old Rogaum to his recalcitrant daughter.

style is in some strange way seamless, unimprovable. Her description of it can hardly be bettered and deserves to be quoted at length. She had been asked by Dreiser to correct the text of *Twelve Men:*

> Always he agreed gratefully to the changes, but in the midst of the work he made an excuse of my slowness and finished the revision himself. It was better so. Dreiser lives and has his being in a tangle of qualitative phrases and parentheses, which perhaps an intimate, but no outsider, could change for the better. They are introduced or excused by *to the contrary notwithstanding, which latter, which same, and the like, I could not help but think, at the same time, in other words*—a quantity of clichés apparently agreeable to him. It is his nature to offer *other* words, a clustered choice of them for any one link in his thought, and to subordinate these to a larger cluster of choices. And it is his nature to use the careless diction of his own people, Americans. In that way, he seems to say, they will understand me and my idiom will be telltale and pantomimic.

Jack London, Gertrude Stein

Perhaps the most gifted prose talent of this generation, certainly the most prodigally squandered, belonged to Jack London (1876–1916). In the decade and a half of his headlong career he wrote fifty books; went the course of several different "philosophies" (Darwin, Herbert Spencer, Nietzsche, socialism, racism, nihilism); became one of the first victims, self-appointed, of the ruthless system of modern democratic publicity; and died correspondingly (a suicide, in ambiguous circumstances), a sacrifice to an exorbitant personal legend. A best seller from the time of two early naturalist thrillers, *The Call of the Wild* (1903) and *The Sea Wolf* (1904), he is a striking example of the popular writer who establishes his relation with a mass audience as much by seeming to provoke and offend it as by flattering its official tastes. An element of charlatanism hangs about London's work (it is of a piece with his life, which increasingly was passed—mate-hunting, sea-voyaging, house-building in the Valley of the Moon, the publication of each new book—in the glare of mass notoriety), and it is no small part of his immense success. He had a shrewd instinct for the chronic main currents of middle-class hallucination, especially a kind of retributive daydreaming about acts of pure domination or unconditional conquest. He appealed most strongly to readers who wanted their day-dreams explained a little, dignified by an overglaze of objective theory; readers for whom, around 1910, pseudo-ideas like the Yellow Peril, the natural supremacy of the strong, the Kiplingesque code of the pack, were the stuff of common wisdom. Darker, more complex intuitions, as of the spreading panic and emptiness of modern life, also inform his work, and these, too, it may be said, obscurely confirmed his appeal. Fifty years after his death it is uniquely Jack London among the popular authors of his day who still holds his place—though we note that he does so as, first, a writer for boys and, second, a master of "socialist realism," the American author most widely circulated in the Soviet Union.

London's attitude to his work was bluff and unfussy. "I have no unfinished stories," he told an interviewer. "Invariably I complete every one I start. If it's good, I sign it and send it out. If it isn't good, I sign it and send it out." He considered himself a novelist of ideas and regularly padded his adventure narratives with intimations of arcane philosophic truth. The actual quality of his thinking, however, is fairly represented by this statement, in the autobiographical *Martin Eden* (1909), of how all experience can be explained by "biology": "I mean the real interpretive biology, from the ground up, from the laboratory and the test-tube and the vitalized inorganic right on up to the widest aesthetic and sociological generalizations." This is the thought—and style—not merely of the self-taught but of the invincibly self-satisfied. As such, in modern writing, it is a positive portent. It represents, in fact, a kind of technical discovery, a means of naturalizing formally, without any serious concession to truth or even plausibility, what passes for reflective thought in the unreconstructed majority consciousness. Any reader of the mass of contemporary American fiction or sociological journalism will recognize its persistence. For London's emphatic, no-nonsense colloquialism (even down to his oddly reductive use of the past tense for utmost generalization—"The aim of life was meat. Life itself was meat. Life lived on life") has survived and prospered as the basic idiom of the straight-talking mass-market fantasy-realists of the 1950s and 1960s, whose individual variations on this style, even sometimes in the work of so enterprising a writer as Saul Bellow, only emphasize its fundamental inertness; it has remained usable only when rather freely parodied, as by Perelman or Thurber.

Jack London's stock in trade as a novelist was the doubly perishable one of a wholly calculated and manufactured sensationalism. In his handling the naturalist novel stands revealed as one more renewal of the durable genre of the Gothic, which since the late eighteenth century has been the most flexible of literary instruments for expressing the range and depth of middle-class disaffection and hysteria. The obvious savoring of physical punishment and torture, brutality and animal terrors, even the crude myth-fantasy of conspiratorial revolution dramatized in *The Iron Heel* (1907), have a long ancestry in popular and Gothic convention. Yet London was more than a popular hack. When he was not straining after sensation and shock, he could write a natural, easy, pungent descriptive style, and he could develop passages of narrative action with a genuine flair for proportion and emphasis. Even during the hectic last years of his life certain straightforward stories of solitary physical adventure achieved an admirable cleanness of form and concentration of emotional effect. His most satisfying books, however, are not his novels. Rather they are works of personal reporting like *The Road* (1907), a chronicle of tramp life, and in particular *The People of the Abyss* (1903), a record of experiences and conditions in the East End of London which anticipates George Orwell's *Down and Out* and *Wigan Pier* of the 1930s and which has the advantage over Orwell's books of an uninhibited American-democratic capacity to participate in working-class life without self-conscious embarrassment. The one form Jack London's talent could not really manage was that of the novel; for the novel requires nothing so much as a firm imaginative grasp of actual social norms and relationships such as this documentary poet of the assault of alien forces upon the unformed individual consciousness almost totally lacked.

Much the same severance from an actually constituted social order circumscribes the work in fiction of Gertrude Stein (1874–1946). In the life histories she unwinds, the circumstances of civil existence, the dimensions of the communal and historical, seem systematically excluded. (As she wrote in "The Gradual Making of *The Making of Americans*," "it may be history but it is not historical.") Places are named— "Bridgepoint," "Gossols," "Europe," "Cincinnati"—and people are said to have moved back and forth from one to another; some live in the part of town "where rich people were living," some in the part of town "where no other rich people were living," and some in hotels; one is musical, another attends college, and now and then all meet one or two others in a park or a kitchen; also, there are marriage, business, governesses, doctors, teachers, and—between persons—"enticements" and "realizations." But all these particular details are only names; they have no substantial existence in the narrative record. They compose a screen of abstractions upon which the personality units of Gertrude Stein's fiction (they are hardly "characters") are described running their parallel courses. Society and history, even personal history, are abstractions to her. Time, in *The Making of Americans* especially (written 1906–1908; published 1925), is essentially biological. There is "daily living," which divides into "growing young," "middle living," and "growing old," with important subdivisions like "just about beginning the ending of her middle living." Otherwise, "all living" is "always repeating." Moreover, it all takes place indoors—or between doors (the doors of solid family houses), traveling or walking about. Gertrude Stein's fiction rarely moves out of the household; and what to our surprise we discover in reading her is that it is the same household as that of the sentimental family romances of the women's magazines, then and since. But it is described rather less wishfully—the parasitic, homoerotic substructure of middle-class relationships is not finally disputed—and altogether more lovingly.

Gertrude Stein's development as a writer of fiction was wholly technical. All that she had to say as a story-teller and moralist is clearly set out in her first and least unconventional book, *Three Lives* (1909). But however we measure her subsequent work—and not a great deal of it charms us into sitting up all night to read it through—the intelligence of her concern for style and form, and the general usefulness, are undeniable. From the first she put herself in the main line of innovation and experiment in modern letters. An obvious model for *Three Lives* and its spare, direct, repetitive presentation of the lives of submerged souls is Flaubert's "Un Coeur Simple"—and Gertrude Stein had in fact, as a kind of preliminary exercise in narrative style, already begun a translation of the *Trois Contes*. By her own later account her chief instigator was William James, who at Radcliffe College had first given her, she said, the idea "that I would get a sense of immediacy if I made a description of every kind of human being that existed, the rules for resemblances and all the other things, until really I had made a description of every human being" ("How Writing Is Written," 1935). With his momentous definition of consciousness as a "stream" William James launched her search for an appropriate method as well.[8] Still another model is suggested by her admiration for the eighteenth-century masters of English fiction, particularly Richardson; Gertrude Stein was the first of several post-Jamesian novelists in English whose effort to escape the nineteenth-century trap of dramatic realism and the well-made story led them back toward the descriptive and psychological immediacy which was that earlier era's great technical invention. In content *Three Lives* is not very different from the genre realism of the '90s or of Dreiser's earlier work. In form, however, dramatic movement has already half dissolved into abstract patterns of notation rhythmically repeated. The results endorse the experiment; Melanctha Herbert in particular, subtle, intelligent, attractive, dependent, self-abasing, is surely one of the few wholly believable women in American fiction. In *The Making of Americans*, even more in the arrangements of "Objects Food Rooms" in *Tender Buttons* (1914), these rhythmic patterns of resemblance and repetition—which now begin to appear as verbal patterns first of all—are increasingly dominant. The different stages of "living" dissolve into phases of timeless being. Change, causal sequence, action of any sort tend to disappear altogether. What Gertrude Stein said to ex-

8. Gertrude Stein's use of "resemblances" in this formulation—a key word with Wallace Stevens, too—confirms one's sense that she belongs with that constellation of young writers, Robinson, Frost, Stevens, Eliot, Aiken, Cummings, whose exposure to Harvard philosophy between 1890 and 1914 is one of the central episodes in modern literary history.

plain the form of her comic opera, *Four Saints in Three Acts* (1929), that it was "written about as static as I could make it," applies to her work in general between, say, *Portrait of Mabel Dodge at the Villa Curonia* (1911) and her return to conventional narration in *The Autobiography of Alice B. Toklas* (1932). "The fact that a saint is there," she had decided, "is enough for anybody."

In short passages Gertrude Stein's sense of the interior shape of individual lives or objects can be penetrating and charmingly precise. Her shorter exercises in portrait-explanation make the best case for her experiments with narrative technique. They speak well, also, for her moral sense. Against the willful, distracted world of masculine events she puts forward an emphatic, distinctly feminine dissent. What she writes is not social criticism, but it invariably defines the point that an effective social criticism would have to rise to.[9] Her balance sheet of values is not easily faulted. She is for art, beauty, originality, genius—she is rather snobbish about genius—and she is against adulteration and sheer pragmatic busyness. But she is not highbrow; she is for work and for results however achieved. And she has not soured on the legendary promise of her native land; she is positively afflicted with old-fashioned American idealism. Her delight in the GIs who flocked to see her after the liberation of Paris in 1944 should not have surprised anyone. The longer she lived in France the more "American" she became. In the extraordinary address to the reader early in *The Making of Americans* she stated a per-

9. Thus, of the sad young men to whom the novelists of the 1920s would in due course give names and histories, she wrote this prophetic epitaph just after the first World War: "A young man is in a position of great responsibility. He can decide about men and women. He has nothing to do with children. Work does not agree with him. What can we do to make him realise that work does not agree with him. I am afraid, nothing." ("Three Moral Tales," 1920–1921.)

sonal allegiance that she never retracted: "I throw myself open to the public,—I take a simple interest in the ordinary kind of families, histories, I believe in simple middle class monotonous tradition, in a way in honest enough business methods." She admits the worst—"middle class is sordid material unillusioned unaspiring and always monotonous for it is always there and always to be repeated"—but cannot be torn loose from her prayerful commitment to this American style of life she had grown up with (getting and spending and generally providing, in humane, ingenious, energetic, domesticated ways of one's own apparently free devising):

> and yet I am strong, and I am right, and I know it, and I say it to you and you are to listen to it, yes here in the heart of a people who despise it, that a material middle class who know they are it, with their straightened bond of family to control it, is the one thing always human, vital, and worthy it—worthy that all monotonously shall repeat it,—and from which has always sprung, and all who really look can see it, the very best the world can ever know, and everywhere we always need it.

The passage supports an impression that the influence of Gertrude Stein upon contemporaries like Sherwood Anderson and even the young Hemingway was not only technical. She sees life in the traditional American-transcendentalist way, as consisting in "efforts to secure one's true vocation" (*The Making of Americans*). It is more important to her that these efforts "make more completeness in individual life" than that they prove "useful to the world," though she will be happy if they do that, too. To the work she set herself—expressing this ethical commitment through novelties of form that would continuously validate it—she brought a vigorous critical intelligence.[10] But as a story-teller, a novelist, her old-fashioned

10. It may well be that her later critical papers, such as *Composition as Explanation* (1926), *Narration* (1935), and "How Writing Is Written" (1935), will prove her most durable work.

ethical idealism three-quarters blinds her. Potentially a comic writer of genuine force and point, Gertrude Stein is unable to grasp the major traditional occasions of prose comedy, which have to do with human behavior as shaped not only by the biological and perceptual rhythms she was preoccupied with but also by economic obligation, in the broadest sense, and by the social contract, which she ignored. In one of the best episodes in *The Making of Americans,* the marriage of Philip Redfern and Martha Hersland, she interrupts an acutely compassionate analysis of private relationships to say, in all earnestness, that "in our American life . . . there is no coercion in custom and it is our right to change our vocation as often as we have desire and opportunity." The gulf between that understanding and Dreiser's is hardly bridgeable, and there is little doubt which side the practical truth of the matter lies on.

But one reads Gertrude Stein for other reasons than one reads Dreiser. The best use to make of her work she herself pleasantly suggests at the end of the section, "Food," in *Tender Buttons:*

> Next to me next to a folder, next to a folder some waiter, next to a foldersome waiter and re letter and read her. *Read her with her for less.* [Emphasis added]

Just so: in such matters the modest principle of *with*-though-*for-less* can become a whole interior way of life—if not transforming in itself, then the cause that transformations are in others. Beyond question the forms and the language of contemporary literature are healthier because Gertrude Stein played her honest and reasonable games with them. If her example also had the effect, historically, of endorsing a certain imaginative complacency in the younger writers who put themselves to school with her—Hemingway for one—their failure to grow out of that complacency is not, strictly, her fault.

Ellen Glasgow, Willa Cather

With the realistic novel and its step-by-step involvement with our immediate consciousness of the flow and pressure of life, judgment of seriously conceived new work is peculiarly vulnerable to time and change. The misadventures of critical opinion in this regard are notorious, and they are usually collective. Down nearly to the time of her death, Ellen Glasgow (1874–1945) still ranked, by general agreement, as one of the solider and more accomplished talents of her generation. If she appeared to stand apart from the livelier currents of experiment and innovation in her time, that was only further proof of her special integrity as an artist. One could speak of her ironic elegies to the older order of Virginia life in the same breath with Chekhov; one could take her at her word that in her later novels especially the illusion-haunted American South had indeed been administered the stiff dose of "blood and irony" it had long needed; also one could trace, from her first novel, *The Descendant* (1897), to her last, *In This Our Life* (1941), a steady advance in objectivity of presentation and in formal control, exactly the kind of advance particularly prized by literary opinion between the two World Wars. Now this reputation has nearly vanished. Posthumous publications—of an autobiography, *The Woman Within* (1954), and a volume of letters (1958)—have not restored it. Paradoxically Ellen Glasgow may even seem at present not a great deal more seriously readable than the costume romancers like Thomas Nelson Page whom she meant to displace. She made a positive and lifelong vocation out of her own honorable fight to break away from the evasions and hypocrisies, the denial of life, of the insulated Richmond gentility she grew up among; but more and more it seems apparent that that part of her imagination which was not paralyzed by the dead weight of her inheritance was trapped and deformed in the tortuous effort to escape it. (The constraint put upon her private sense of life and of human responsiveness by her deafness, which she always tried to disguise, must also be taken into account.) In short, what once seemed an exemplary career in the service of a steadily maturing art now presents itself as one more monotonous case history in the pathology of American undevelopment.

Two melancholy themes dominate the long succession of Ellen Glasgow's novels. One is the destructiveness of romantic illusions about worldly life, past or present. The second is waste—erosion and sterility, social, moral, psychological; the turning of the prospect of life into "barren ground" (the title chosen for the novel which represented, she felt, the final "liberation" of her capacities). Both themes rise naturally enough out of the life of her home region and follow from her early-formed ambition to write its true history; she comes by them honestly as a turn-of-the-century Virginian. (It could even be argued that she discovered these themes for modern southern writing in general.) But as she develops them, we sense more and more that they are being mechanically inflicted on the fictional scheme of events. They represent prejudgment and personal bias rather than the necessary consequence of a consistent narrative demonstration. The buried vein of authenticity in Ellen Glasgow's work is almost entirely subjective and emotional, referring to nothing else so surely as to the pathos of her own undeliverance. For that reason it is possible to think that she is at least as persuasive, as a novelist, in the more unguardedly sentimental life histories that round out the first half of her career— *Virginia* (1913), *Life and Gabriella* (1916)—as in the astringent social comedies (*The Romantic Comedians*, 1926; *They Stooped to Folly*, 1929) and the naturalistic dramas of stoic endurance (*Barren Ground*, 1925; *Vein of Iron*, 1935) which have come to be considered her best work. As social history and social criticism her novels are well-bred fantasy. From first to last their carefully matched and counterpointed characterizations—chivalrous first families, underbred shopkeepers and business agents, homespun farmers, Negro servants—remain the stereotypes of the older Southern romancers. These stereotypes may be ironically inverted or, increasingly, treated with malice and contempt, but the change of tone is superficial. They do not at any time come forward, and are not permitted to, into the diverse options of actual life, the life we know. For this reason they are all too easy targets for their creator's once-celebrated wit and irony in defining them. The ethical severity of Ellen Glasgow's wit, along with the somber themes it serves, represents a more attractive creative intention than the preening cleverness of her fellow townsman, James Branch Cabell (1879–1958), but its products have tarnished almost as badly. Even her carefully rendered Virginia landscapes are so much painted scenery, as monotonous and mechanical as the plots they furnish. One may dislike falling out of sympathy with Ellen Glasgow's work and the effort of character, of spirit, it embodies. In the endless and dispiriting process of moral reformation, against the raging main current, which continues to be the grudged public calling of the American consciousness in literature, she played in her time her limited part; nevertheless one is compelled to think that a freer, more responsive imagination would have released its inward energies and got to the bottom of its view of things once and for all in two or three books nearer the truthfulness of self-validating art than any of her twenty-odd volumes ever managed to come.

It is just this kind of imaginative release, in two or three of her dozen novels, that has given Willa Cather (1873–1947) the surprisingly firm place she continues to hold in critical appraisals of her generation's work. The waste and wear of life, the eventual barrenness, the human cost of success, the embittering frustration of early prospects, the estranging burdens of natural feeling and desire: these things are as central to her understanding of life as to Ellen Glasgow's—and as indeed to that of more than a few women of spirit and imagination in the feminist era, and before, and since. The question is: how did she herself, as a writer, overcome their circumscription? Of those books of hers which still persuade us—*O Pioneers!* (1913), the first half, roughly, of *The Song of the Lark* (1915), *My Ántonia* (1918)—two facts may be noted at once. First, they were written over a relatively brief period following the first opening out of her long career: about a decade after she began publishing the poems and stories represented, respectively, by *April Twilights* (1903) and *The Troll Garden* (1905), but some years before that dry, irritable hardening of sentiment and prepossession which—beginning with the oddly tactless novels, *One of Ours* (1922) and *A Lost Lady* (1923)—deadens nearly all her later work. She matured late and hardened early, in the American fashion. Second, these books all deal with the country and circumstance of her prairie childhood, which gave her her liberating subject as a story-teller and which alone seem to have exacted from her the special patience and forbearance of inward understanding that, beyond moral earnestness and a noted devotion to style, brought her a measure of fulfillment as an artist.[11]

"To the query whether it is possible for an artist to exist

11. Born in Virginia, Willa Cather moved with her family to Red Cloud, Nebraska, when she was nine. Her Virginia (Winchester, in the Shenandoah Valley) was not Ellen Glasgow's; nevertheless, leaving Virginia, as Ellen Glasgow did not, and at just that age—not too soon to be unaware of the change nor too late to be consciously prejudiced against her new life—was clearly her good fortune as a writer.

in the United States," T. K. Whipple wrote in 1928, "the best answer would be: Go read Miss Cather." This was indeed the first meaning of her work to her contemporaries in a period, 1910–1930, which was reading all the new American books in the shadow of an obsessive concern for American literary culture's "coming-of-age." Not surprisingly the explicit message of much of her own later writing has to do with maturity of spirit or the want of it. For Willa Cather such maturity is invariably a condition to be attained by way of surrendering the self to some heroic and transcendent service. Self-indulgence, of sense or desire, even of natural human hopefulness, is the abyss to be avoided; from the pathetic early story, "Paul's Case," through the clumsy parable of *Alexander's Bridge* (1912), her first novel, to the vindictive cartoon harassment which at fifty she chose to inflict upon her "lost lady," this abyss yawns before her characters as the very earnest of degradation and spiritual disaster. Opposed to it—radiant and redemptive for all this author's studied coolness in defining alternatives (and clearly the opposition projects a division in her own nature which she could not resolve except wishfully)—is the moral discipline Willa Cather particularly admired, the idealized self-discipline of, interchangeably, the artist and the saint. It is for her a total dedication of being, a conscientious withdrawal from worldly pleasures and benefits into the heaven-haven of a liberating spirituality.

The patently idealized Father Hector of *Shadows on the Rock* (1931) defines this discipline categorically in declaring that nothing "worth while" is ever accomplished "except by that last sacrifice, the giving of oneself altogether and finally." It is of course a noble thought—but in Willa Cather's later work we gradually discover that it operates to hold life at arm's length, and at no small cost to our belief in its relevance to the life around us. By the time she had formulated this thought in so many words, it served her not as an instrument of imaginative exploration and measurement but as a protective screen against the unnerving disorder of common experience. Her plea for a fiction stripped of naturalistic detail (in an essay of 1922, "The Novel Démeublé") and, some years later, her reversion to radically simplified representations of the historical past for fictional settings—territorial New Mexico in *Death Comes for the Archbishop* (1927), colonial Quebec in *Shadows on the Rock*—are symptomatic. The ideal of an uncontaminated and immunized art led her steadily away from the kind of recollective realism she had settled upon in the brief prime of her career. Yet it is this work of her prime which really illustrates her moral-aesthetic principle of self-surrender. For it was only when, just at mid-life, she turned back to the Nebraska of her childhood—turned back, that is, to that one life to which she had already surrendered her unguarded private consciousness beyond recall—that she did in fact free her imagination to accomplish something wholly "worth while" and (as a novelist) recreate a substantial and convincing fictional world.[12]

Willa Cather's secure work is recollective and memorial. Except as a register of incontrovertible past impressions her moral intelligence is uninteresting; her direct moral precepting invariably surrounds itself, in her work, with a kind of vacuum of demonstration. (Her natural sensibility is anything but uninteresting and is, in an honorable way, her undoing in a number of works—the long story, "Coming Aphrodite," reprinted in *Youth and the Bright Medusa*, 1920; the ambitious novel of 1925, *The Professor's House*—in which certain intense passages and episodes not only tear loose from the

12. She did return later to these materials in the three long stories, life histories really, of *Obscure Destinies* (1932), and in them, as David Daiches remarks, regained something of "the richness of texture and clear emotional pattern" of all her more directly autobiographical work.

larger moral design but are the first means of exposing that design as false and willful.) As a craftsman Willa Cather has surely been overpraised or praised for the wrong things. Her architectural sense is limited and easily overtaxed; indeed her rather narrow and uncertain talent for story-telling seems to flourish in the degree that she departs from the requirements of coherent dramatic representation and orderly plotting. *O Pioneers!* and *The Song of the Lark* are episodic and discontinuous, and her best book, *My Ántonia*, is not a novel at all but a loose chronicle of community remembrance. But in this way, one feels, all three are so much the more open to the free flow of uncoerced observation through which, in the writing, Willa Cather's intensely personal confrontation of life could be creatively reabsorbed into the collective history of a world she had had no choice not to participate in and without reserve.

O Pioneers!—her second novel—is social history of an irreplaceable kind. Woven into the collective record which it composes, the pathos of obscure individual destinies gains both mass and representativeness. In the raw struggle for life on the prairie frontier that the book holds up to view, there are moments of extraordinary beauty and spiritual grace, but the struggle itself is not sentimentalized; the cost in suffering and despair, the defeats as well as victories of the spirit, are also made plain and in fact become dominant as the narrative reaches its end. A tendency to idealize certain characters, particularly a figure of endurance and "impervious calm" like the heroine, Alexandra Bergson, is balanced by a concrete knowledge both of the hard conditions of prairie settlement and, equally, of the strange, unaccountable differences in temper and fortune that result in one life's flourishing among these conditions and another's failing. The writing in *O Pioneers!* registers a distinctly feminine sensibility; yet it must be said that Willa Cather on her home ground, among her uprooted Scandinavians, Czechs, Russians, French, and not less displaced and migratory "Americans," knew as much about the actual course of life of both men and women in American society as any writer of her period. Inevitably many of her homesteaders, who had not been farmers at all but craftsmen in the old country—"tailors, locksmiths, cigar-makers"—are beaten in the struggle, and those who succeed, and the children they raise, appear brutalized by it; Alexandra Bergson's father and her loutish, sullen older brothers, Lou and Oscar, are cases in point. The new life they are building scarcely seems worth the effort. It does not require the special perspective of Crazy Ivar, the old "queer" recluse who has withdrawn into a hillside cave house out in the open solitude of uncultivated land, to dislike "the litter of human dwellings: the broken food, the bits of broken china, the old wash-boilers and tea kettles thrown into the sunflower patch," representing the establishment of civilization on the prairie. Among the many books signalizing a "revolt from the village" in this period of American writing—nearly all are by mid-westerners—Willa Cather's have the special merit of a per-spective in time which frames a whole cycle of regional (and national) history: the rich early promise, the grinding descent into meanness and standardization. It is this perspective that gives a saving depth to the melodramatic violence which cli-maxes O Pioneers! The nightmarish killing of Marie Shabata and her lover, Alexandra's younger brother, by Marie's hus-band is contained within the commonplace general tragedy the book strikes through to, the regular sacrifice of the young and most promising to the destructive fatality of a particular historical process. The "disgust of life" which weighs down even Alexandra Bergson's spirit, returning home from her interview with poor Frank Shabata in the state prison (half-crazed and scarcely human, he now seems to her), and the image of the prison itself, round out a chronicle of effort and change that began, we remember, with an image of a different sort—an image as ambiguous as it is heroic and hopeful—closing the first chapter: the lantern of the Bergson wagon at nightfall, "making a moving point of light along the highway, going deeper and deeper into the dark country."

In *The Song of the Lark* community history is subordinated to the story of Thea Kronborg's emergence into the talent and vocation that lead eventually to a great opera career. The later, professional stages of her story are carried off more persuasively than one might expect—Willa Cather's knowledge of the world of young artists and their metropolitan patrons was also at first hand—but the imaginative power of the book is concentrated in the earlier sections dealing with Thea's childhood among her guardians and first sponsors in the Colorado town she grows up in. (Moonstone, Colorado, is Red Cloud, Nebraska, only slightly disguised, with Mexicans and Germans replacing the Scandinavians and Czechs.) Maxwell Geismar is surely right in finding the climax of the book in the last big Moonstone scene, toward the end of Part II, rather than in Thea's Wagnerian triumph at the Metropolitan. This is the scene in which she sings through the night among her friends in the Mexican quarter and takes strength directly for the last time from that home ground which has nourished her talent though it cannot train it—that "naive, generous country that gave one its joyous force, its large-hearted, childlike power to love, just as it gave one its coarse, brilliant flowers."

In *My Ántonia*, the last and strongest of these fundamentally autobiographical books, Willa Cather returned to the looser narrative design of *O Pioneers!* An "Introduction" warns us, in fact, that the narrative that follows has no form at all beyond the natural flow of musing recollection. There is no proper plot and little sustained drama. The book finds its form rather in certain repeated alternations of tone and feeling developed through the casual succession of narrative incident.[13] Through these alternations the contrast between countryside and town takes on the weight of a moral argument, and it merges with other contrasts which embody, together, the book's themes: contrasts between the grassy draws and meadows, sunflower-bordered roads, and tree-shaded rivers of the open land and the "growing piles of ashes and cinders in the back yards" of Black Hawk; between the "fine, well-set-up country girls," with Norwegian and Czech names, who hire out to work in town and whose blooming natural beauty is held to be a "menace to the social order," and the perfect characterlessness of the brushed, smoothed, pitiably "refined" daughters of town families; between the unforgettable "freemasonry" (as it is called in the "Introduction") of, at once, childhood and the first hard stages of prairie settlement and the drab, guarded life of "evasions and negations," repressed, conforming, wasteful, which we watch taking its place; between the lyric vision of a life cast within the harshly beautiful determinations of the natural order and the sour mockery of the failed civilization which rapidly supersedes it.

These contrasts and progressive changes take on, as the book develops, the resonances of legend and folk memory. *My Ántonia* is suffused with that provisional myth-making by which the victims of a fixed historical process come to

13. The nearest formal precedent in American writing is Sarah Jewett's *The Country of the Pointed Firs* (see above, pp. 97-99). It is worth recalling the personal encouragement and good counsel Sarah Jewett gave Willa Cather at the beginning of her career.

In being as unified, imaginatively, as any novel, and yet not a novel, *My Ántonia* resembles two of the most original and accomplished American works of the next decade, *Winesburg, Ohio* (1919) and *In Our Time* (1925), and like them it looks back to a nineteenth-century masterpiece, Turgenev's *Sportsman's Sketches*, which served as a model for this whole genre of the regional story-chronicle in early twentieth-century American writing.

terms with their gradually discovered fate. The main scenes and episodes are shadowed by legends of earlier migrants—the Mormons on their trek west to a promised land, who scattered the sunflower seeds now blooming along the country roads; the Spaniards before them who left a swordblade under the sod for a homesteader to plow up three centuries later. The events overtaking Àntonia's father, a suicide during the terrible first winter and buried at a country crossroads (with "propitiatory intent"), renew the great story of Coronado himself, who "died in the wilderness, of a broken heart." Dark tales from the Old World—as of the farmers Pavel and Russian Peter, said to have thrown a young bride to pursuing wolves—are renewed and naturalized, old barbarisms that disquietingly blend into the fresh untamed landscape. The story of the Nativity, read aloud at Christmas, makes only one legend more: "as we listened it all seemed like something that happened lately, and near at hand." These overtones and analogues are at the heart of the book's power of truth. When Willa Cather attempts to formulate them explicitly, when she speaks of Àntonia, in middle age among her children, as "a rich mine of life, like the founders of early races," an element of sentimental assertiveness sometimes threatens—but cannot really violate—the imaginative integrity of the whole. In American writing of this period *My Àntonia* possesses a rare steadiness of formal apprehension, an achievement back of which we may recognize the liberating conjunction of two decisive factors: unstinted personal emotion and a remarkably firm and objective knowledge of an actual pattern of regional, and national, history.

The "New" Poetry: Robinson and Frost

For poetry the important consequences of the renewed impulse toward "realism" in this rising generation were formal and stylistic. It is hard now, after the experimental novelties and triumphs of another half-century, to imagine the indifference of established critical taste around 1900 to the kind of poetic language Edwin Arlington Robinson and Robert Frost (thirty-one and twenty-six respectively at the turn of the century) had begun teaching themselves to write in. It is also hard to imagine how unsure they themselves could be as to when in fact they had achieved what they wanted—in Robinson's case the "sense of reality" (letter to Harry de Forest Smith, February 3, 1895) which he had found in no poet of his time so much as in the prose of Hawthorne and Thomas Hardy; in Frost's, those "effects of actuality and intimacy," communicating the special thrill of "sincerity," which he once called (letter to W. S. B. Braithwaite, March 22, 1915) "the greatest aim an artist can have."

A more direct and substantial confrontation of actual experience than can be found in the propriety-ridden verse of the preceding thirty years in American writing—the period of Edwin Rowland Sill, Joaquin Miller, Sidney Lanier, John Boyle O'Reilly, Father Tabb, James Whitcomb Riley, Edwin Markham, Lizette Woodworth Reese—is surely a main part of Robinson's and Frost's achievement. But the language for embodying it in poems was not created all at once. It is curious to leaf through Frost's first collection, *A Boy's Will* (published in 1913 but consisting mostly of poems written six, ten, even fifteen years earlier) and discover how little Frostian the run of it sounds. His early poems, Malcolm Cowley has remarked, "gave his own picture of the world, but in the language of the genteel poets." Surely verbal texture was not what encouraged Frost to go on reprinting poems beginning, "Thine envious fond flowers are dead, too,"* or "Lovers, forget your love,/ And list to the love of these,/

---

* From "My Butterfly" from *Complete Poems of Robert Frost*. Copyright 1934 by Holt, Rinehart and Winston, Inc. Copyright © 1962 by Robert Frost. Reprinted by permission of Holt, Rinehart and Winston, Inc., and Jonathan Cape Limited.

She a window flower,/ And he a winter breeze."* The first
example dates back to 1895, but the point, historically, is that
even then Frost knew better. His twenty-year struggle to
establish a satisfactory verse language is one of the significant
episodes in modern literary history. "I was under twenty,"
he wrote in the letter already quoted,

> when I deliberately put it to myself one night after good
> conversation that there are moments when we actually touch
> in talk what the best writing can only come near. The curse
> of our book language is not so much that it keeps forever to
> the same set phrases (though Heaven knows those are bad
> enough) but that it sounds forever with the same reading
> tones. We must go out into the vernacular for tones that
> haven't been brought to book. We must write with the ear
> on the speaking voice.

—we must achieve, he said in the same letter, and was saying
in all his correspondence and conversation of the time, not
merely fine sounds or important sense but something more
vital than either: the very "sound of sense," caught as if at
the instant of its coming alive.

Robinson's command of tone (so defined: the "sound of
sense") does not seem as supple and varied or as distinctly
individual as Frost's came to be, but it is perhaps more consistently "major" in the body of his work, just as the body of
his work represents a more abundant and a steadier creative
energy. We observe that he secured his verse style sooner than
any of his nearer contemporaries—Masters, Frost, Amy
Lowell, Sandburg, Wallace Stevens; "modern" poetry in the
United States begins with Robinson's volumes of 1896 and
1897, *The Torrent and The Night Before* and *The Children
of the Night*. Yet he too had his troubles breaking through the
flaccidity of contemporary verse conventions. Two versions

* From "Wind and Window Flower" from *Complete Poems of
Robert Frost*. Copyright 1934 by Holt, Rinehart and Winston, Inc.
Copyright © 1962 by Robert Frost. Reprinted by permission of
Holt, Rinehart and Winston, Inc., and Jonathan Cape Limited.

of one of his early successes, the much-anthologized villanelle, "The House on the Hill," show him groping toward the characteristic style of his maturity, distinguished (though the advance is slight and uncertain in this instance) by a more concentrated specification of feeling and, coincidentally, a provocative obliquity of statement. The first version, written out in a letter of February, 1894, antedates the second and published version by more than two years:

I.*   II.

They are all gone away,
  The house is shut and still:
There is nothing more to say.
	They are all gone away,
	  The House is shut and still,
	There is nothing more to say.

Malign them as we may,
  We cannot do them ill:
They are all gone away.
	Through broken walls and gray
	  The winds blow bleak and shrill
	They are all gone away.

Are we more fit than they
  To meet the Master's will?—
There is nothing more to say.
	Nor is there one to-day
	  To speak them good or ill:
	There is nothing more to say.

What matters it who stray
  Around the sunken sill?—
They are all gone away,
	Why is it then we stray
	  Around that sunken sill?
	They are all gone away.

And our poor fancy-play
  For them is wasted skill:
There is nothing more to say.
	And our poor fancy-play
	  For them is wasted skill:
	There is nothing more to say.

There is ruin and decay
  In the House on the Hill:
They are all gone away,
There is nothing more to say.
	There is ruin and decay
	  In the House on the Hill:
	They are all gone away,
	There is nothing more to say.

Two versions of his rendering in sonnet form of Horace, Book I, Ode XI, which can be dated to May, 1891, and December, 1895, show the same development toward verbal plainness, emotional concentration, dramatic obliquity.

A morally serious apprehension of life joined to a steady determination to make poetry once again an adult calling: these motives are fundamental to Robinson's and Frost's progress beyond the dead level of competent verse rhetoric of the '80s and '90s. Yet other ambitious young poets of the same generation worked from the same motives—in particular the group of university poets, mostly Harvard-educated, among whom William Vaughan Moody (1869–1910), Trumbull Stickney (1874–1904), and William Ellery Leonard (1876–1944) seem now the most gifted, and Santayana (who published *Sonnets and Other Verses* in 1894 and a verse tragedy, *Lucifer*, in 1899) appears as a kind of unofficial senior tutor. The special historical interest of this group has been pointed out by Malcolm Cowley, in remarking how the "tradition" they participated in, with its classical learning, its use of myth-themes, its French exposure, and its assumption that verse drama is the supreme literary form, is the local tradition that nourished T. S. Eliot.[14] Through Eliot we can see that these allegiances were not necessarily stultifying. But reading the published work of these undoubtedly thoughtful and sincere poets we can also see the essential inertness of their verse language, in syntax, in phrase cadence, in diction and metaphor. Perhaps we can see, too, why certain ideas—an "objective correlative" for emotion; artistic creation as an "escape from personality"—gained a special prominence in

14. *The Literary Situation*, 1955, p. 244.

Robinson and Frost were also at Harvard briefly in the '90s, but with this difference: both matriculated when already into their twenties and when—so it appears from early letters—they had already learned to read and to think critically for themselves; and both came away before having to commit themselves to the pursuit of a degree.

Eliot's early thinking. It is in technique first of all, in the securing of a fresh voice and a greater concentration of form, that the poetic renaissance of the early 1900s declares itself. For Robinson and Frost not less than for Eliot and Pound, technique becomes the critical test of a poet's "sincerity." Certainly nothing is more fundamental to the actual creation of a "new" poetry than this: the transfer of ambition from the lining out of important subjects and weighty themes to the achievement of a disciplined, freshly viable craftsmanship.

In feeling and in imaginative grasp there is a narrowness and monotony about the poetry of Edwin Arlington Robinson (1869–1935) which, at first encounter, may make nearly inexplicable the ranking which more than one commentator has felt it impossible to withhold from him: the foremost talent in American poetry between Whitman and Eliot. Reading one after another of his severe narrative portraits, with their dry skepticism and sensuous bareness, we may wonder whether he was not himself a leading victim of that American blight which seems his central, perhaps obsessive, subject. Robinson is the poet of casualties; of broken lives and exhausted consciences; of separateness;[15] and of the calm that comes with resignation and defeat—perhaps only with death. He writes of an "ethical unrest" ("Flammonde") or "querulous selfishness" ("Captain Craig") undercutting every philosophic reassurance, every visionary refuge, men may think to guard their lives with. Robinson's sense of life has, of course, its regional sources. His links with the older New England consciousness—the "folk atmosphere of the upper levels of New England society," in Yvor Winters's phrase—

15. More separateness than isolation: his most compact monologues and analyses invariably assume a listener or observer, the irony of whose uncomprehending presence intensifies dramatically the suggested emotion.

and also the timing of his absorption into it, at the dry climax of its long dissolution, have not gone unremarked. The Puritan concept of life as a wearing state of spiritual probation; the Puritan-Transcendentalist passion for "the light" and for right relationship; the inexhaustible, humanly exhausting concern of both Puritan and Transcendentalist for defining the sovereign laws of life ("lords of life," in Emerson's phrase) through the minutely detailed testimony of certain representative men: these motives receive perhaps their last direct expression in Robinson's poems. But it is typical of the state of the New England tradition when he came to inherit it that the opening lines of an early sonnet called "Credo" should affirm only negations—"I cannot find my way: there is no star. . . ."—and that thirty years later his address to this tradition in another sonnet, "New England," should be derisively ironic.

Inheritance, temperament, imaginative consciousness blend almost indistinguishably in Robinson. His most casual words are suffused with the tones and accents of his best poems. At twenty-four he remarked in a letter to Harry de Forest Smith: "I am afraid that I shall always stand in the shadow as one of Omar's broken pots. I suspect that I am pretty much what I am, and that I am pretty much a damned fool in many ways; but I further suspect that I am not altogether an ass, whatever my neighbors may say." The damned and the fooled—these are the recurring subjects of Robinson's verse portraits; and a great part of his strength as a poet is his ability to specify as if from interior knowledge both the magnitude and the inscrutability of the forces that have prevailed over them. His poems convey a real awe, a sense of the actual mystery and translatedness, of those who have met and endured these forces to the full. A few poems celebrate the even more mysterious and select company of those who have themselves somehow prevailed in their lives, though such figures, typi-

cally, are all but nameless in the poems devoted to them—
"The Master" (Lincoln), "Walt Whitman," "Ben Jonson
Entertains A Man From Stratford"; the fine "Rembrandt to
Rembrandt" is the exception in this respect, and there the
speaker, unhonored, is left to name himself. These heroes
survive not as imaginable persons but as "flying words," as
"piercing cadences" too pure and triumphant to be heard
directly, as vanished yet unforgettable impressions.

Words and cadences rather than generalizing argument;
the emotion not to be contested rather than the thought seeking to complete itself—these (almost against his intellectual
will, it seems) are the particular means of Robinson's accomplishment. In his first maturity he accepted the notion that
the duty of the learned man was to consider what it was that
he "believed"; to search out a system of philosophic or religious truth which he could give a proper name to, perhaps
even live by. So we find Robinson at the time of his first
book trying to define his religion—"a kind of optimistic desperation" was his own early description of it—and earnestly
considering the merits and claims of "idealism" over against
"materialism" as "the one logical and satisfactory interpretation of life." We note how Christian Science attracted him
until he came up against its theological and sectarian pretensions, and how late in life he was still pointing out (to an
interviewer in 1932) the "Transcendentalism" in certain
poems. What bearing do such matters have upon his achievement as a poet? Robinson's "thought," we can say, was neither
more nor less impressive than that of many sensitive and
serious-minded contemporaries. Neo-Darwinist generalities
and post-Protestant absolutes concerning human fate and the
order of the cosmos rumbled through his head as monoto-
nously as may be imagined, given his times and background—
and that might indeed be the principal interest of his poems
if he had not written them out so carefully; if he had not, that

is, coincidentally committed himself to that other way of truth-seeking which is the vocation of the artist. Robinson matters as a poet, not as a philosopher. His thought counts as it is articulated in the words, measures, serial figures of his verse. He is not even a philosophical poet, really—certainly not so much of one as, say, Eliot or Stevens. His saving grace is that he will not say what he cannot take technical possession of; he is sincere and pursues truth within his capacity to complete the expressive figures he composes in.

That would seem to be the point of Frost's charming, scarcely improvable tribute in a preface to the posthumous *King Jasper* (1935): "For forty years it was phrase on phrase on phrase with Robinson"—and every one, Frost added, "the closest delineation of something that *is* something." Phrase rather than image: Robinson's language is notoriously abstract and unsensuous. His metaphors tend to be apparitional; they are verbal signals not so much embodying the theme or the emotion in concrete detail as lighting up its progress through the bare statement of the poem. Dark, light, gleams, voices, fire and flame, music, years, waves, dreams: this basic vocabulary is composed almost entirely of the familiar "dead" metaphors of common rhetoric (and of Romantic wisdom verse in its decadence). But one sign of Robinson's rather powerful tact as a poet is that half the time such metaphors are used parodistically, to cover with doubt or irony or pathos the turns of thought and feeling that commonly lean on them. A case can be made, in fact, for their special appropriateness in poems so many of which are built upon the imaginative setting of the congregated American village and its befogged way of looking at things (whether Gardiner, Maine, or the New York City of his 1910 volume, *The Town Down the River*); poems which consistently produce, as Conrad Aiken once suggested, the effect of something deviously known rather than directly seen. But the basic strength of Robinson's poetic language resides in something even more elemental than this use of metaphor. Robinson surely has the most flexible working vocabulary in modern American poetry—and has it (in contrast to poets like Pound and Stevens) entirely within the framework of the plain style. In large part it is sheer unaided verbal and denominative resourcefulness that enlivens his poems, restoring the full vocabulary of ordinary prose discourse to verse statement, and that serves him as a main defense against argumentative monotony (with imperfect success) in the long verse narratives of his later career.[16] The elaborations, the refinements, the suspended complexities of stated meaning would be quite strangling in Robinson's longer poems without this continual infusion of fresh linguistic oxygen.

Robinson's poetic authority involves something more of course than this ordinary verbal resourcefulness, though that is a notable part of it. What it centrally consists in is a matter at once of argumentative syntax and of prosody. Frost seems to have had his eye on one aspect of it in praising Robinson for "the way the shape of the stanza is played with [in the developing statement], the easy way the obstacle of verse is turned to advantage." The young poet and critic Jane Flanders has discussed it in more specific detail:

> Although Robinson was at ease with a variety of forms (one criterion for a major poet), including blank verse and the sonnet, his ear was most naturally tuned to balanced cadences, the ballad measure, and the resolution of true rhymes. Into

16. About this later work—the Arthurian poems, *Merlin* (1917), *Lancelot* (1920), and *Tristram* (1927), and the psychological verse novels like *Roman Bartholow* (1923), *The Man Who Died Twice* (1924), *Cavender's House* (1929), and *Matthias at the Door* (1931)— the comment has been made more than once that, whatever else may be said about them, it cannot be said that they are badly written. Almost any passage, tested at random, will show the same resourceful competence at phrase-balancing and verse-making.

lyric stanza forms he forced studied analyses, composing an abstract, bony kind of verse the elements of which remain constantly in tension and reflect in their actual construction the tension of the characters they portray.

Within the chosen measures of his verse it is always the firmly wrought phrase- and sentence-figure—"phrase on phrase on phrase"—that carries attention forward. This is the means by which his apprehensions reach us. Figures of predication and address, metrical and stanzaic figures, figures of expression and description: they come into being together and cannot be dissevered. They act along the line of their own advance; they are how his poems speak. Like any settled way of speaking, of course, this of Robinson's creates its own dangers. The capacity to produce these basic figures of statement in consistent abundance, the "formulary ingenuity" in Robinson that Yvor Winters speaks of, is also what frequently creates, especially in long poems, the damping impression of a kind of automatic writing. Certain devices become mannerisms and begin to seem self-proliferating: in particular the use, like a speech tic, of abstract relative clauses for primary statement (thus, successfully enough, in "Flammonde": "How much it was of him we met/ We cannot ever know; nor yet/ Shall all he gave us quite atone/ For what was his, and his alone"*),[17] and also a corresponding trick of negative identification (not this, not this, not even this, but possibly that, though perhaps

17. It is characteristic of Robinson, whose verse idiom is grounded in the broad range of Romantic and Victorian poetry, to have spotted an occasional fine effect in a poet like Longfellow and adapted it to his own uses. See the fourth stanza of Longfellow's "The Fire of Driftwood": "We spake of many a vanished scene,/Of what we once had thought and said,/Of what had been, and might have been,/ And who was changed, and who was dead. . . ."

* Reprinted with permission of The Macmillan Company from *Man Against the Sky* by E. A. Robinson. Copyright 1916 by E. A. Robinson, renewed 1944 by Ruth Nivison.

not that either). Sometimes these devices are precisely suited to the unfolding of the argument; sometimes they are the means to what seems a willful obscurity, a pointless circumlocution. But in the main Robinson's predicative style, as we may call it, is a style equal to the most demanding occasions in his poetry. It is the instrument, for example, which makes "The Man Against the Sky" (1916), his meditative ode on the mysteries of mortal being and the shadow our consciousness of mortality throws over the reasoned conduct of life, one of the most fitly eloquent of modern poems; here as elsewhere it seems an admirable vehicle for expressing the restless yet finely balanced skepticism of Robinson's mind.

His best-remembered poems are mostly the shorter dramatic monologues and narrative portraits or biographies: "Luke Havergal," "Charles Carville's Eyes," "Cliff Klingenhagen," "Richard Cory," "Eros Turannos" (justly praised), "Mr. Flood's Party," "Flammonde," to name only the most frequently anthologized. But anthologies are a means of forgetting as well as remembering. They are also a means of simulating critical principles where lack of space is what really decides; so they regularly conspire to perpetuate Poe's curiously long-lived thesis that the coherent long poem is a practical impossibility. In any case nobody anthologizes Robinson's 2016-line poem of 1902, "Captain Craig," the climactic work of his first maturity. Yet it is possible to think that this "rather particular kind of twentieth century comedy," as he called it, is his greatest achievement. Most of the poem's effort goes into defining—which is to say, surrounding, blanketing, wholly occupying—an attitude or mind style of which the Captain himself is first spokesman and, in his reported life, chief exemplar. Space is lacking to suggest the variety and energy and sheer surface interest of the line-by-line fashioning of the poem. It must do to say that this effort of definition goes forward by contrasts, dialectically; Robinson's ironic humor has the firmness of syllogism, of argument pursued until it has embraced, or disarmed, its invoked opposite. Humor is the determining mode. Captain Craig, by his own account, is above all a "humorist"—"Shrewd, critical, facetious, insincere." What he propounds is propounded with "an ancient levity/ That is the forbear of all earnestness." A stoical, derisive, yet garrulous and congenial humor is his refuge from impossible alternatives: from "altruism," for example, for which the actual world is never quite ready; or from "sincerity"—the poem is a kind of anatomy of failed or overworked sincerity and thus bids for a place among the classics of skeptical or third-stage romanticism; or from a state which both altruism and sincerity will come down to in any case, that oppressive and irreversible exhaustion of spirit from which so much of modern literature (and modern catastrophe) takes its rise:

> . . . the spiritual inactivity
> Which more than often is identified
> With individual intensity,
> And is the parent of that selfishness
> Whereof no end of lesser *tions* and *isms*
> Are querulously born.

The abounding wordiness of "Captain Craig" (even these few lines display it) is both reinforced and moderated by the facetious, mock-pedestrian tone of the Captain's discourse. *Wordiness* becomes, in fact, the active metaphor for the mode or style of life, always inadequate, which the poem defines. In the metaphoric substructure of "Captain Craig" wordiness is set against the ideal mode of *music* (a conjunction is made at the end, ironically, in the presumptuous music of the brass band, blaring "indiscreetly," which marches the Captain to his grave). Appropriately, then, throughout the poem, counterpointing all its knotted figures of primary statement, the music of older poetic formulas sounds—cadences from Shakespeare, Milton, the Bible, Emerson, Byron, Wordsworth, Tennyson, Swinburne. Greece and Provence are mentioned: "Captain Craig" is one more early modern work—Pound's "Hugh Selwyn Mauberley" (1920) is another—that finds in allusions to the Greeks both a source of metaphor for its skeptical, ironic lamentation and also a kind of litany of consolation in its knowledge of their names. The Wordsworthian echoes are particularly significant with regard to the theme of "the Child"—the phoenix life within the overshadowed adult consciousness—which the Captain's comfortless, perilously insistent humor justifies itself by keeping in view.

Whether "Captain Craig" succeeds greatly or not and finds and entirely fulfills its own proper laws of form, it is historically of the greatest interest. Its moral and stylistic comedy stands, in American literature, midway between Melville's "Marquis of Grandvin" and Wallace Stevens's "The Comedian as the Letter C" (a poem surely influenced by it), and is stronger and steadier in running its course than either of those—as one may say with all due admiration for Stevens's copiously witty poem. A remarkable quantity of subsequent American writing seems an elaboration of the manner of address perfected in "Captain Craig." One may mention in particular all the ironic narratives—shifting between the facetiously verbose and the cynically proverbial—of what it is that lies beneath middle-class respectability, or of the doings of certain mortally disaffected though perhaps transfigured heroes who approach some rarer knowledge of the spirit's capacity for truth but go to ruin as a consequence: the fiction, that is, of writers like Cozzens, Penn Warren, Styron, Bellow, Wright Morris, Salinger and, as Louis Coxe has observed, of Robert Lowell in his verse narrative, *The Mills of the Kavanaughs;* of Henry Miller and of Faulkner when he gives rein to the compulsive talkers of his later stories; of, supremely perhaps, the Eugene O'Neill of *The Iceman Cometh* and

Long Day's Journey Into Night. "Captain Craig" is a poem whose working co-ordinates embrace no small part of the expressive tradition it energetically advances.

Frost's talent, less resourceful and abundant though hardly less fine, developed more slowly than Robinson's, coming into its majority only in the closing years of our period. At thirty-eight Robert Frost (1874–1962) had published not a dozen short lyrics. The story of his emergence—years of practice and experiment carried on in virtual isolation, his poems regularly rejected by the established literary monthlies; association with a group of younger Georgian poets during three years in England between 1912 and 1915; acceptance finally by an English publisher (still a matter of prestige in the United States); the support of favorable first reviews by Ezra Pound and Edward Thomas, among others—is well known, and it is well worth knowing as part of the general emergence of modern American literature. But the qualities that gave first readers of *A Boy's Will* (1913) the surprise and pleasure of a genuinely accomplished new talent are hard now to specify exactly. They were hard to specify in 1913. Pound's initial review (in *The New Freewoman*), acknowledging that "Mr. Frost's book is a little raw, and has in it a number of infelicities," claimed for it no virtue more definite than an "utter sincerity," and he remarked: "One reads the book for the 'tone,' which is homely, by intent, and pleasing, never doubting that it comes direct from his own life, and that no two lives are the same." The critical emphasis is worth noting. Frost, we may say following the terms of Pound's praise, had managed to do in a miscellaneous verse collection something of what his best contemporaries in the novel were attempting to do through the heavier forms of realistic fiction: he had articulated an identifiable life, and manner of life, in a language of statement and incident that was both truthful and formally appropriate. He had become a poet by becoming, in choice of theme, a biographer. ("Theme alone can steady us down," he wrote later.) A few of the poems in his first book have become anthology regulars: "Mowing," "Storm Fear," the parabolic "A Tuft of Flowers." But the Frost who uniquely among modern American poets was to build up a notable popular following as well as the critical respect of his peers is very much more plainly in view in *North of Boston* (1914). This second collection consists almost entirely of narrative poems; ten in fact are short stories (though only one of these, the touching "A Servant to Servants," is a dramatic monologue), while five of the remaining six offer the kind of forty- or fifty-line meditative narrative-lyric in the first person in which Frost is most nearly the master. It was with these expertly figured, cadenced, *spoken* poems—"Mending Wall," "After Apple Picking," "The Wood Pile," "The Death of the Hired Man," "The Black Cottage" in particular —that Frost staked his claim to major recognition. With these and with the corresponding verse narratives ("An Old Man's Winter Night," "Birches," "Out, Out—") and the fine sonnets ("Meeting and Passing," "The Oven Bird," "Putting in the Seed") of *Mountain Interval* in 1916, he made authoritatively familiar the "speaking tone of voice" he had gone in search of. It is the prime technical resource of all his poetry.

In recent years more and more of Frost's early thinking about poetry—as in letters to friends and to his first admirers —has been made available in print, and the interesting revelation, at least for literary history, has been its nearness in practical outlook to the programmed verse revolution Ezra Pound was concurrently conducting. Frost's voice in various statements of intention, a voice already thoroughly artful and mannered in its folkish wit and plainness, would never be mistaken for Pound's or for Eliot's; but the positions taken or assumed—the idea of the poem as an organized figure of statement; the notion of a dramatic necessity as basic to poetic truthfulness; the attack on the superfluous word, the inert phrase, the singsong rhythm; even the reasoned sense of the vital relationship between traditional forms (in Frost's case chiefly metrical) and individual originality—substantially correspond. "The object in writing poetry," so Frost summed up his thought in the preface to his *Collected Poems* of 1939, "is to make all poems sound as different as possible from each other." That remark assumes that two conditions of poetic virtue have already been secured: technique and voice. And with respect to these Frost's achievement is unarguable. A natural individuality of temper and sensibility has been endorsed and verified by a corresponding individuality of completed form, communicating without interruption that indispensable "sound of sense" which was the earliest and steadiest of his goals.

This double individuality, at once personal and technical, Frost always cherished—but at the expense, it may be felt, of another kind of development that can best be described as imaginative and moral. His individuality is the prime source of, at once, his strength as a verse-maker and rhetorician and his otherwise indefinable limitation as a poet. Technical strength, sophistication, and harmony; imaginative narrowness and oversimpleness—the case, so characterized, again recalls that of Pound, and we observe that with both Frost and Pound critical admiration has often frozen into a particularly illiberal kind of cult worship. To see either of these curiously self-contained figures in perspective, we need the measure of their greater contemporaries in Anglo-American poetry, of Eliot, of D. H. Lawrence, of Yeats, even—within the severe limits of his accomplishment—of Hart Crane. Then we can see more clearly, for example, how Frost carried through half, but only half, of the job of remaking his own poetic practice which we recognize with Yeats to have been the means of his achieving the graver, more complex authority of his magnificent later work. Frost saw the need of reforming his style earlier in his career than Yeats in his; saw this need almost before he had a style to reform; but he never could admit the need of reforming, enlarging, reopening his imagination. His poems are most satisfactory when dealing with the secondary emotions of human life—anxiety, apprehension, regret, ironic reconsideration—or with emotion at a certain remove: love examined and calculated as a resource,[18] fear anticipated and withdrawn from, loneliness become policy and safeguard. These poems celebrate fine virtues and worthy states of mind: endurance, humor, grit, reasoned submission, self-respect, natural integrity, the wary alertness of the creature to all that is problematical in its regular existence. Yet what we are persuaded of in them is more often (let us admit it) the rightness of having respect for such states of mind, and the right-mindedness of the poet's concern for them, than their full moral truth or necessity. The English critic A. Alvarez has described very well the felt quality of Frost's best poems: "They are perfect, but they haven't very much weight." They are, we notice, fundamentally anecdotal, poems of occasion and comment; there is simply less searching out of imaginative possibilities than is the case with poetry of the first rank. There is less concern for the impersonal truth of things. But as these poems of Frost's do have the genuine charm, in voice and design, of properly finished work, they were at once rightly recognized as a real addition to our small stock of durable literature, and they have rightly been prized and

18. So in "Storm Fear": "I count our strength,/Two and a child. . . ."*

* From "Storm Fear" from *Complete Poems of Robert Frost.* Copyright 1934 by Holt, Rinehart and Winston, Inc. Copyright © 1962 by Robert Frost. Reprinted by permission of Holt, Rinehart and Winston, Inc., and Jonathan Cape Limited.

loved. Their wide popularity is a further source of interest, having grown up around the skillfully idealized projection of the ethos of American individualism in its guarded, sly, New England aspect. To have defined satisfactorily for a significant segment of our population, as well as for a whole geographical region, a life-style to live by at least from one day to the next under the discouraging east wind of modern civil existence, is not an unworthy achievement.

The "New" Poetry: Sandburg, Lindsay, Masters

Though Robinson and Frost were both promptly enlisted into the poetic renaissance of 1912 and after, they had little to do with its progress as a self-conscious movement. As a movement the "new" poetry had its active centers in London and Chicago, and spread its influence chiefly through the successive Imagist anthologies issued (under Pound's and then Amy Lowell's direction) between 1914 and 1917 and through the Chicago-based monthly, *Poetry: A Magazine of Verse* (founded 1912). Only two of Frost's poems and two of Robinson's appeared in *Poetry* between 1912 and 1920. But in the same years the magazine printed more than fifty poems by Carl Sandburg (b. 1878) and as many by Amy Lowell (1874–1925); it featured a series of spectacular novelties by Vachel Lindsay (1879–1931), including "General William Booth Enters Into Heaven," "The Sante Fé Trail," "The Chinese Nightingale," and the "Booker Washington Trilogy"; it regularly found room for the progressive experimentation of Ezra Pound and William Carlos Williams; also, it repeatedly emphasized the special contribution of midwestern writers to this poetic coming-of-age by publishing, for example, a dozen post-Spoon River effusions by Edgar Lee Masters (1869–1950) and, in September, 1917, a typically evangelistic sequence by Sherwood Anderson of six "Mid-American

Songs." The liberal taste of *Poetry*, and its generosity—for which both Harriet Monroe, its founder, and Ezra Pound, foreign editor in its early years, were responsible—to freshness and originality of any kind from any quarter, made it a showcase for new work. It opened its pages not only to Lindsay's gospel music and Sandburg's free-verse mood pieces but to "The Love Song of J. Alfred Prufrock" and "Sunday Morning," to Yeats's "Ego Dominus Tuus," to James Joyce, D. H. Lawrence, and Rabindranath Tagore. But the dominant image of the "new" which *Poetry* publicized and settled upon American verse for at least a decade was one formed around the poets of its home province, the Illinoisans Sandburg, Lindsay, and Masters.[19]

Yet the "newness" of the midwestern poets strikes us now as having more to do with the newer prose realism of their generation (itself conspicuously regional) than with the major development of twentieth-century poetry. They were Dreiser's, Sherwood Anderson's, Jack London's contemporaries more than they were Frost's or Stevens's or Pound's; and where they subsequently proved influential, it was by

19. Amy Lowell's description of the "new" movement, on the other hand, in her *Tendencies in Modern American Poetry* (1917), gave roughly equal emphasis to three main groups: the New Englanders Robinson and Frost, the midwesterners Masters and Sandburg, and the Imagists H. D. and John Gould Fletcher.

The poets themselves—at least at first—were more conscious of their participation in a common effort of reform and renewal than of their differences. Pound welcomed all three Illinois poets and beat drums for them, though he began soon enough in private letters to point out their characteristic limitations, while Sandburg, in the February, 1916, issue of *Poetry*, published an essay praising Pound as that poet "who, in the English language, by means of his own examples of creative art in poetry, has done most of living men to incite new impulses." Sandburg shrewdly remarked that it was Pound's poems rather than his articulated theories that were chiefly inspiring his fellow poets.

way of suggesting to younger prose writers some fresh source of material or method of treatment—so Masters' *Spoon River Anthology* helped Anderson toward the freehanded design of his Winesburg collection four years later; so Lindsay's vaudeville-show *montages* of American folkways and folk noises may be counted among the native forerunners of Dos Passos' experiments in the novel or of Thornton Wilder's in drama during the next generation. Even their improvisation of new forms—Sandburg's declamatory public speaking, Lindsay's revival hymns and circus-parade rhythms—are essentially a reaching out for new material. This, too, is "poetic," they seem to be demonstrating: these sights and sounds, these colloquialisms, these popular rituals, these memories. As with their contemporaries in the novel, their effort is not really to change and advance the art they practice so much as to democratize its uses. Their poetry is egalitarian and populist—the spell-binding performance Sandburg and Lindsay could give their own work before popular audiences may in fact be taken as a faithful expression of its leading motives.

These poets belong with the realistic novelists of 1900–1920 in a further respect: their best poems tend to be those in which they surrender their intention most completely to the data of life they know best as historical persons. Their good work is fundamentally documentary, their effective style a kind of rhythmic ventriloquism. What is curious is that when, seeking some final earnestness and sincerity, they write instead in their own poetic voices, all three should so regularly lapse into variations of the period style we associate mainly with Amy Lowell and with "feminine" poetry, which is to say that loose, mood-sketching imagism that had replaced ideality and high-mindedness as the staple of magazine verse during these years. No style has blurred faster (its very successes, such as they were, destroyed it): the fog on little cat feet, once greatly admired for delicacy and precision, seems approachable now only by way of bluff parody.

Of the Illinois poets Sandburg and Lindsay were the more conspicuously gifted and achieved the greater contemporary reputations. Now, however, we find it hard to escape the impression that their work is finally contingent and occasional, a poetry of moods and wishful sentiments rather than completed emotional knowledge. It requires not only that we suspend disbelief but that, so to speak, we already believe absolutely in the value of the sentimental-humanitarian gestures it offers in place of accurate perception and clear imaginative understanding. That is why it depends so heavily for effectiveness on the kind of re-creative performance of which Sandburg and Lindsay were both masters, and is itself rarely more than the occasion, the text, for such performance. "General William Booth" is a case in point. Its assertive language gains life and form as much from the musical rendering it explicitly calls for as from its own slapdash tones and relationships—and though the poem would obviously have been more impressive when chanted by its author from a public platform than in the relative silence of print, it is perhaps even better when cut down to serve as a text for Charles Ives's extraordinary musical setting, which lends its words a composed power and solemnity they do not really achieve for themselves.

The solid literary monument left by the Illinois poets is surely Masters' *Spoon River Anthology* (1915). As against collections like Sandburg's *Chicago Poems* (1916) and *Cornhuskers* (1918), the titles of which stake out rather grander imaginative claims than the diffuse contents quite deliver, Masters' dense volume of epitaph-portraits has the strength of its bulk and plan. Like some minor masterpiece of local-color fiction it embraces not only the present condition but the whole shaping history of its locale; the life stories it sets out (in the simple, compact free-verse cadences Masters adapted from models like the *Greek Anthology* and Sandburg's early poems) are mutually reinforcing and take on, in part through their very monotony, the weight and pathos of a collective truth, an impersonal and objective necessity. The themes and situations in *Spoon River* are the conventional ones of village realism—failure, isolation, the buried life, the unacknowledged talent, the febrile self-deluding character of success—and the dominant emotions (see the opening poem, "The Hill") are those of American regionalism in general: nostalgia and regret, the elegiac and the memorial. Masters was in no sense an originator or discoverer, and the rest of his work—he had published eleven books before *Spoon River* and continued producing poems, plays, novels, biographies, declarations, for another thirty years—has mostly dropped out of sight.[20] His singular achievement in *Spoon River* testifies first of all to the fertilizing power of the two central impulses in American writing during the early 1900s: the impulse to "make it new," which encouraged him to trust his poetic argument to the discipline of an experimental verse form; and the impulse to tell not just "the truth" in one's work, but, specifically, those peculiar home truths which the full course of the commonest American lives uniquely revealed.

20. Two exceptions are his biography of Vachel Lindsay, inspired by his own sense of the pathos of being a poet in the United States, and his autobiography, *Across Spoon River*, a period piece in the history of post-Victorian liberation.

It is our faith and the faith of many, that we are living in the first days of a renascent period, a time which means for America the coming of that national self-consciousness which is the beginning of greatness. In all such epochs the arts cease to be private matters; they become not only the expression of the national life but a means to its enhancement.

—Editorial, *The Seven Arts*,
I, 1 (November, 1916)

P.S. Any agonizing that tends to hurry what I believe in the end to be inevitable, our American Risorgimento, is dear to me. That awakening will make the Italian Renaissance look like a tempest in a teapot! The force we have, and the impulse, but the guiding sense, the discrimination in applying the force, we must wait and strive for.

—Ezra Pound to Harriet Monroe,
18 August 1912

Until 'we' accept what I've been insisting on for a decade, i.e., a universal standard which pays no attention to time or country—a Weltlitteratur standard—there is no hope.

—Ezra Pound to Harriet Monroe,
7 November 1913

I fear for the ultimate intelligence of America, which in all conscience, judged by world standards, is low enough.

—Theodore Dreiser, "Life, Art and America,"
The Seven Arts, February, 1917

5. RENAISSANCE:
1912 AND AFTER

EXCEPT in poetry[1] no special concentration of new work distinguishes the years 1910 to 1919 in American literature. Of the prose writers whose books fill out the productive history of this decade, Willa Cather is perhaps the only one whose essential talent was not already formed by 1910; the good work after that date not only of

1. A considerable exception, to be sure, in a decade that saw the emergence of Pound, Frost, Lindsay, H. D., Stevens, Williams, Jeffers, Ransom, Marianne Moore, and Hart Crane, among others, and that closed with "Gerontion" and "Hugh Selwyn Mauberley." For the sake of argumentative unity the subject of their emergence, including critical assessment of their first books, has been relinquished to the next volume in this history.

Howells, James, and Henry Adams but also of Veblen, Santayana, Edith Wharton, Dreiser, follows from earlier developments. Nevertheless the legend of an American renaissance during these years—a climactic leap forward into full cultural possession of the bountiful American promise of "youth and life" (the manifesto-like title of Randolph Bourne's essay collection of 1913)—is grounded in abundant fact. Renewal in literature and the arts after 1910 is as tangible, historically, as progressivism and reform in civil life and opinion. In both spheres gentility and pharisaism remained powerfully obstructive, but the backlash tactics they were being driven to—from the high-minded abstractions of a new academic humanism to the grosser hysteria of police censorship and the prohibition amendment—merely confirm our impression of the irrepressible strength of new currents. In a suddenly more favorable creative climate high American purposes no longer seemed quite so deeply at odds with the enabling American energies. America at large could still be called—as Dreiser called it, with unexpected wit—"the land of Bottom the Weaver," but to writers of sufficient nerve and purpose the obduracy of common taste had become more challenge than deterrent. "The stamina of stupidity," Ezra Pound assured *Poetry*'s editors, "is weaker."

For literature there is no turning point so definite as, for painting and sculpture, the famous Armory Show of 1913—unless perhaps the Armory Show itself, which for all the arts gave the general cause of newness, modernism, and creative freedom an extraordinary backing of original technical authority. It is characteristic of the period that after 1910 a whole cluster of new magazines committed in one way or another to cultural renewal came into existence—the socialist *Masses* in 1911 and the progressivist *New Republic* in 1914 (both chiefly concerned with politics but programmatically hospitable to new trends in the arts), *Poetry* in 1912, *The*

Little Review in 1914, *The Smart Set* as reorganized in 1913 by Willard Huntington Wright and in 1914 by Mencken and Nathan, *The Seven Arts* in 1916, the new *Dial* of 1917–1918. It is equally characteristic, however, that none of them spoke so clearly for new standards of judgment and performance as did Ford Madox Ford's *English Review* (founded 1908) or the *Nouvelle Revue Française* of Gide and Jacques Rivière, to say nothing of avant-garde explosions like Tristan Tzara's *Dada* of 1917. Ezra Pound, serving as an auxiliary foreign editor, did briefly help to give a more precise critical direction to both *Poetry* and *The Little Review*, after they had begun publication. But for the most part the new American literary journals of 1910–1919 did not so much define and sponsor new developments as open their pages to some of those discovered to be already in progress.

If at their foundation these magazines shared any single premise, it was that set out in the *Seven Arts* editorial quoted at the head of this chapter: the premise that great literature and an organic cultural maturity (or "national self-consciousness") were one and the same cause, with a first corollary that in the evolutionary process of American development both fulfillments lay just around the corner and had only to be resolutely reached for. The critical history of the decade of 1910–1920 might well be written in terms of two opposing responses to this premise: first, its enthusiastic general acceptance among various younger writers and editors, and then (in a development intensified by the cultural crisis of the war but already taking shape, as in Pound's quick mind, before 1914) a small but singularly violent and infectious revolt against it. (So the rhetorical assertion borrowed from Whitman and printed each month on the cover of *Poetry* concerning the necessity of "great audiences" for the production of "great poets" is remembered chiefly for Pound's prompt and fundamentally realistic repudiation.) In any event it is the energetic confusion of cross-purposes rather than any clear-cut critical debate that characterizes the rising tendency of the decade. For a time youth and idealistic hopefulness were enough to make comrades in arms of writers who in due course would discover themselves moving toward quite different if not basically incompatible goals—but only for a time. *The Seven Arts,* we can see now, never managed to translate its prophetic vision into a viable editorial policy; month by month its practical contribution to a "new" American literature was in fact negligible. Its editors spoke glowingly of some ideal future harmony of corporatively engaged artist-prophets, but their practical commitment was still to romantic individualism and personal sincerity; thus, in their lead editorial, a few sentences after stating their basic faith in the onset of an epoch in which "the arts [would] cease to be private matters," they could announce with equal positiveness, "What we ask of the writer is simply self-expression without regard to current magazine standards." The whole inconsistent complex of motives at work in this new American renaissance was caught up, with an intellectual unembarrassment that amounts to a kind of genius, by Sherwood Anderson in an evangelizing manifesto (or advertising blurb) contributed to the first number of *The Little Review,* entitled "The New Note" (1914). In quick succession Anderson appealed to "craft love," then to the "comradely spirit" prerequisite to the giving and receiving of new formulations, then to the "unbelievably difficult task" at the center of the whole business of imaginative art—which is simply "to catch, understand, and record your own mood." "In the trade of writing," Anderson postulated,

> the so-called new note is as old as the world. Simply stated, it is a cry for the reinjection of truth and honesty into the craft; it is an appeal from the standards set up by money-making magazine and book publishers in Europe and Amer-

ica to the older, sweeter standards of the craft itself; it is
the voice of the new man, come into a new world, proclaim-
ing his right to speak out of the body and soul of youth,
rather than through the bodies and souls of the master
craftsmen who are gone.

Nearly all the muddled main currents of the period's will to
renewal flow through this declaration. Realism, we note, is
centrally reaffirmed, and once more as a fundamentally moral
cause, a purification of spirit; the acquisitive, merchandising
society of modern times is defined as the enemy; the ancient
discipline of self-governing craftsmanship is brought forward
in opposition; at the same time it is suggested that the actual
received traditions and fruits of this craft discipline are somehow as dangerous as the standard of cash success; finally, the
newness that is wanted turns out to be more than anything
else the uncontaminated (and thus as nearly as possible un-
informed) self-expression of youth—youth speaking to youth
for youth's sake.

It is an appealing faith, but it was not one by which writers
were likely to get their proper practical education and come
into their mature growth. Indeed the most interesting new
departures in American writing after 1910 had little enough
to do with it. The freshest work in the novel during the next
few years is, with regard to form, conspicuously derivative
and traditional: not, for example, Ernest Poole's *The Harbor*
(1915), a shapeless though boisterously sincere expression of
the double cause of socialism and self-deliverance, but Sinclair
Lewis's *Our Mr. Wrenn* (1914) and Ring Lardner's *You
Know Me Al* (1916)—the one an American copy of H. G.
Wells's *The History of Mr. Polly,* the other a worthy heir
to a long American line of newspaper-colloquial parody-
extravaganzas and coincidentally the freshest exercise in the
genre of the epistolary novel since Smollett and Fanny
Burney. Sherwood Anderson's own case is representative.

The opening sections of his first two books, the novels *Windy McPherson's Son* (1916) and *Marching Men* (1917), are alive with the qualities that distinguish his best later stories—the narrative originality, the keen sense of place and atmosphere, the concrete awareness of sensual human presences. But he was at a loss how to apply these gifts to the job of building up a substantial work of fiction; and it was only in recovering the secure compositional forms of traditional American regionalism—vernacular story-telling and the episodic substantiation of conflicting emotional judgments (pity and ironic revolt, nostalgia and despair)—that Anderson found his way to the purified artistry of *Winesburg, Ohio*.

Perhaps the central achievement of the years after 1910 was the consolidation of a *critical* context in which good new work was promptly recognized and assimilated; a professional milieu in which a writer of Anderson's gifts and ambitions *could* be properly encouraged, helped toward some encompassable end. It is symptomatic, surely, that several of the most notable figures of this decade were critics and polemicists: Van Wyck Brooks, H. L. Mencken, Randolph Bourne, Ezra Pound in his role of *maître d'école* for the new poetry, and, toward the end of the decade, younger men like Waldo Frank, whose prophecy-analysis, *Our America*, appeared in 1919, and Paul Rosenfeld, whose sympathetic studies of various contemporaries in *Port of New York* (1924) are saturated with the creative spirit of the new age. What is also symptomatic, with this whole group of critics, is the element of personal involvement with the best new imaginative work of their time. Mencken (b. 1880) made more of a mark, one can say, by his championing of his friend Dreiser's novels than by his early primers on Shaw (1905) and Nietzsche (1908), while Brooks (b. 1886) and indeed nearly the whole *Seven Arts* board personally adopted Anderson as their prototypical new man in American letters: a writer incontestably rooted in American realities, and incontestably original, whose struggle for maturity as an artist was a drama worth assisting at. The critical idealism of Brooks's early writings—in particular *The Wine of the Puritans* (1908), *America's Coming-of-Age* (1915), and *Letters and Leadership* (1918)—descends straight from long-standing New England, and Harvard, critical tradition; but with earlier inheritors of that tradition, with Charles Eliot Norton, for example, or even John Jay Chapman, we do not find anything like Brooks's practical apprenticeship at the painter John Butler Yeats's conversational table or his dialogue-correspondence—in which both sharpened their sense of their separate tasks—with Anderson. What American letters had always lacked, even in the great days of Transcendentalism, was a *school*—"a national school of our own generation," as Henry Adams had imagined it fifty years earlier; "a national set of young men like ourselves or better, to start new influences not only in politics, but in literature, in law, in society, and throughout the whole social organism of the country," the effect of which might be to keep American talent from dissipating itself in "random, insulated work" for merely "special and temporary and personal purposes";[2] and a great part of the excitement and practical confidence of 1912 and after derived from the sense that some such happy development was more and more a matter of fact.

Yet it was a development which, precisely as it meant to establish a self-renewing *critical* consensus, was also self-undermining. The higher the excitement over future prospects, the sharper the disappointment at the actual meagerness and imperfection of new work, as well as at its obvious failure to effect any real change in the common consciousness. For the first time a class of writers emerges in the United States whom

2. Letter to C. F. Adams, Jr., London, November 21, 1862.

we may call, who call themselves, "intellectuals"; writers whose specific function is not to produce novels or plays or poems or learned treatises or even critical elucidations but to guide literate opinion, to formulate goals and channel energies, above all to stand guard moment by moment over the nation's faltering communion with its own creative destiny; a clerisy without portfolio, one may fairly say. Characteristically, however, this class's most acute perceptions rise from its anxious communion with itself. Its chief occupation turns out to be that of identifying its own weaknesses and denouncing its own failures. This, pre-eminently, became the part played by Randolph Bourne (b. 1886) between 1912 and 1918. Bourne in particular, among his generation, seemed to speak for its leading motive—its intense desire, in Van Wyck Brooks's summary, "for a new fellowship in the youth of America as the principle of a great and revolutionary departure in our life . . . creating, out of the blind chaos of American society, a fine, free, articulate cultural order."[3] Thus the shock which toward the end of Bourne's brief life moved him to his most forceful writing was his discovery of the treasonableness of the American clerisy with regard to its own proper critical function. The decisive moment for this class, to Bourne's mind, was America's entrance into the great powers' war. And though it was as a pacifist that he himself responded to this crisis, the bitterest revelation was not merely the near-unanimity of American intellectuals ("socialists, college professors, publicists, new-republicans, practitioners of literature") in supporting American belligerency. It was their giving themselves up *as intellectuals* to the war mind and war spirit—giving themselves up, moreover, joyfully and with self-satisfaction to this ultimate betrayal of the dream of an

3. "Introduction," *The History of a Literary Radical and Other Papers by Randolph Bourne*, edited by Van Wyck Brooks, New York, 1920.

organic national renaissance; propagandizing, publicly rationalizing their submission to the rule of *staatsräson,* scolding deviants and conniving in their punishment.[4] Bourne was specific about the significance of this betrayal. The intellectuals, he pointed out, had had clear and honorable alternatives:

> They could have used their energy to force a just peace or at least to devise other means than war for carrying through American policy. They could have used their intellectual energy to ensure that our participation in the war meant the international order which they wish. *Intellect was not so used* [emphasis added]. It was used to lead an apathetic nation into an irresponsible war, without guarantees from those belligerents whose cause we were saving.

It was this apparent failure of intellect to be true to its own proper task of critical leadership that especially absorbed Bourne's attention, and, correlatively, the moral failure of that intellectual elite upon whose collective wisdom and integrity the whole confident idea of a national coming-of-age had been based—too easily based, he now understood. Thenceforth if the revolutionary promise of American life and American letters was to be substantially realized, it would have to be through the dissident courage and constancy of individual men. The collective optimism which had fed the hopes of his generation, Bourne felt, might very well have been a means of escaping the real challenges of its high calling, and he attached what remained of his own hopefulness about American

4. "The War and the Intellectuals," *Seven Arts,* June, 1917. See also "A War Diary," September, 1917, and "Twilight of Idols," October, 1917. The last of these, with its naked attack on John Dewey and on Dewey's social philosophy as one of mere accommodation to worldly power, was an immediate cause of *Seven Arts'* losing its sponsorship and ceasing publication. All three papers are reprinted in *The History of a Literary Radical,* more recently in *War and the Intellectuals,* edited by Carl Resek (1964).

prospects to the "more skeptical, malicious, desperate, ironical mood" ("Twilight of Idols") that he sensed the end of the decade and of the national war adventure was bringing to pass among certain younger writers. So far, between 1912 and 1918, had he been carried by his initial faith in the great chances of his times.

Bourne, following his own course as an "intellectual" and as the conscience of the Young America of his day, had thus arrived at a position not unlike that which Pound and Eliot had already come to occupy as poets and men of letters: that the business of original creation was more difficult and problematical than its official custodians ever quite admitted, and that a national society produced literature, art, philosophy of real and enduring value to the commonwealth not by defining a collective purpose—noble as that might be—and conscripting individual talents into its service, but by freeing them to get their proper education where they could and to make their own way however far from any approved starting point it might take them. Bourne's disillusionment in 1917–1918 is as representative as the generous but unfocused hopefulness of his *Youth and Life* essays of 1913 and played its part in precipitating the mood of the 1920s. American letters had been waiting for a national "school," an organized community of mind and purpose within which American genius would flower as never before. But now that something of the kind had been brought into being, its best prospective members abruptly turned away. Like the most gifted Irish writers of the same era they were discovering that the ritual satisfactions of a self-promoting provincial "renaissance" would not get their work done for them; would even, perhaps, keep them from it. It was not simply postwar restlessness or—in the era of Prohibition and the Society for the Suppression of Vice—the irritated nostalgia of former ambulance drivers for a less angular civilization that, after 1919, took the newest American writers off to Paris (or Munich, or Vienna, or even London) in droves. It was specifically the collapse of the dream of 1912, the dream of a distinctively American *âge d'or* with one or another American town (Chicago, Springfield, Greenwich Village) a new Athens and all the world more and more like an American town. It was the practical intuition that for a writer bent on artistic maturity and freedom a company of true masters—and Paris in 1919 was first of all the gathering place of the internationally recognized masters of modern art—was infinitely more valuable than a mere local society of fellows.

Or perhaps it was simply a matter of dressing out the dream of 1912 in new and more suitable clothes. For all extraordinary differences, the "Paris" actually created by the expatriate American writers of the early '20s was at bottom perilously like the idyllic American village, the timeless, comradely, all-licensing Boystown, which had pacified the imaginative distempers of an earlier, simpler generation. The idea of "salvation by exile" (Malcolm Cowley's phrase) was not intrinsically different from the idea it displaced, salvation by a bootstrap cultural nationalism. And it could be just as easily abused. The salvation complex itself was what, after 1919, the best of the newest generation were revolting against. For major literary history the neo-Progressivist argument that now began to rage concerning the nourishing qualities of American civilization is finally immaterial. The great question upon which much of this transatlantic coming and going was based —whether American civilization would produce a great literature by fulfilling itself or by escaping from itself—had little bearing on the practical problems of learning to write. The important practical division that did in fact open up during the second half of the decade after 1910 was between (as we might call them) the "Americans" and the "new men of letters"—between those who still somehow thought that because America was a special place created by a special providence its art not only would reflect a different consciousness but also would come into being in some fundamentally different, some morally purer and technically simpler way, and those others who exercised their peculiarly American freedom by deliberately setting out to make themselves at home, as artists, in a wider and more authoritative world, asking at every step (some publicly, some to themselves only) not, "How can I be American and real?" but, "How would Flaubert have done it, or Balzac, or Jules Laforgue, or Mann or Joyce or Valéry or Strindberg, or [seen no longer as library monuments and schoolroom relics but as living masters of a continuous artistic tradition] Dante or Shakespeare or Catullus or Euripides?" Into this second party went, each in his own way, Eliot, Pound, Stevens, Conrad Aiken, Hart Crane, Hemingway, Fitzgerald, Faulkner, Edmund Wilson, Eugene O'Neill. And though there remained with each a certain distinctively American ingenuousness about their choice, who now can doubt, half a century later, their literary intelligence and practical good sense in making it?

Select Bibliography

Bibliographic listings for American literature are now so thoroughgoing and so easily accessible that only a minimum selection of titles is offered here.

REFERENCE WORKS:

BIBLIOGRAPHICAL

For the period covered in this volume, as for the whole span of American literature, the *Literary History of the United States*, ed. Robert E. Spiller, *et al.* (1948; 2nd edition, 1953), remains the standard general survey, and its bibliographical third volume, together with *Bibliography Supplement*, ed. Richard M. Ludwig (1959), the standard general reference work. *The Literature of the American People*, ed. Arthur Hobson Quinn (1951), is also useful. Marcus Cunliffe, *The Literature of the United States* (1954), is still the best short history and is written with notable critical tact. James D. Hart, ed., *The Oxford Companion to American Literature* (3rd edition, 1956), is indispensable. The choice of titles in Howard Mumford Jones and Richard M. Ludwig, *Guide to American Literature and Its Backgrounds*

Since 1890 (3rd edition, 1964), emphasizes the "intellectual and sociological" context of the era's work. The relevant chapters in Frank Luther Mott, *Golden Multitudes: The Story of Best Sellers in the United States* (1947), and James D. Hart, *The Popular Book* (1950), are instructive on the special problem of popular taste. Frank Luther Mott, *A History of American Magazines, Volume IV: 1885–1905* (1957), is a mine of information concerning this sector of the literary market, as is the "Historical Introduction," on the publishing houses of D. Appleton and Company and The Century Company, in *Fruit Among the Leaves*, edited by Samuel C. Chew (1950).

Two journals, *American Literature* and *PMLA*, maintain running bibliographies of periodical articles in the field. For current works of literary criticism and scholarship the reviews in *Journal of English and Germanic Philology* and *Modern Language Review*, as well as *American Literature*, are particularly informative. Lewis Leary, ed., *Articles on American Literature, 1900–1950* (1954), and James D. Woodress, *Dissertations in American Literature, 1891–1961* (1962), are essential checklists.

REFERENCE WORKS:
CRITICAL AND HISTORICAL

Roughly half the material in Philip Rahv, ed., *Literature in America* (1957), in Lewis Leary, ed., *American Literary Essays* (1960), in Morton Dauwen Zabel, ed., *Literary Opinion in America* (3rd edition, 1962), and in Edmund Wilson, ed., *The Shock of Recognition* (1943), concerns the period of this volume. Alfred Kazin, *On Native Grounds* (1942), gives a vivid panoramic impression of motives and impulses operating throughout the period; so also do Van Wyck Brooks, *The Confident Years, 1885–1915* (1952), and, in a narrower focus, Brooks's charming memoir, *Scenes and Portraits* (1954). Various essays in Joseph Warren Beach, *The Outlook for American Prose* (1926), T. K. Whipple, *Spokesmen* (1928), Malcolm Cowley, ed., *After the Genteel Tradition* (1937), Malcolm Cowley and Bernard Smith, eds., *Books That Changed Our Minds* (1939), and Conrad Aiken, *A Reviewer's ABC* (1958), give near-contemporary evaluations of early twentieth-century writing. Grant C. Knight, *The Critical Period in American Literature, 1890–1900* (1951) and *The Strenuous Age in American Literature, 1900–1910* (1954), offer serviceable descriptions, while Larzer Ziff's forthcoming study of the '90s should provide a definitive account. Bernard I. Duffey, *The Chicago Renaissance in American Letters* (1954), is a reliable survey of careers and purposes involved in that turn-of-the-century episode; a comparable study of New Orleans as a literary center remains to be written.

A good introduction to the underlying currents of social and political opinion between the 1880s and the 1920s, and to the context of populism and progressivism, is provided in Richard Hofstadter, *The Age of Reform* (1955). Louis Filler, *Crusaders for American Liberalism* (1939), also is valuable. Among innumerable accounts of the small-town, petty-bourgeois background of American regionalism, the opening chapters of Irving Howe, *Sherwood Anderson* (1951), are outstanding. Kenneth S. Lynn, *The Dream of Success* (1955), lists, incidentally, some odd symptoms of the breakdown of common morale during the period and the spread of neurasthenic compensations. The emergence of a class of dissident "intellectuals" in American life is described in Christopher Lasch, *The New Radicalism in America: 1889–1963* (1965).

Everett Carter, *Howells and the Age of Realism* (1954), offers a detailed study of the course of the main theoretical program of the '80s and '90s in American letters. The critical foundations of "realism" as an international movement are well presented in George J. Becker, ed., *Documents of Modern Literary Realism* (1963). On "naturalism," Charles Child Walcutt, *American Literary Naturalism* (1956), may be supplemented by Malcolm Cowley, " 'Not Men': A Natural History of American Naturalism," *Kenyon Review*, Summer, 1947, reprinted in Stow Persons, ed., *Evolutionary Thought in America* (1950).

Most individual authors of consequence in this period are included in the Twayne United States Authors Series and in the University of Minnesota Pamphlets on American Writers, both current. Both series contain up-to-date bibliographies.

NOVELS AND NOVELISTS:
HOWELLS AND CONTEMPORARIES

The standard biography of Howells is E. H. Cady, *The Road to Realism: the Early Years, 1837–1885* (1956) and *The Realist at War: the Mature Years, 1885–1920* (1958). Van Wyck Brooks, *Howells: His Life and Work* (1959), is a sympathetic appreciation. *Mark Twain–Howells Letters: The Correspondence of Sam-*

uel L. Clemens and William Dean Howells, 1872–1910, ed. William M. Gibson and Henry Nash Smith, 2 volumes (1960), documents a unique literary friendship.

For Mark Twain, Albert Bigelow Paine's official biography (3 volumes, 1912) is indispensable. Paine also edited *Mark Twain's Letters*, 2 volumes (1917). Two well-known and, at one time, controversial studies, Van Wyck Brooks, *The Ordeal of Mark Twain* (1920), and Bernard DeVoto, *Mark Twain's America* (1932), are prime evidence of the special tenderness and exaggeration of judgment, pro and con, which American critics of Mark Twain have always been subject to. Bernard DeVoto, *Mark Twain at Work* (1942), brilliantly illuminates the inward habit of Twain's creative imagination. Henry Nash Smith, *Mark Twain: the Development of a Writer* (1962), perceptively traces various key themes and obsessions from book to book, while Professor Smith's study of *A Connecticut Yankee, Mark Twain's Fable of Progress* (1964) and also Robert A. Wiggins, *Mark Twain: Jackleg Novelist* (1964), throw light on the difficulties of Twain's later career. Collections of critical essays on Twain, which in any case mostly repeat one another, have become too numerous to mention.

There is little good criticism of Ambrose Bierce; an exception is Edmund Wilson's chapter on Bierce in *Patriotic Gore: Studies in the Literature of the American Civil War* (1962). Elizabeth Stevenson, *Lafcadio Hearn* (1961), is excellent on Hearn's American years. The best of Hearn's critical writing during his New Orleans period is collected in *Essays in European and Oriental Literature*, ed. Albert Mordell (1923), and *Essays on American Literature*, ed. Sanki Ichikawa (1929). Arlin Turner, whose biography of George Washington Cable (1956) is standard, also has edited a collection of Cable's short fiction, *Creoles and Cajuns* (1959), and another of social and political essays, *The Negro Question* (1958). Guy A. Cardwell, *Twins of Genius* (1953), describes Cable's association with Mark Twain; Philip Butcher, *George W. Cable: the Northampton Years* (1959), deals with his later career. The discussion of Cable in Edmund Wilson's *Patriotic Gore* is first rate, while another section of the same book is responsible for the revival of interest in Kate Chopin and a reprinting (1964) of *The Awakening*. On local-color writers,

W. P. Randel, *Edward Eggleston* (1946), Clyde E. Henson, *Joseph Kirkland* (1962), and Edward Foster, *Mary E. Wilkins Freeman* (1956), are serviceable guides. Recent reprintings of E. W. Howe's *The Story of a Country Town* and of Hamlin Garland's *Main-Travelled Roads* and *Crumbling Idols* contain critical introductions. F. O. Matthiessen, *Sarah Orne Jewett* (1929), may be supplemented by Richard Cary's biography (1962).

Books and articles about Henry James continue to pour forth, as do new editions of his work. F. W. Dupee, *Henry James* (1951), is a first-rate critical biography; D. W. Jefferson's shorter study (1960) in the British *Writers and Critics* series is also to be recommended. Simon Nowell-Smith, ed., *The Legend of the Master* (1947), is an entertaining compilation of personal anecdote. F. O. Matthiessen, *The James Family* (1948), is required reading. Leon Edel's biography—three of its projected four volumes have appeared (1953–1962)—is standard, though far from definitive. Professor Edel also has edited a selection of James's letters and two excellent anthologies of James's criticism, *The American Essays of Henry James* (1956) and *The Future of the Novel* (1956); more recently he has put all readers of James in his debt by editing *The Complete Tales of Henry James*, 12 volumes (1962–1964). James's earlier, mostly journalistic criticism has been collected in *Literary Reviews and Essays*, ed. Albert Mordell (1957); his theater criticism in *The Scenic Art*, ed. Allan Wade (1948). *The Notebooks of Henry James*, ed. F. O. Matthiessen and Kenneth B. Murdock (1947), is fundamental to understanding James's working methods.

Among critical assessments the brief comments on James in E. M. Forster, *Aspects of the Novel* (1927), and Edwin Muir, *The Structure of the Novel* (1928), are extremely suggestive. The more comprehensive essays by Yvor Winters in *Maule's Curse* (1938), by Edmund Wilson in *The Triple Thinkers* (1938), and by R. P. Blackmur in *Literary History of the United States* (1948), are all distinguished for style and critical tact as well as for interpretive judgment. F. W. Dupee, ed., *The Question of Henry James* (1945), remains a model for all such anthologies of critical essays. F. O. Matthiessen's study of the great trilogy of 1902–1904, *Henry James: The Major Phase* (1943), retains its value; a comparable study of the work of 1896–1901—perhaps the one period which the vast corpus of Jamesian commentary has not yet come to terms with—would be equally profitable. Marius Bewley, *The Complex Fate* (1952), examines the "Hawthorne aspect" informatively. Quentin Anderson, *The American Henry James* (1957), deals provocatively with the rich question of James's American inheritances. Although afflicted with the thesis-pushing and the mandarinish complication of argument that characterize a great deal of incidental James criticism, recent books by Dorothea Krook, *The Ordeal of Consciousness in Henry James* (1962), and Laurence B. Holland, *The Expense of Vision* (1964), are notable examples of the detail and reverent dedication James induces in close students of his work.

Minor realists and humorists of the turn-of-the-century period are dealt with in Thomas F. O'Donnell and Hoyt C. Franchere, *Harold Frederic* (1961), Warren I. Titus, *Winston Churchill* (1963), Clarence A. Glasrud, *Hjalmar Hjorth Boyesen* (1963), Elmer Ellis, *Mr. Dooley's America: A Life of Finley Peter Dunne* (1941), and Lee Coyle, *George Ade* (1964). No book-length study of Henry Blake Fuller has appeared since Constance M. Griffin's University of Pennsylvania dissertation of 1939. Herrick has been better served: Blake Nevius, *Robert Herrick: the Development of a Novelist* (1962), sympathetically reviews the whole career, and there have been new editions of *The Memoirs of an American Citizen*, ed. Daniel Aaron (1963), and *Together*, ed. Van Wyck Brooks (1962). Rumors of critical neglect of Edith Wharton have been exaggerated. The most detailed assessment is Blake Nevius, *Edith Wharton: A Study of Her Fiction* (1953); the best shorter estimates are assembled in *Edith Wharton: A Collection of Critical Essays*, ed. Irving Howe (1962). Percy Lubbock, *Portrait of Edith Wharton* (1947), is a sympathetic though not wholly candid biographical evocation, while Louis Auchincloss's pamphlet, *Edith Wharton* (1961), offers an appreciative study of her achievement by a "New York" novelist of a later generation.

LITERATURE OF ARGUMENT

Richard Hofstadter's monograph, *Social Darwinism in American Thought, 1860–1915* (1944), remains an admirable introduction to the evolutionist factor in turn-of-the-century writing. Philip Wiener, *Evolution and the Founders of Pragmatism* (1949), is both critical and historical. A kind of natural history of the "Progressive" impulse is outlined in Daniel Aaron's *Men of Good Hope* (1951; re-issued 1961), which contains chapters on George, Bellamy, Lloyd, Howells, Veblen, and Brooks Adams, as well as a convenient bibliography. The complementary topic of visionary and prophetic pessimism is treated, less satisfactorily, in F. C. Jaher, *Doubters and Dissenters: Cataclysmic Thought in America, 1885–1918* (1964). Perry Miller, ed., *American Thought: Civil War to World War I* (1954), is a serviceable introductory anthology.

For Veblen, Joseph Dorfman, *Thorstein Veblen and His America* (1934), is essential. Important miscellaneous papers and reviews of Veblen's, including the reply to Cummings, are reprinted in *Essays in Our Changing Order*, ed. Leon Ardzrooni (1934). *The Portable Veblen*, ed. Max Lerner (1948), is a wide-ranging selection with a stimulating "Editor's Introduction." David Riesman, *Thorstein Veblen: A Critical Interpretation* (1953), lacks seriousness.

Ralph Barton Perry's monumental biography, *The Thought and Character of William James*, 2 volumes (1935), is a classic of modern scholarship. A two-volume edition of *The Letters of William James* appeared in 1920; *Selected Letters of William James*, ed. Elizabeth Hardwick, in 1961. F. O. Matthiessen, *The James Family* (1948), throws light on William James's literary sensibility.

Nothing like Perry's great work exists for the other leading philosophic writers of the period, although Sidney Hook, *John Dewey* (1939), and W. B. Gallie, *Peirce and Pragmatism* (1952), are to be recommended. The Library of Living Philosophers has issued *The Philosophy of John Dewey*, ed. P. A. Schilpp (1939), and *The Philosophy of George Santayana*, ed. P. A. Schilpp (1940). Vincent Buranelli, *Josiah Royce* (1964), contains a useful bibliography. Santayana's essays on James and Royce, in *Character and Opinion in the United States* (1920), are critical assessments of the highest interest. Various chapters in the first two volumes of Santayana's *Persons and Places*, 3 volumes (1944–1953), deal with the author's American life and contacts. Daniel Cory has edited *The Letters of George Santayana* (1955). Milton Berman, *John Fiske: The Evolution of a Popularizer* (1961), is an effective survey. Martin Halpern, "Henry Brewster (1850–1908): An Introduction," *American Quarterly*, XIV (Fall, 1962), opens the way to further consideration of this neglected figure.

The principal historians of the period are examined critically in *The Marcus W. Jernegan Essays in American Historiography*, ed. William T. Hutchinson (1937). On Turner as a writer, Ray Allen Billington's "Foreword" to a new edition of the *Rise of the New West* (1962) is illuminating. For the Adamses, Brooks Adams's long, tendentious essay, "The Heritage of Henry Adams," prefacing an edition of his brother's theoretical papers, *The Degradation of the Democratic Dogma* (1919), should be supplemented by Charles Beard's lively "Introduction" to a reprinting of *The Law of Civilization and Decay* (1943). Both Thornton Anderson, *Brooks Adams: Constructive Conservative* (1951), and Arthur T. Beringause, *Brooks Adams: A Biography* (1955), are critical and interpretive. Ernest Samuels's three-volume biography, *The Young Henry Adams* (1948), *Henry Adams: The Middle Years* (1958), and *Henry Adams: The Major Phase* (1964), makes full use of the Adams papers held by the Massachusetts Historical Society. Elizabeth Stevenson's briefer *Henry Adams* (1955) is a reliable portrait-chronicle. Outstanding in a vast and growing critical literature are William H. Jordy, *Henry Adams: Scientific Historian* (1952), J. C. Levenson, *The Mind and Art of Henry Adams* (1957), and a series of essays by R. P. Blackmur: "The Expense of Greatness," *Virginia Quarterly*, XII (July, 1936), reprinted in *The Lion and the Honeycomb* (1955); "Henry Adams: Three Late Moments," *Kenyon Review*, II (Winter, 1940); "Harmony of True Liberalism: Henry Adams's *Mont-Saint-Michel and Chartres*," *Sewanee Review*, LX (Winter, 1952); "Adams Goes to School," *Kenyon Review*, XVII (Fall, 1955).

Recent studies of leading literary critics of the period include Arnold T. Schwab, *James Gibbons Huneker: Critic of the Seven Arts* (1963); Arthur Hazard Dakin, *Paul Elmer More* (1960); Harry Levin, "Irving Babbitt and the Teaching of Literature": *The Irving Babbitt Inaugural Lecture* (1960); Howard Mumford Jones, "Introduction," in W. C. Brownell, *American Prose Masters* (new edition, 1963); Richard B. Hovey, *John Jay Chapman: An American Mind* (1959). *The Selected Writings of John Jay Chapman*, ed. Jacques Barzun (1957), has a critical introduction.

THE CLASS OF THE '70S

On the newer currents in American fiction between 1890 and 1920, two books by Maxwell Geismar are of particular interest: *Rebels and Ancestors: The American Novel, 1890–1915* (1953) and *The Last of the Provincials: The American Novel, 1915–1925* (1947). See also R. W. Schneider, *Five Novelists of the Progressive Era* (1965), and Louis Auchincloss, *Pioneers and Caretakers* (1965). Critical biographies of Frank Norris have been written by Franklin Walker (1932), Ernest Marchand (1942), and Warren French (1962); more concentrated assessments may be found in the introductions to various recent reprintings of *McTeague* and *The Octopus*. Stephen Crane continues to elude critical definition, although John Berryman, in *Stephen Crane* (1950), and Daniel G. Hoffman, in *The Poetry of Stephen Crane* (1957), approach his work with the insight and tact to be expected of scholars who are also accomplished poets. *Stephen Crane: Letters*, ed. R. W. Stallman and Lillian Gilkes (1960), is indispensable. A listing of recent editions of *The Red Badge of Courage* would fill a page in itself; nearly all are equipped with introductions and short bibliographies.

Robert H. Elias, *Theodore Dreiser: Apostle of Nature* (1949), and F. O. Matthiessen, *Theodore Dreiser* (1951), are standard, to be supplemented by *Letters of Theodore Dreiser*, ed. Robert H. Elias, 4 volumes (1959); but for literary history the most valuable biographical study is Dorothy Dudley, *Forgotten Frontiers: Dreiser and the Land of the Free* (1932), reissued as *Dreiser and the Land of the Free* (1946). Much of the best criticism of Dreiser has been written by other novelists. *The Stature of Theodore Dreiser*, ed. Alfred Kazin and Charles Shapiro (1955), collects the best earlier essays. More recent appraisals, as yet uncollected, by Nelson Algren, Saul Bellow, Irving Howe, Alfred Kazin, and Robert Penn Warren, among others, indicate that Dreiser has resumed his place in the first rank of American novelists and that his creative influence is, if anything, increasing.

Continuing interest in Jack London's writing, perhaps stronger in Europe than in the United States, is reflected in two current British publishing ventures, *The Fitzroy Edition of the Works of Jack London* and *The Bodley Head Jack London*. On Gertrude Stein, various recent studies offer conflicting judgments: Elizabeth Sprigge, *Gertrude Stein: Her Life and Work* (1957); B. L. Reid,

Art by Subtraction: A Dissenting Opinion of Gertrude Stein (1958); John Malcolm Brinnin, *The Third Rose: Gertrude Stein and Her World* (1959). As critical guides none of these supplants Donald Sutherland, *Gertrude Stein: A Biography of Her Work* (1951). Frederick J. Hoffman's pamphlet, *Gertrude Stein* (1961), contains a helpful select bibliography. The fullest survey of Ellen Glasgow's novels is Frederick P. W. McDowell, *Ellen Glasgow and the Ironic Art of Fiction* (1960); briefer studies are Blair Rouse, *Ellen Glasgow* (1962), and Louis Auchincloss's pamphlet, *Ellen Glasgow* (1964). Blair Rouse has edited *Letters of Ellen Glasgow* (1958). The most serviceable book-length study of Willa Cather is E. K. Brown and Leon Edel, *Willa Cather: A Critical Biography* (1953). Still deflected by the need to come to terms with the overextended reputation she enjoyed during her later career, criticism of Willa Cather has not yet managed to define very clearly the imaginative strength of her best work.

In the absence of satisfactory fuller treatment (which probably must wait until papers in the Houghton Library, Harvard, may be opened), Yvor Winters' short *Edwin Arlington Robinson* (1946) provides the firmest critical survey of the poetry. Emery Neff, *Edwin Arlington Robinson* (1948), and Ellsworth Barnard, *Edwin Arlington Robinson: A Critical Study* (1952), lack critical focus. Robinson's technical resources and education are admirably set out in Edwin S. Fussell, *Edwin Arlington Robinson: The Literary Background of a Traditional Poet* (1954). Perhaps no one has written better about Robinson than Conrad Aiken, during the 1920s, in three short pieces collected in *A Reviewer's ABC* (1958), although Louis Coxe's pamphlet, *E. A. Robinson* (1962), is discerning on general issues. There are two important collections of letters: *Selected Letters of Edwin Arlington Robinson*, ed. Ridgely Torrence (1940), and *Untriangulated Stars: Letters of Edwin Arlington Robinson to Harry de Forest Smith, 1890–1905*, ed. Denham Sutcliffe (1947). Charles T. Davis's edition of *Selected Early Poems and Letters* (1960) facilitates study of Robinson's beginnings as a poet.

Book-length studies of Robert Frost abound and multiply; most, however—such as those by Sidney Cox, Lawrance Thompson, Reginald Cook, John Lynen, George Nitchie, and Reuben Brower—testify more to the seductiveness of the poet's voice and remarkable public presence than to any clear critical perspective. Elizabeth Shepley Sergeant, *Robert Frost: The Trial by Existence* (1960), which quotes generously from letters and prefaces, seems, so far, the most useful general treatment. Volumes of letters are cropping up on all sides, but a proper collected edition appears unlikely for several years to come. *The Letters of Robert Frost to Louis Untermeyer,* ed. Louis Untermeyer (1963), and *Selected Letters of Robert Frost,* ed. Lawrance Thompson (1964), are the most important to date. A fine early volume of critical appreciations, *Recognition of Robert Frost,* ed. Richard Thornton (1937), has not been superseded.

The patchiness of scholarly work on the Illinois poets confirms one's sense of abruptly declining reputations. Contemporary assessments, beginning with Amy Lowell's *Tendencies in Modern American Poetry* (1917), remain the best sources of critical opinion. Amy Lowell herself has been rather better served in Horace Gregory's *Amy Lowell: Portrait of a Poet in Her Time* (1958). On Lindsay, two biographical studies deserve mention: Edgar Lee Masters, *Vachel Lindsay: A Poet in America* (1935), and Eleanor Ruggles, *The West-Going Heart: A Life of Vachel Lindsay* (1959).

RENAISSANCE: 1910–1919

The materials for a proper study of the literary history of the decade, 1910–1919, are only now beginning to be available. (For these years recent periodical articles, establishing basic data, are particularly worth examining.) So far the best published sources of information and critical insight are volumes of memoirs and letters by active participants. Foremost among these—besides Frost's letters, listed above—are *The Letters of Ezra Pound,* ed. D. D. Paige (1951); *Letters of Sherwood Anderson,* ed. Howard Mumford Jones and Walter B. Rideout (1953); *Letters of H. L. Mencken,* ed. Guy J. Forgue (1961); Margaret Anderson, *My Thirty Years War* (1930), along with *The Little Review Anthology,* ed. Margaret Anderson (1953); Harriet Monroe, *A Poet's Life: Seventy Years in a Changing World* (1938); also, for its description of the legacy of this decade as the writers of the '20s received it, Malcolm Cowley, *Exile's Return* (1934; revised, 1951).

Henry F. May, *The End of American Innocence: 1912–1917*

(1959), is an attempt to define, for these years, an essential turning point in cultural history. Herbert Howarth, *Notes on Some Figures Behind T. S. Eliot* (1964), is a model for the introductory presentation of biographical and critical data about a writer whose work is still in process of settling into the status of a classic. The context of Ezra Pound's early career is presented in Patricia Hutchins, *Ezra Pound's Kensington: An Exploration, 1885–1913* (1965). The opening pages of William Wasserstrom, *The Time of the Dial* (1963), provide valuable information, as do the first sections of Stanley K. Coffman, *Imagism: A Chapter for the History of Modern Poetry* (1951). The standard work on the leading figure of the *Seven Arts* group is Louis Filler, *Randolph Bourne* (1943)—but nothing is more likely to contribute to study of this group, in a practical way, than the recent reprinting of the whole two-year run of the magazine itself.

The narrowness of perspective that has characterized rather too much American scholarship in the field of American literature and American studies particularly needs correction for the modern period. As a first antidote to parochialism of this sort, two wide-ranging essays may be suggested: Harry Levin, "What Was Modernism?" *Massachusetts Review*, I (Summer, 1960), and R. P. Blackmur, *Anni Mirabiles: 1921–1925* (Washington: U.S. Government Printing Office, 1956).

Index

Names and Titles

Aaron, Daniel, on Henry George, 206

Abbott, Lyman, *Christianity and Social Problems,* 208n.; *The Evolution of Christianity,* 152n.

Acton, John Emerich Edward Dahlberg (Baron Acton), 189–90

Adams, Andy, *The Log of a Cowboy,* xiv

Adams, Brooks, 187–9, **190–3,** 193n., 194, 194n., 195, 198, 199; bibliography, 306; *America's Economic Supremacy,* 191, 193n.; *The Emancipation of Massachusetts,* 190–1; *The Law of Civilization and Decay,* 21, 39, 68n., 187, 192–3; *The New Empire,* 191; *The Theory of Social Revolutions,* 191–2

Adams, Charles Francis, Jr., 185, 194n., 293n.

Adams, Charles Kendall, 194n.

Adams, Henry, 12, 49, 124, 167–8, 181n., 183, 184, 185, 187–9, 190, 191n., 192, 193n., **193–205,** 288; on an American "school," 293, 293n.; bibliography, 306; letters, 204, 204n.; "American Character," 198; *Democracy,* 128; *Documents Relating to New England Federalism,* 196; *The Education of Henry Adams,* 12, 148, 194, 195, 200–1, 202–4; *Esther,* 9, 9n., 27, 128–30; *Historical Essays,* 194; *History of the United States During the Administrations of Jefferson and Madison,* 39, 129, 187–8, 191n., 195, 195n., 196–9; *John Randolph,*

~ 313

Selected Topics

capitalist democracy, the culture of, 11, 11*n.*, 15–22, 28*n.*, 33–4, 46–7, 60, 90–1, 186, 201, 206, 209–11, 220, 291; Bierce on, 77–8; Boyesen on, 102–3; Dreiser on, 15–6, 238–40, 242; Eggleston on, 92–3; Gertrude Stein on, 251–2; Henry Adams on, 199, 203; Henry Blake Fuller on, 17, 136–8; Henry Demarest Lloyd on, 207–8; Henry James on, 13–4*n.*, 18, 36, 124, 216; Howells on, 19–22, 60; and Jack London, 244–5; John Dewey on, 172; Veblen on, 37, 156; Whitman on, 21; Willa Cather on, 18, 260, 262

Darwinism, 25, 40, 82, 89, 153, 169, 177, 184, 244; in *The Education of Henry Adams*, 203; in Veblen, 156, 158

determinism (and fatalism), 24–5, 34, 40, 46, 226, 232; in Dreiser, 239–40; in Howells, 21–2

egalitarianism, 92, 94*n.*, 283; in Howells, 58; in Mark Twain, 67

evangelicalism, 27–9, 102*n.*, 132, 171, 177, 178–9, 205, 205*n.*

genteelism and ideality, 9–11, 52*n.*, 140–1, 253–4, 288; in Cable, 85–6; in Willa Cather, 257–8

historicism, 182–3, 189–90, 192–3

humanism, 212–5

imperialism (and anti-imperialism), 14, 154–5, 185, 191, 203

individualism, 33–4, 88, 123, 181–2, 221–2; and Frost, 279–81

~ 329